The Play of Allegory
in the *Autos Sacramentales* of
Pedro Calderón de la Barca

Volume 2

Contexts and Literature

General Editor: Virgil Nemoianu

The Play of Allegory in the *Autos Sacramentales* of Pedro Calderón de la Barca

Barbara E. Kurtz

The Catholic University of America Press

Washington, D.C.

Publication of this book has been funded in part by a grant from
The Program for Cultural Cooperation between Spain's Ministry
of Culture and United States Universities.

The Play of Allegory in the Autos Sacramentales *of*
Pedro Calderón de la Barca
was composed in Granjon
by World Composition Services, Inc., Sterling, Virginia
and designed and produced by Kachergis Book Design,
Pittsboro, North Carolina

Library of Congress Cataloging-in-Publication Data

Kurtz, Barbara Ellen, 1950–
    The play of allegory in the *autos sacramentales* of Pedro Calderón
de la Barca / by Barbara E. Kurtz.
        p.   cm.
    Includes bibliographical references and index.
    1. Calderón de la Barca, Pedro, 1600–1681. Autos sacramentales.
2. Religion in literature. 3. Allegory.   I. Title.
PQ6317.R4K87   1991
862.3—dc20
ISBN 0-8132-0733-9 (hardcover : alk. paper)
90-36829

Contents

This book is dedicated to
Ruth House Webber and
George Haley

🦋 Introduction

🦋 At one point in Sheridan's *The Rivals,* that infamous lexicographer Mrs. Malaprop engagingly declares: "O, there's nothing to be hoped for from her! she's as headstrong as an allegory on the banks of the Nile."[1]

Mrs. Malaprop could certainly be forgiven her lexical and allegorical confusion if she were set down in the current critical landscape. These days there are innumerable allegories on the banks of the Nile—and everywhere else in twentieth-century academia, too. For, in recent years a certain all-inclusiveness has come increasingly to characterize discussions of allegory, making for some very strange allegorical bedfellows—everything from works traditionally considered allegories (such as medieval debate poems) through picaresque romances, westerns, and detective stories,[2] everyone from Chaucer to Thomas Pynchon, from Vladimir Nabokov to Plato.[3] Current theory stretches the boundaries of allegorical literature as traditionally defined—almost, it would seem, to the very limits of man's imaginative activity. Allegory's most basic attributes are nowa-

1. Richard Brinsley Sheridan, *The Dramatic Works of Richard Brinsley Sheridan,* ed. Cecil Price, 1 (Oxford: Clarendon, 1973): 113.

2. Angus Fletcher categorizes these (and other) forms as allegory in *Allegory* (Ithaca: Cornell University Press, 1964), 3.

3. Maureen Quilligan considers these writers (and others) as allegorists in *The Language of Allegory* (Ithaca: Cornell University Press, 1979).

days a matter of some uncertainty. Is allegory a mode? Is it a genre? What on earth is it?

Unlike vacillating modern theoreticians, the seventeenth-century Spanish dramatist Pedro Calderón de la Barca (1600–1681) seems to know what allegory is (or to think he does, at any rate). Calderón was Spain's premier dramatist of the *auto sacramental,* commonly defined as a one-act allegorical drama intended for performance at the annual Corpus Christi festivities. The *auto's* theme or ostensible subject matter and pretext is the celebration of the Eucharist, and its form is generally personification allegory. Calderón's *autos* deal with Eucharistic doctrine and its significance for man's spiritual life through analogies drawn between sacred history and the realm of human, mundane activities: the world is metaphorized as stage or marketplace or labyrinth, for example; life as pilgrimage or trial; Christ himself is represented as soldier or secular prince; and so forth. The *auto* usually ended with what is termed a "discovery," a ritual disclosure of a host and chalice that merges play into liturgy. Calderón wrote over seventy *autos* in a career that spanned some fifty years (from before 1630 until the writer's death). Of all the many dramatists who worked in this genre, he was inarguably the most successful, as well as the most artistically sophisticated and inventive. Perhaps more importantly, he remains one of the most acute and subtle theoreticians ever to consider the workings and the import of allegorical discourse, that most specialized and esoteric of art forms.

Paradoxically (in view of the statement just made), Calderón left no treatise on allegory; indeed, he produced no single, sustained piece of writing on the subject comparable, say, to Spenser's letter to Raleigh.[4] What he did leave us are dozens of com-

4. See Edmund Spenser, in *The Faerie Queene,* "Letter of the Author expounding his whole intention in the course of this work . . . ," ed. J. C. Smith and E. de Selincourt (London: Oxford University Press, 1970), 407.

ments on allegory scattered throughout his allegorical *autos*. One of the curiosities, and one of the charms, of Calderón's *autos* is the frequency with which the personified characters pause in the midst of their spiritual and theological travails to discourse learnedly, and often at some length, about the definition and nature of allegory, of personification, of rhetorical tropes in general, elucidating volubly as they go.[5] It is by culling from the plays the personifications' *obiter dicta* on allegory, and by analyzing their implications, that the allegorical theory implicit or partially explicit in Calderón's *autos* can be extrapolated and reconstructed.

Despite their brilliance and originality, Calderón's *autos,* and even more his allegorical theory, have never really attracted the critical attention they deserve. The general indifference to Spain among scholars of European literature, and most particularly scholars of European allegory, doubtless explains the *autos'* absence from those critics' work. More surprising is the relative neglect of the Calderonian *auto* among Hispanists (with notable and honorable exceptions).[6] Relatively few *calderonistas*

5. In the edition by Valbuena Prat see, for example, as definitions of allegory, 427 and 1242, and as a definition of personification, 1189. All references are to this edition, Angel Valbuena Prat, *Don Pedro Calderón de la Barca, Obras completas*, vol. 3, *Autos sacramentales*, 2d ed. (Madrid: Aguilar, 1967); page numbers will be indicated within the text at the end of quotations. For the dating of the plays I follow Kurt Reichenberger and Roswitha Reichenberger, eds., *Bibliographisches Handbuch der Calderón-Forschung*, 3 vols. (Kassel: Thiele, 1979).

6. Other general studies of the Calderonian *auto* include Lucien-Paul Thomas, "Les jeux de scène et l'architecture des idées dans le théâtre de Calderón," in *Homenaje ofrecido a Menéndez Pidal*, 2 (Madrid: Hernando, 1925), 501–30; Jutta Wille, *Calderóns Spiel der Erlösung: eine spanische Bilderbibel des 17. Jahrhunderts* (Munich: C. Kaiser, 1932); Sister M. Francis de Sales McGarry, *The Allegorical and Metaphorical Language in the Autos Sacramentales of Calderón* (Washington, DC: The Catholic University of America Press, 1937); Lucy E. Weir, *The Ideas Embodied in the Religious Drama of Calderón* (Lincoln, NE: The University, 1940); Eugenio Frutos, *La filosofía de Calderón en sus Autos Sacramentales* (Saragossa: Institución "Fernando el Católico," 1952); Donald Dietz, "Toward Understanding Calderón's Evolution as an *Auto* Dra-

have studied the dramatist's *autos* within the European contexts and traditions that did so much to shape the plays. Even fewer have studied his theory of allegory, to my mind his major

---

matist: A Study in Dramatic Structure," in *Studies in Honor of Ruth Lee Kennedy,* ed. Vern G. Williamsen and A. F. Michael Atlee (Chapel Hill: Estudios de Hispanófila, 1977), 51–55, "Conflict in Calderón's *Autos Sacramentales,*" in *Approaches to the Theater of Calderón,* ed. Michael D. McGaha (Washington, DC: University Press of America, 1982), 175–86, and "Liturgical and Allegorical Drama: The Uniqueness of Calderón's *Auto Sacramental,*" in *Calderón de la Barca at the Tercentenary: Comparative Views,* ed. Wendell M. Aycock and Sydney P. Cravens (Lubbock: Texas Tech University Press, 1982), 71–88; F. C. Lacosta, "Los autos sacramentales de Pedro Calderón de la Barca," *Archivo hispalense* 42 (1965): 9–26; Bruce W. Wardropper, "The Search for a Dramatic Formula for the *Auto Sacramental,*" *Publications of the Modern Language Association* 65 (1950): 1196–1211; José María Díez Borque, "El auto sacramental calderoniano y su público: Funciones del texto cantado," in Kurt Levy, Jesús Ara, and Gethin Hughes, eds., *Calderón and the Baroque Tradition* (Waterloo: Wilfrid Laurier University Press, 1985), 49–67, "Teatro y fiesta en el barroco español: El auto sacramental de Calderón y su público: Funciones del texto cantado," *Cuadernos hispanoamericanos* 396 (1983): 606–42, and the introduction to *Una fiesta sacramental barroca* (Madrid: Taurus, 1983), 7–120, which contains extensive bibliography; Louise Fothergill-Payne, "The World Picture in Calderón's *Autos sacramentales,*" in Kurt Levy et al., eds., *Calderón and the Baroque Tradition,* 33–40; Julio Rodríguez Puértolas, "La transposición de la realidad en los autos sacramentales de Calderón," in Luciano García Lorenzo, ed., *Calderón: Actas del Congreso internacional sobre Calderón y el teatro español del Siglo de Oro* (Madrid: Consejo Superior de Investigaciones Científicas, 1983), 751–58; Hans Flasche's numerous, magisterial studies, including, for example, "Calderon als 'magister religionis' im Auto Sacramental," in *Sonderdruck aus Europäische Lehrdichtung: Festschrift für Walter Naumann zum 70. Geburtstag* (Darmstadt: Wissenschaftliche Buchgesellschaft, 1981), 143–58; "Die Struktur des Hof-Laudatio in den Loas der *Autos* Calderóns," in August Buch, Georg Kauffmann, Blake Lee Spahr, and Conrad Wiedemann, eds., *Europäische Hofkultur im 16. und 17. Jahrhundert: Vorträge und Referate gehalten anlässlich des Kongresses des Wolfenbütteler Arbeitskreises für Renaissanceforschung und des Internationalen Arbeitskreises für Barockliteratur in der Herzog August Bibliothek Wolfenbüttel vom 4. bis 8. September 1979* (Hamburg: Hauswedell, 1981), 277–86; Kurt Reichenberger, "Calderóns Welttheater und die Autos Sacramentales," in Franz Link and Günter Niggl, eds., *"Theatrum Mundi": Götter, Gott und Spielleiter im Drama von der Antike bis zur Gegenwart* (Berlin: Duncker & Humbolt, 1981), 161–75. On the *auto sacramental* in general, see also Ricardo Arias, *The Spanish Sacramental Plays* (Boston: Twayne Publishers, G. K. Hall, 1980). On Corpus Christi drama in general, see

achievement.[7] It is to address this twofold neglect, and this two-fold audience, that I undertook this work.

The following study does not include all the *autos* Calderón wrote, nor does it take up, obviously, all the issues raised by this most complex corpus of plays.[8] Rather, I concentrate on those *autos* or groups of *autos* that implicitly or explicitly address questions that are important in the traditions of Western allegory, material to Calderón's theory of allegory, or significant for allegorical theory in general.

In Chapter 1, "Defining Allegory: Introduction to *Auto* and Allegory," I consider the *autos* as personification allegory within the conventions of that most maligned, and frequently misunderstood, of modes.[9] I conclude that the Calderonian *auto* far surpasses in complexity and profundity most earlier person-ification allegories and that it challenges as well many of liter-ary theory's most accepted tenets concerning allegorical dis-course. Chapter 2, "Myth and Truth: *Auto* as Allegoresis," is an examination of the mythological *autos,* those plays that allego-

V. A. Kolve, *The Play Called Corpus Christi* (Stanford: Stanford University Press, 1966). The history of criticism and critical approaches to Calderón (primarily, how-ever, as *comediógrafo*) can be reviewed in Manuel Durán and Roberto González Echeverría, *Calderón y la crítica* (Madrid: Gredos, 1976). See also *Critical Essays on the Theatre of Calderón,* ed. Bruce W. Wardropper (New York: New York Univer-sity Press, 1965); Frederick A. de Armas, David M. Gitlitz, and José A. Madrigal, eds., *Critical Perspectives on Calderón de la Barca* (Lincoln, NE: Society of Spanish and Spanish American Studies, 1981); and McGaha, ed., *Approaches to the Theater of Cal-derón.* Studies of individual *autos* will be footnoted throughout the present study.

7. The outstanding exception is the pioneering study by Alexander A. Parker, *The Allegorical Drama of Calderón* (Oxford: Dolphin, 1943).

8. Hispanists will doubtless note my omission of *El gran teatro del mundo*, the best known of the *autos*. The explanation for its absence is simple; I find it overstudied, and perhaps overrated as well.

9. On personification allegory, especially in the Hispanic tradition, see Barbara E. Kurtz, "'With Human Aspect': Studies in European Personification Allegory with Special Reference to the Hispanic Contribution," (Diss., University of Chicago, 1983).

rize classical myth as prefigurative of Christian truth. These *autos,* in explicitly thematizing the divine Word as source and guarantor of pagan myth, as well as of language and illuminated interpretation, embody a powerful allegory of the assumed divine origin and sacral significance of myth and allegory. Chapter 3, "History and Time: *Auto* as Kerygma," concerns the historical *autos,* which typically allegorize events of secular history by contemporizing and individualizing Christian *Heilsgeschichte.* In Calderón's vision, the historical *auto* proclaims, and indeed embodies, the homology of sacred history, national history, contemporaneous event, *auto,* and Eucharist as manifestations of divine providence. In so doing, the historical *auto* converts allegorical drama into kerygma, into contemporary witness to sacred truth. In Chapter 4, " 'In Imagined Space': *Auto* as Spiritual Exercise," I take up the implications of one of Calderón's most explicit, yet paradoxically puzzling, statements concerning his *autos.* In his prologue to the 1677 edition of the plays, Calderón recommends to his public a "composition of place" as imaginative aid in understanding the *autos.* This recommendation, an apparent allusion to the famous Ignatian *compositio loci,* may be an exhortation to true meditative reflection upon the *autos,* to the use of real meditative technique in apprehending and interpreting the plays. This is a hypothesis that, if Calderón's recommendation is viewed in light of contemporaneous theological and aesthetic doctrine concerning the work of art, may adumbrate a virtual paradigm for the cognition of allegorical discourse itself. The Afterword synthesizes the different conceptions of the *auto* presented in a vision of the plays and of Calderón's allegorical theory (or theories) as quasi-sacramental, grounded in an explicit homology of *auto,* allegory, and the Eucharist and an implicit and radical logocentrism.

As we shall see, I trust, Calderón's allegory and its theory is varied, often subtle, always inventive, frequently brilliant. Most provocatively of all, the very fact that these allegories define themselves as allegories and, in fact, define themselves as modes of definition, constitutes a radical, and radically logocentric, vision of the fundamental sacramentalism of allegory as manifested in the *auto sacramental.*

From Calderón's headstrong allegories, there is much to be hoped for, indeed.

Some methodological and theoretical caveats are in order. In the first place, I should hasten to note that the approach adopted to Calderón's allegory and allegorical theory—examination of the characters' theoretical *obiter dicta*—is not ingenuous. Certainly modern literary theory, from New Criticism on, has taught us to guard against the intentional fallacy and has thoroughly inculcated (at least in academic readers) the need to avoid confounding what characters say with what their authors mean. Nevertheless, the approach, however fraught with pitfalls, seems legitimate in the case of the *autos.* The plays' didacticism should largely guarantee the instructional validity and utility of any theoretical excursuses interpolated within the plays; if the *autos* are to fulfill the homiletic, quasi-liturgical role their author envisioned for them, their doctrinal presuppositions must be, one would assume, fairly transparent. Furthermore, Calderón's vision of the *autos'* dramaturgy seems to entail, as will be shown, a profoundly logocentric conception of artistic and specifically allegorical creation, a conception that posits divine intentionality itself as the ultimate source and guarantor of the sacred meaning presumed immanent in these plays. Some of the fuller implications of these problems are considered in Chapter 1 and the Afterword.

In the second place, it must be noted that the varying conceptions of the Calderonian *auto* outlined above are not mutually exclusive. More importantly, none was entirely determinative or configurative of the whole corpus or even, in some cases, of individual plays. In particular, the vision of the *auto* as analogous in certain respects to an Ignatian *compositio* is evident only late, and somewhat sporadically, in the *autos*. The analogy's value for Calderón is primarily, one would suppose, analeptic legitimization of the plays' quasi-liturgical status, and analeptic supposition of a paradigm capable of giving the *autos* theoretical cohesiveness. Its value for us is, I hope, made clear in Chapter 4.

Finally, Calderón's own conception of his *autos* evidently varied. Occasionally, that conception was almost simplistically banal, as when in a moment of didactic reductionism he defines the *auto* perfunctorily as versified sermon.[10] Occasionally, however, and increasingly in the later years of his career, the dramatist's vision is more profound, and more profoundly theological, grounded (as suggested above) in a conception of the *auto* as quasi-sacramental and of allegory as intrinsically numinous.[11]

The *auto sacramental* which Calderón codified with such artistic and theoretical brilliance is intimately connected with Spanish soil and the Catholic Counter-Reformation which found in Spain one of its staunchest defenders.[12] The Spanish provenance of the *autos* notwithstanding, the dramas are closely related to dramatic and allegorical traditions of European diffusion.[13] The *auto*'s remote origin may, indeed, be the

10. Although even in this case, the definition may have some heretofore unrecognized implications. See Ch. 1 of the present study.

11. Chronological considerations, while not ignored in these pages, have not been paramount in shaping the conclusions reached. As a general rule, it can be stated that allusions to and consideration of allegory within the *autos* themselves do increase in frequency, length, and detail over the course of Calderón's career. However, the actual *content* of such theoretical dicta varies considerably less, with exceptions duly noted throughout the present study.

12. On this relationship, see especially Marcel Bataillon, "Essai d'explication de l'auto sacramental," *Bulletin Hispanique* 42 (1940): 193–212. Bataillon also studies the historical development of the pre-Calderonian *auto*. See also "Ensayo de explicación del 'auto sacramental,'" in *Varia lección de clásicos españoles* (Madrid: Gredos, 1964).

13. The question of the origin of the *auto sacramental* is not without controversy. In this exposition I follow Bruce W. Wardropper, *Introducción al teatro religioso del*

medieval morality and the Pastoral mystery plays associated with the Christmas liturgy.[14] These early genres share many of the distinctive features that were later to characterize the *auto sacramental:* scenes from the Old and New Testaments, allegorical figures or universal types, liturgical overtones.

The prototypical *auto* before about 1520 presents the shepherds of the first Christmas Eve, who witness an angel's or other character's exposition of the Incarnation. Around 1520 occurred a milestone of capital importance in the evolution of the *auto sacramental:* the transfer and adaptation of the prototype to the feast of Corpus Christi.[15] The dramatist responsible for this change was probably Hernán López de Yanguas (c. 1470–c. 1540), whose *Farsa sacramental* was probably the first *auto* to adapt Christmas liturgical drama to Eucharistic ends.

From the second half of the sixteenth century dates a collec-

---

Siglo de Oro (Salamanca: Anaya, 1967). For an alternative view, see Jean-Louis Flecniakoska, *La formation de l'"auto" religieux en Espagne avant Calderón* (Montpellier: P. Déhan, 1961). In Wardropper's view it was the Pastoral Christmas play, transformed to realize Eucharistic ends and modified by contemporary dramaturgy, that originated the *auto sacramental*. Flecniakoska, on the other hand, sees the contemporaneous flowering of the secular *comedia* as the preponderant influence on the development of the *auto*. He notes that the *auto* achieved the plenitude of its form at the very moment that the *comedia* also reached its maturity, and he ultimately defines the *auto* as a devout comedia in one act (p. 446). On the origins and evolution of the *auto*, see also A. A. Parker, "Notes on the Origins of the 'Auto Sacramental,'" *Modern Language Review* 30 (1935): 170–82, and the excellent brief overview of problems concerning the issue by Dietz, "Liturgical and Allegorical Drama." Dietz's article is also important in disputing the view, traditional in Calderonian criticism, that the Eucharist is the principal or central theme of all the *autos*; Dietz maintains, on the contrary, that the theme is the divine presence in human history. He also asserts that the *auto sacramental* "originated with Calderón de la Barca because his genius allowed him to wed theology and drama in a creation of a new art form" (80).

14. In Spain, it appears, true examples of the medieval morality were virtually nonexistent. However, shorter, less complex works, what Wardropper calls "pseudomoralities," were relatively common in the later Middle Ages, the product of dramatists such as Gil Vicente and Diego Sánchez de Badajoz.

15. On Corpus Christi, see the bibliography in Wardropper, *Introducción*, 51, and Díez Borque, *Una fiesta sacramental*, 73, nn. 79 and 80.

tion of anonymous religious pieces, among which figure a number of Eucharistic works. The *Códice de autos viejos* consists for the most part of dramatizations of biblical episodes, intended for representation at any ecclesiastical festival, including Corpus Christi.[16] Some thirty works, whose theme is specifically the Eucharistic sacrament, belong exclusively to Corpus Christi. These so-called *farsas del Sacramento* or *farsas sacramentales,* immediate progenitors of the *auto sacramental,* make more extensive use of allegory and intensify the role of dogma.[17]

It was during this half century that the *auto sacramental* began to attain dramatic and theological maturity in the hands of professionals of increasing dramatic talent and allegorical skill. The Valencian Joan Timoneda is generally considered the first professional writer to compose *autos sacramentales.* He wrote five such dramas; three were collected in 1558 in the *Ternario espiritual,* and one additional *auto* appeared in the *Ternario sacramental* of 1575.[18] His works are the key to the transformation of the anonymous *farsa sacramental* into the pre-Calderonian *auto sacramental.* Timoneda sought to refine and regularize Corpus Christi drama; he also expanded the role of allegory and treated theological questions with greater care and subtlety than the authors of the *farsas.*

During the course of the *auto*'s subsequent evolution, a number of contemporaneous events played an influential role. The Council of Trent (1545–1563), which reaffirmed traditional

16. For the *Códice,* see the edition by Léo Rouanet, *Colección de autos, farsas y coloquios del siglo XVI* (Madrid: Biblioteca Hispánica, 1901).

17. Dietz clarifies as follows the relationship among *auto viejo, farsa,* and *auto sacramental*: "[T]he miracle plays in Spain were simply called '*autos*' or '*coloquios,*' whereas the morality-type plays of an allegorical nature were called '*farsas.*' The *auto sacramental,* as it eventually evolved, . . . is really more akin to the '*farsa*' than to the '*auto*' or '*coloquio.*' " See Dietz, "Liturgical and Allegorical Drama," 80.

18. See vol. 58 of the *Biblioteca de Autores Españoles,* ed. Eduardo González Pedroso (Madrid: M. Rivadeneyra, 1865). Timoneda's entire corpus has been edited by Eduardo Juliá Martínez, *Juan de Timoneda, Obras* (Madrid: Sociedad de Bibliófilos Españoles, 1947–48).

doctrine in so many spheres, invested Corpus Christi with new prestige and authority, and it recommended that the festival be celebrated as a manifestation of the triumph of truth over heresy. This new aspect of Corpus Christi—arm of the Counter-Reformation—significantly influenced the development of the *farsa sacramental* in the second half of the sixteenth century.[19] It seems probable that, even if it was not directly responsible for creating the *auto sacramental,* the Tridentine defense of the Mass did tend to endow the genre with its special sacramental and symbolic character.

More problematic is the possible influence of two contemporaneous situations that, in J. L. Flecniakoska's view, contributed to the *auto*'s development: the flourishing of devotional poetry, and the promotion of theater in the colleges of the Jesuits. As Flecniakoska points out, the universe of contemporaneous devotional poetry is much the same as that of the *autos;* in it we find the same didactic and dogmatic preoccupations, and a similar interest in the Eucharist.[20] Although the *auto* certainly did not originate in such religious poetry, some relationship between the two genres does seem probable.

The same could be said as well of the university theater. The Jesuits of the time sponsored dramatic presentations, student compositions actually, which share with the contemporaneous *auto* a frequent basis in sacred history, characters and principal themes, the use of allegory, and didactic, catechistic objectives.[21]

19. Bataillon sees in the *auto* a phenomenon of the Catholic Reformation, which sought to rectify religious life. According to this view, the dramatic pieces were a highly appropriate means of reforming the Corpus Christi festivities. Wardropper and Flecniakoska, on the other hand, deny any direct influence of Tridentine dogmatics on the actual origin of the *auto sacramental,* because the genre began to develop before the promulgation of the Council's decrees. On this point, see also Dietz's discussion, "Liturgical and Allegorical Drama," 75–76.

20. Flecniakoska, Ch. 12.

21. The history and characteristics of the university theater during this period have been studied by Flecniakoska; Justo García Soriano, "El teatro de colegio en

Nevertheless, there is little or no evidence that Calderón directly imitated any of these dramas; as of now, any mutual influence between *auto* and Jesuit theater remains a hypothesis, although a highly probable one, especially given Calderón's close association with the Society.[22]

In the decades of Spain's so-called Golden Age many of the country's leading dramatists—Rojas Zorilla, Lope de Vega, Mira de Amescua, Tirso de Molina[23]—tried their hand at the sacramental dramas, with varying (and usually indifferent) results.[24] Some of the finest *comediógrafos* made the switch from reasonably verisimilar *comedia* to allegorical *auto* with a rather dismal lack of artistic distinction. It was not until Calderón began writing *autos* that the genre reached the plenitude of its dramatic, allegorical, and scenographic potentialities. So successful was Calderón that in 1649 he received from Madrid a monopoly in writing the plays.

España," *Boletín de la Real Academia Española* 14 (1927): 235–77, 374–411, 535–65, 620–50; 15 (1928): 62–93, 145–87, 396–446, 651–69; 16 (1929): 80–106, 223–43; 19 (1932): 485–98, 608–24; I. Elizalde, S.I., "San Ignacio de Loyola y el antiguo teatro jesuítico," *Razón y Fe* 153 (1956): 289–304; Balbino Marcos Villanueva, S.I., *La ascética de los jesuitas en los autos sacramentales de Calderón* (Bilbao: Universidad de Deusto, 1973); and Louise Fothergill-Payne, "The Jesuits as Masters of Rhetoric and Drama," *Revista canadiense de estudios hispánicos* 10 (1986): 375–87. Fothergill-Payne provides additional, valuable bibliography on Jesuit drama, 386, n. 2. See also below, Ch. 4.

22. On Calderón's contacts with the Society, and the possible influence of Jesuit writing on his *autos*, see Ch. 4 of the present study.

23. On these dramatists of the *auto sacramental*, see especially Wardropper. More limited in scope but valuable is Donald Thaddeus Dietz, *The Auto Sacramental and the Parable in Spanish Golden Age Literature* (Chapel Hill: University of North Carolina Dept. of Romance Languages, 1973). See also Kurtz, " 'With Human Aspect,' " Ch. 4.

24. It is a dramatist of the second rank, José de Valdivielso, who wrote perhaps the finest *autos sacramentales* before Calderón. His *Doze autos sacramentales y dos comedias divinas* was published in 1622 and reproduced in vol. 58 of the BAE (1865). The best recent edition is the *Teatro completo*, ed. Ricardo Arias y Arias and Robert V. Piluso (Madrid: Isla, 1975).

For the most part, the *autos* were performed out of doors, on the very carts used to transport the stage machinery.[25] However, throughout the sixteenth century, and especially in the second half, the *auto* became progressively more elaborate in both dramaturgy and stagecraft; stage decor came to be quite splendid, even ostentatious.[26]

The linkage of *auto* and pageantry or spectacle mirrored the *auto*'s growing popularity. Parker points out that "in Valladolid, for example, Calderón's *autos* were regularly performed from 1681 [the year of the playwright's death] to 1765, and not only at Corpus Christi. . . . And public taste demanded the performance of his *autos* during the next eighty years—after these plays had forfeited the esteem of the 'intellectuals'—and would have demanded them for longer still."[27] Praise for the Calderonian *auto* was almost universal among the dramatist's contemporaries.[28]

Nevertheless, this admiration began to fade with the onset in the eighteenth century of different tastes and dramatic norms.[29]

25. This description is an oversimplification of what was in reality an exceedingly and increasingly elaborate scenography. For further detail, see especially N. D. Shergold, *A History of the Spanish Stage from Medieval Times until the End of the Seventeenth Century* (Oxford: Oxford University Press, 1967), 1–112 and 415–504; also Wardropper, Chs. 3–8.

26. "[L]as escenas pintadas en los carros, los efectismos mecánicos, los aderezos escénicos demostraban mucha ingeniosidad y unos esfuerzos tremendos por pasmar al público" ["the scenes painted on the carts, the mechanical stage effects, and the scenic decor demonstrated much ingenuity and a tremendous effort to astonish the audience"] (Wardropper, 66).

27. Parker, 10.

28. Parker quotes a number of the panegyrics common at the time; see, for example, the judgment of Fray Manuel Guerra y Ribera, cited on p. 15.

29. On the history of Calderonian criticism in general, see especially Durán and González Echevarría, *Calderón y la crítica*, 1, 13–123. On the history of the reception of Calderón's theater, see Martin Franzbach, *El teatro de Calderón en Europa* (Madrid: Fundación Universitaria Española, 1982); and the numerous studies by Henry W. Sullivan, "Calderón's Appeal to European Audiences in the Enlightenment and

The neoclassicists were virtually united in their contempt for the *auto* and their denunciation of Calderón as the preeminent writer in the genre.[30] In 1749, Blas Antonio Nasarre attacked the plays as "la interpretación cómica de las Sagradas Escrituras, llena de alegorías y metáforas violentas, de anacronismos horribles; y lo peor es, mezclando y confundiendo lo sagrado con lo profano" ["the comical interpretation of Sacred Scripture, full of violent allegories and metaphors, of horrible anachronisms; and the worst of it is (their) mixture and confusion of sacred and profane."][31] Several years later the director of the Madrid theaters, José Clavijo y Fajardo, would attempt to obtain from the government complete prohibition of the *autos sacramentales*, which he saw as a scandalous profanation of Christianity and Christian values.[32] Clavijo's contemporary Nicolás Moratín denounced the genre more specifically for what he considered the inherent inverisimilitude of its personification allegory:

> ¿Es posible que hable la Primavera? ¿Ha oído usted en su vida una palabra al Apetito? ¿Sabe usted cómo es el metal de la voz de la Rosa? . . . ¿Juzgará nadie posible que se junten a hablar personajes divinos y humanos de muy distintos siglos y diversas naciones, v.gr., la Trinidad Suprema, el demonio, San Pablo, Adán, Jeremías y otros tales, cometiendo horrorosos e insufribles anacronismos?[33]

Romantic Eras: 1738–1838," *Ottawa Hispánica* 5 (1983): 41–58, "Calderón's Reception in Spain during the Romantic Era, 1800–59," *Ottawa Hispánica* 4 (1982): 27–54, "A Select Bibliography of Calderón's Reception in Holland and Germany," *Ottawa Hispánica* 3 (1981): 91–101, and *Calderón in the German Lands and the Low Countries* (Cambridge: Cambridge University Press, 1983).

30. A general overview of the neoclassicists' reactions to Calderón is R. Merritt Cox's "Calderón and the Spanish Neoclassicists," *Romance Notes* 24 (1983): 43–48.

31. Quoted by Parker, 20.

32. "A la verdad parece increíble que una nación tan cristiana pueda ver sin horror profanados los misterios de su religión" ["In truth, it seems incredible that so Christian a nation should tolerate without horror the profanation of the mysteries of its faith."] Quoted by Parker, 21.

33. Quoted by Parker, 24.

Is it possible for Spring to speak? Have you ever in your life heard a word out of Appetite? Do you know the timber of Rose's voice? . . . Could anyone judge it possible to commingle personages divine and human, from different centuries and diverse nations, for example, the Holy Trinity, the devil, St. Paul, Adam, Jeremiah, and so forth? These are horrible, insufferable anachronisms.

The increasing prevalence of such views led Charles III to issue a 1765 decree of prohibition against the *auto sacramental:*

[T]eniendo presente S.M. que los autos sacramentales deben . . . prohibirse, por ser los teatros muy impropios y los comediantes instrumentos indignos y desproporcionados para representar los sagrados misterios de que tratan, se ha servido S.M. de mandar prohibir absolutamente la representación de los autos sacramentales.[34]

Since Your Majesty considers that the *autos sacramentales* ought to be prohibited, for theaters are highly improper for representing their sacred mysteries and actors most unworthy instruments, Your Majesty has seen fit to order the absolute prohibition of performances of the *autos.*

The neoclassical reaction against Calderón met with contrary reevaluation at the hands of the German Romantics,[35] a reexamination that followed the publication in 1865 of the first modern edition of the Calderonian *autos.* The Schlegels, August Wilhelm and Friedrich, were primarily students of the secular *comedia;* however, their enthusiasm for the *autos,* although somewhat overwrought, did help to resuscitate the Spanish dramatist's foundering reputation as allegorist and playwright. The Schlegels, whose prestige and translations helped to diffuse interest in Calderón throughout Europe, also helped to promote the idea, popular (and rather misleading) in subsequent criticism, that Calderón shares with Dante the place and honor of supreme Christian poet.

34. Quoted by Parker, 24.
35. See Parker, 27–28, Durán and González Echevarría, 38–64, and Franzbach, 127–40.

The Romantic approbation of Calderón (Shelley was a notable enthusiast) was unfortunately somewhat ill founded, or at least poorly thought out, swamped in a rather misty excess of ardor and crippled by a shortage of analytical rigor. August Wilhelm Schlegel, for example, found that Calderón could make the universe "glow in purple flames of love."[36] The Romantic poet Joseph Freiherr von Eichendorff, who translated a dozen of the *autos,* likewise cloaked approbation in overheated, somewhat tinny, mysticism.[37] Wagner found Calderón superior to the more "realistic" Shakespeare; Liszt, a model hymn of divine love; and so on.

The Romantics' Calderonian mysticism was, however, only one critical stance in the era's scholarly thought, most of which continued to be hostile to Calderón on grounds both aesthetic and theological.[38] Menéndez y Pelayo, the dominant critic of nineteenth-century Spain, wrote in the centenary year of 1881 that the *auto sacramental* is "una no sé si llamar aberración o excepción estética" ["aberration or aesthetic deviate"].[39] The plays possess, in his opinion, only "toda la frialdad inherente al arte alegórico, la yerta monotonía que comunican siempre al arte las alegorías y las abstracciones" ["all the coldness inherent to alle-

36. Quoted by Parker, 27.
37. See Parker, 55, n. 36.
38. Parker summarizes the dominant critical stance as follows:
    "This nineteenth-century criticism has ... fallen roughly into two schools: the first is the period of romantic exaltation in which critics are swept off their feet by what they thought was a dazzling revelation of a transcendent world; the second in which all the emphasis is on the truth or falsity of Calderón's doctrines, and in which criticism enters into alliance with controversial apologetics. The third school, which flourished in the last thirty years of the century, overlapping well into the twentieth, is characterized mostly by critical preoccupations of a more 'aesthetic' nature and by a theory of literature in which romanticism is superseded by 'realism.' Though the standpoint is different we return to something very close to neo-classical criticism. The whole technical basis of the *autos* is dismissed either as primitive and therefore outmoded or, more commonly, as in fundamental contradiction to the established laws of art." (p. 41)
39. Quoted by Parker, 41–42.

gorical art, all the inert monotony with which allegories and abstractions always infect art"].[40]

Modern restoration of Calderón's dramatic and allegorical reputation can be traced to the work of Angel Valbuena Prat, who wrote his doctoral dissertation on Calderón's *autos* and who produced as well the most available and utilized edition of the plays.[41] His valuable critical labor was followed by A. A. Parker's seminal study of Calderón's allegorical dramaturgy. Parker's work constituted the first truly sensitive appreciation of the plays' allegory and the first historical overview of the varying critical valuations of the corpus.[42] His *Allegorical Drama of Calderón* has remained authoritative to the present day. However, Parker closely analyzes only three of the *autos,* and, of course, his work could not benefit from the critical and theoretical advances in the study of allegory made in the years since it was published. Nonetheless, I am indebted throughout this monograph to Parker's pioneering scholarship and insights. I can only hope to follow the path he first and so ably laid down.

40. Quoted by Parker, 42.

41. See above, n. 7.

42. For additional material on the historical background of the *auto*, see E. Cotarelo y Mori, *Bibliografía de las controversias sobre la licitud del teatro en España* (Madrid: Revista de archivos, bibliotecas y museos, 1904); Carlo Rossi, "Calderón en la polémica del XVIII sobre los 'autos sacramentales,'" and "Calderón en la crítica española del XVIII," in *Estudios sobre las letras en el siglo XVIII* (Madrid: Gredos, 1967), 9–40 and 41–96, respectively; Juan Manuel Rozas, "La licitud del teatro y otras cuestiones literarias en Bances Candamo, escritor límite," *Segismundo* 1 (1965): 247–74; Ramón Torres Esquer, "Las prohibiciones de comedias y autos sacramentales en el siglo XVII," *Segismundo* 2 (1965): 187–226; Edward M. Wilson, "Nuevos documentos sobre las controversias teatrales: 1650–1681," in *Actas del Segundo Congreso de la Asociación Internacional de Hispanistas* (Nijmegen: University of Nijmegen Press, 1967), 155–70; N. D. Shergold and J. E. Varey, *Los autos sacramentales en Madrid en la época de Calderón, 1637–1681: estudios y documentos* (Madrid: Ediciones de Historia, Geografía y Arte, 1961); and Ansgar Hillach, "El auto sacramental calderoniano considerado en un relieve histórico-filosófico," *Hacia Calderón, Quinto Coloquio Anglogermano, Oxford 1978,* ed. Hans Flasche and Robert D. F. Pring-Mill (Wiesbaden: Franz Steiner Verlag GMBH, 1982), 20–29.

The intended (perhaps hoped-for) audience for this study has dictated some of the expository and editorial choices made. In the first place, I have often reflected while preparing this work that in literary criticism as in politics one cannot hope to please all or even some of the people all of the time. To aim at a varied audience of disparate interests and specialties, I have made what I feel are necessary compromises. Scholars familiar with the critical literature on allegory may find the theoretical discussion occasionally obvious; Hispanists will already know much if not all the background material on the *auto sacramental* in general and Calderón's *autos* in particular. Of both communities I would request temporary indulgence at those moments when discussion finds its way onto their own scholarly terrain.

In the second place, my desire to bring Calderón's *autos* and allegorical theory as wide a public as possible necessitated translation of all quotations. That task proved a daunting one, since the playwright's Spanish is often formidably (and sometimes deliberately) difficult. Prudence being the better part of translation as well as of valor, I opted in almost every case, although with frequent regret, for literal accuracy rather than poetic justice to the original. I can only hope that fidelity and clarity can compensate somewhat for the losses inevitable with such a choice.

Finally, I should like to acknowledge the encouragement that friends and colleagues have offered at every stage of this project. In particular, I thank Ruth House Webber and George Haley, professors and friends during my graduate student days at the University of Chicago. To their patience with my earliest attempts to work with allegory, and to their kindly interest and support throughout my professional career, I owe more than I can ever express, much less repay. To them I dedicate this book in deepest gratitude.

1. Defining Allegory
Introduction to *Auto* and Allegory

. . . soy
. . . .
docta Alegoría . . .
  (Prologue to *El sacro Parnaso,* 1659)

Allegorists, as a breed, are notable for many moral and ethical qualities and much literary virtue; modesty, however, is not typically one of them. Jean de Meun, for example, writes of his *Roman de la Rose* that "[l]a matire en est bele et noive."[1] Edmund Spenser, in his famous letter to Sir Walter Raleigh "expounding his whole intention in the course of this worke,"[2] confidently asserts that the "conceit" of the *Faerie Queene,* which might seem "tedious and confused,"[3] actually "giueth great light to the Reader."[4] John Bunyan is perhaps the most sanguine of all, reiterating over and over again the value and profit to be derived from his "little book,"[5] maintaining rather grandiosely that he "[s]eek[s] the advance of Truth,"[6] and comparing his

1. Guillaume de Lorris and Jean de Meun, *Le Roman de la Rose,* ed. Daniel Poirion (Paris: Garnier-Flammarion, 1974), v. 39: p. 44.

2. Edmund Spenser, "Letter of the Authors. . . ," in *Poetical Works,* ed. J. C. Smith and E. de Selincourt (London: Oxford University Press, 1970), 407.

3. Spenser, 408.

4. Spenser, 407.

5. John Bunyan, *The Pilgrim's Progress,* ed. Roger Sharrock (Middlesex, England: Penguin Books, 1965), 33.

6. Bunyan, 35.

style and method to the "types, shadows and metaphors," the "Dark figures, allegories"[7] of Scripture itself.

Jean de Meun, Spenser, and Bunyan write of their allegories with rather lofty self-assertion, even magniloquence. However, the pretension is more apparent than real. The allegorist, typical didact, is commonly at some pains to elucidate his goals in part because he may thus help ensure their attainment. In affirming the value of their allegories, such writers merely confer upon their writing proleptic confirmation of the edifying effect they hope to have on the audience.

Like these (and other) allegorists, Calderón composed a statement of purpose, which hints at a similar apologetic note: "[S]i en lo dicho o por decir hubiere una sola voz que disuene a la pureza de la fe a al decoro de las buenas costumbres, desde luego, la delato, la detesto y la retracto, y de ella pido el perdón y a ti la enmienda" (42); ("[I]f in what has been said or may be said in the future there should be a single word inconsistent with purity of faith and the decorum of seemly custom, I denounce it, I abominate it, and I retract it; and I ask pardon for it, and request that you [the reader] amend it.")[8]

Although Calderón affirms his *autos'* religious orthodoxy and moral propriety, at least as partially achieved *desiderata,* he is otherwise refreshingly self-effacing, even tentative, in advancing claims of value and efficacy for his work. He admits to hesitancy in publishing "these poorly polished drafts" ("estos mal limados borradores" [41]); acknowledges that some of their passages may be "tepid" ("Parecerán tibios algunos trozos . . ." [42]); and, most interestingly, cordially invites the public's imaginative and even editorial collaboration in the plays:

> [E]l papel no puede dar de sí ni lo sonoro de la música, ni lo aparatoso de las tramoyas, y si ya no es que el que lea haga en su

7. Bunyan, 34.

8. The statement appears in the prologue Calderón prepared for the printed edition of the *autos.*

> imaginación composición de lugares, considerando lo que sería sin entero juicio de lo que es . . .
>
> Si a ti se te ofrecen otras [objeciones], te suplico me las adviertas para que en la segunda parte o las satisfaga o las obedezca. . . . (42)

> Paper can convey neither the sonority of the music nor the splendor and ingenuity of the stagecraft. So the reader should make in his imagination a composition of place. . . . If other objections occur to you, I beseech you to warn me of them so that I may satisfy or respond to them in the second part [of the printed plays].

The audience, he suggests, is welcome to make any emendations needed to realize fully the *autos'* dramatic and theological import.

Calderón's elevation of the *autos'* public to "authorial" status partly reflects the genre's occasional pretext. The *auto's* quasi-liturgical role, its devotional exaltation of the Eucharist, gives the play something of the ceremonial and cultic function of Communion itself; by extension, it confers upon the audience a participatory role analogous to that of the congregant or communicant.[9]

All of which is to say, quite simply, that the *autos* are as much religious ritual as literature. Calderón implicitly acknowledges this ritualism by calling attention to the repetitiveness of the *autos'* allegorical "medios," their devices or resources: "[S]iendo siempre uno mismo el asunto, es fuerza caminar a su fin con unos mismos medios, mayormente si se entra en consideración de que estos mismos medios, tantas veces repetidos, siempre van a diferente fin en su argumento" ("[S]ince the subject matter is always the same, it is necessary to fulfill its objectives through the same means; all the more so in view of the fact that these means, so often repeated, always tend toward a different end in their development within the plot") (42). The individual plays merely ring dramatic changes upon a single sacramental,

---

9. For the fuller theological and literary implications of this relationship between sacrament and *auto,* see Ch. 4 and the Afterword of the present study.

Christological theme, using various dramatic *argumentos,* or plot lines, to allegorize the same Eucharistic *asunto.* The musical analogy I utilize here is not gratuitous; Calderón himself states that parallel passages in the *autos* are not so much "repeated" as "attuned" or "harmonized" ("no como repetidos, sino acordados" [42]), the dominant in this sacramental and dramatic harmony being the Eucharist, the *auto*'s pretext and justification. In the "discovery" of the host and chalice, which triumphally concluded most *autos sacramentales,* the Eucharist gave the play its dramatic coda as well.

The implications of Calderón's prefatory remarks are far-reaching (and will be discussed more fully in later chapters). At the moment it may suffice to point out that the liturgical function makes the *auto sacramental* profoundly difficult, even alien, for the modern (and probably thoroughly secularized) reader. It was the intimate, essential connection between *auto* and liturgy that attracted the obloquy of early commentators;[10] it is probably responsible as well, at least in part, for the critical neglect from which the *auto* still suffers today.

If emotional sympathy for the *autos'* theological context and issues may elude the average twentieth-century reader, intellectual approximation to the texts should still be attainable; for numerous aspects of Calderón's *autos* reflect well-known, well-studied traditions of personification allegory.

To represent or describe his personifications, Calderón frequently exploits the conventionalized devices of medieval personification in relatively straightforward fashion. The early *El gran duque de Gandía* (1639?)[11] incorporates a traditional alle-

10. See Alexander A. Parker, *The Allegorical Drama of Calderón* (Oxford: Dolphin, 1943), Ch. 1, "The Autos and Their Early Critics" and the discussion in the Introduction to the present study.

11. The date given is Valbuena Prat's. Reichenberger does not include the play in his dating of the *autos.*

gory of the four seasons,[12] each of whom is described in terms of representative symbols: Winter appears with "un vidrio de agua" ["a glass of water"], Spring with "un azafate de flores" ["a bouquet of flowers"], Summer with "espigas" ["spikes of wheat"], Autumn with "manzanas" ["apples"] (104). Most of the personifications of *No hay más fortuna que Dios* (1652–53) likewise bear emblems or insignias that characterize their social stations: Power, a crown of laurels and a scepter; Farming, a hoe; Beauty, a mirror; Discretion, a book; Soldiery, a sword; Poverty, a staff.[13] Elsewhere, Calderón links his personifications in those familial galaxies or genealogies so characteristic of medieval tradition.[14] In *Lo que va del hombre a Dios* (1652?–

12. On this tradition, see Eugenio Asensio, "El *Auto dos quatro tempos* de Gil Vicente," *Revista de filología española* 33 (1949): 350–70 and L. Biadene, " 'Carmina de Mensibus' di Bonvesin de la Riva," *Studi di filologia romanza* 4 (1903): 1–130.

13. Such characterizing symbols or representative insignia accompany innumerable medieval personifications—for example, Boethius's Lady Philosophy:

> Her dress was made of very fine, imperishable thread,
> of delicate workmanship: she herself wove it, as I
> learned later, for she told me. Its form was shrouded
> by a kind of darkness of forgotten years, like a smoke-
> blackened family statue in the atrium. On its lower
> border was woven the Greek letter Π, and on the upper,
> Θ, and between the two letters steps were marked like
> a ladder, by which one might climb from the lower
> letter to the higher. . . . In her right hand she
> carried a book, and in her left, a sceptre.

Boethius, *Tracts and De Consolatione Philosophiae*, trans. H. F. Stewart and E. K. Rand, rev. S. J. Tester (Cambridge: Harvard University Press, 1973), 133–35. On the use of this descriptive convention in medieval allegory, see Barbara E. Kurtz, " 'With Human Aspect': Studies in European Personification Allegory with Special Reference to the Hispanic Contribution" (Diss., University of Chicago, 1983), especially Ch. 1, "The people of personification allegory: figurative portraiture."

14. Cf., for example, the *Avaritia*'s baneful entourage in Prudentius's *Psychomachia*:

> Care, Hunger, Fear, Anguish, Perjuries, Pallor, Corruption, Treachery,
> Falsehood, Sleeplessness, Meanness, diverse fiends, go in attendance on the mon-

57?), for example, Nature is the wife of Man; their offspring, she says, are Self-Love and Life (276).

Despite the medieval cast of such figures and their depiction, and despite their more or less denotative or deictic character, most of Calderón's personifications far surpass the simplicities of standard allegorical practice. Indeed, the most complex of them possess a multiplicity of meanings rare in the generally more limited figures of medieval personification allegory. Moon in *El verdadero Dios Pan* (1670), to cite a prominent example, is at one and the same time the personified Moon, Diana, Proserpina, and the human soul, whereas the titular "Pan" is the pagan deity, the Good Shepherd of scriptural parable, and the transubstantiated "pan" or bread of the Eucharist.

Perhaps the outstanding example of such multivalency is Culpa (Sin or Guilt).[15] The character's primary meaning is the natural, expected one: mankind's original sin.[16] But the figure frequently takes on the subsidiary meaning of *culpa actual,* or the particular sins of the individual.[17] This much is straightforward and unsurprising. More intriguing are the links Calderón establishes between this incarnation of sin and such figures as Death[18] and, most significantly of all, the Devil himself.[19]

---

ster; and all the while Crimes, the brood of their mother Greed's black milk, like ravening wolves go prowling and leaping over the field.
Prudentius, ed. and trans. H. J. Thomson (Cambridge: Harvard University Press, 1949), 311.

15. Because the acceptation of Culpa as proper noun, as personified figure, is not univocal, hence not accurately translatable, the Spanish name will be used throughout this study. On the figure's varied meanings, see below.

16. Cf., for example, *El pleito matrimonial del cuerpo y el alma,* in which Pecado, or sin, one of Culpa's alter egos, states, "Yo soy la culpa primera" (79). Cf. also *La segunda esposa y triunfar muriendo, El año santo en Madrid, Las órdenes militares, Tu prójimo como a ti, La nave del mercader, El jardín de Falerina.*

17. Cf., for example, *La segunda esposa y triunfar muriendo* (446).

18. Cf., for example, *La segunda esposa y triunfar muriendo* (431).

19. Cf., for example, *Lo que va del hombre a Dios.* Angel L. Cilveti has very ably studied the complex relationship among all these figures in *El demonio en el teatro de*

The identification of Sin and the Devil is traditional, deriving ultimately from St. Paul and culminating in the Fathers, especially St. Athanasius.[20] Other elements of Calderón's treatment are also conventional, traceable in the apocalyptic current that was transmitted to medieval Christianity principally by Gregory of Nyssa.[21] In numerous *autos* Calderón identifies Culpa with the dragon of Rev. 12:9.[22] In still others he introduces details of popular religious provenance. For example, he frequently describes his Sin-Devil as possessing the face of a woman, a tradition that has no scriptural basis but that apparently derives from popular demonology.[23]

Most interesting of all in Calderón's Culpa is the strongly Manicheistic bent of the conception. In a number of *autos,* Culpa is the antagonist of Grace; this contrast or conflict suggests that the adversaries represent immanent cosmic forces, contending powers of evil and darkness on the one hand and goodness and light on the other.

Although the extent and depth of the dramatist's Manicheism has been, and seems likely to remain, the source of some controversy,[24] the presence of uncomfortably heterodox views

Calderón (Javea, Valencia: Albatros, 1977). On Calderón's Devil, see also E. F. Keating, "El diablo en Calderón de la Barca y John Milton," *Cuadernos hispánicos* 333 (1978): 417–34.

20. See Cilveti, 179.

21. See Cilveti, 169.

22. Cf., for example, *El año santo en Madrid, El valle de la zarzuela, El jardín de Falerina, A María el corazón, La nave del mercader.*

23. See Maximilian Rudwin, *The Devil in Legend and Literature* (La Salle, IL: Open Court Publishing, 1931), 52–53, 232–34, 311.

24. A. A. Parker, for example, asserts that Manicheistic leanings are a characteristic "defect" of the *autos* of Calderón's youth, whereas in his mature works the dramatist avoided this highly unorthodox dualism. See Parker, "The Devil in the Drama of Calderón," in *Critical Essays on the Theatre of Calderón,"* ed. Bruce W. Wardropper (New York: New York University Press, 1965), 3–23. Cilveti convincingly refutes this view, maintaining that "la sugerencia del dualismo maniqueo aparece en los autos tempranos y en los más tardíos" (21–22).

in this apparently most Catholic of writers is undeniable. Nowhere are these Manicheistic tendencies more evident than in
La vida es sueño (1673), where Shadow (one of Culpa's alter
egos) provides a revealing self-portrait:

> símbolo a la Luz harán
> de Gracia, de Culpa a mí.
> Mira si con causa aquí
> místicos sentidos dan
> a mis rencores disculpas;
> pues la Luz, por mi desgracia,
> será imagen de la Gracia,
> y la Sombra, de la Culpa.   (1393)

> Light will be made symbol of Grace, I, symbol of Sin. See if
> mystical meanings don't with good reason excuse my rancor, since
> Light, to my misfortune, will be the image of Grace, and Shadow,
> the image of Sin.

Culpa is both symbol of sin and principle of darkness in eternal
opposition to the light of Grace.

Culpa's complexity, in theological heterodoxy and eclecti-
cism as well as allegorical richness, far exceeds that of most,
generally univocal, medieval personifications. The conflated
ingredients of varying origin make the Calderonian Culpa
polysemous, a metaphor for the nature and source of sin.[25]

In his personifications the dramatist inventively merges old
and new, allegorical convention and often highly original inno-
vation. A similar range distinguishes the *autos*' varied plot lines.
Many of the Calderonian *autos* are based on Christian allegory's

25. Calderón's conception of sin is ultimately Thomistic, as Parker and, most re-
cently, Cilveti have pointed out with a wealth of documentation. Scholastic doctrine
concerning the potentiality of sin in man and the devil's indirect influence on the individual's commission of sin found in the seventeenth-century dramatist one of its
best expositors. Calderón's linkage of Sin and Devil makes vivid dramatic capital out
of concepts that in his theological precursors take the form of abstruse doctrinal ru-
minations.

very oldest themes. The early *El pleito matrimonial del cuerpo y el alma* (before 1651), for example, takes up the competition between matter and spirit, commonly treated in the Middle Ages as the debate of Soul and Body.[26] Calderón skillfully, and humorously, transforms the traditional conflict by bringing it into the divorce court, where Soul, weary of Body's endless carousing, attempts to break off the ill-formed union. Other *autos*— for example, *El gran mercado del mundo* (1634–35?), *Los encantos de la Culpa* (before 1647), *El año santo de Roma* (1650), *El año santo en Madrid* (1652), *A María el corazón* (1664), *Tu prójimo como a ti* (1656?), and *La nave del mercader* (1674)—utilize the

---

26. On this *auto,* see especially *El pleito matrimonial del cuerpo y el alma,* ed. Manfred Engelbert (Hamburg: Cram, de Gruyter, 1969). The bibliography on medieval debate literature is seemingly inexhaustible. For general background, see Pierre Le Gentil, *La Poésie lyrique espagnole et portugaise à la fin du Moyen Age,* in two vols. (Rennes: Plihon, 1949–53), *passim,* and F. J. E. Raby, *A History of Secular Latin Poetry in the Middle Ages,* in two vols., 2nd ed. (Oxford: Oxford University Press, 1953), *passim.* The magisterial study of medieval debate literature is Hans Walther, *Das Streitgedicht in der lateinischen Literatur des Mittelalters, Quellen und Untersuchungen zur lateinischen Philologie des Mittelalters,* vol. 5, pt. 2 (Munich: Beck, 1920). See also David Lampe, "Middle English Debate Poems: A Genre Study" (Diss., University of Nebraska, 1969), 93–110; M. C. Waites, "Some Aspects of the Ancient Allegorical Debate," *Studies in English and Comparative Literature* (Radcliffe College Monographs, no. 15; London and Boston, 1910); Angus Fletcher, *Allegory* (Ithaca: Cornell University Press, 1964), 157–58. On the medieval Hispanic tradition, especially in relation to European precursors and influence, see A. D. Deyermond, *A Literary History of Spain: The Middle Ages* (London: Ernest Benn, 1971), especially pp. 72–76 and 188–90; Deyermond provides extensive bibliographies on specific traditions, such as the debate between body and soul; John G. Cummins, "Methods and Conventions in the 15th-Century Poetic Debate," *Hispanic Review* 31 (1963): 307–23, and "The Survival in the Spanish *Cancioneros* of the Form and Themes of Provençal and Old French Poetic Debates," *Bulletin of Hispanic Studies* 42 (1965): 9–17. Medieval Spanish letters possess a number of examples of the European tradition of the body-soul debate, among them the *Disputa del alma y el cuerpo* (which survives in incomplete form in a manuscript of the early thirteenth century), two versions of an *arte mayor* poem (the *Disputa del cuerpo e del ánima* and the fourteenth-century *Revelación de un ermitaño*), and the late fifteenth-century *Tractado del cuerpo e de la ánima.* See Deyermond, 73 and 189 and the bibliography he includes.

topic of life as pilgrimage or journey[27]; others—*El valle de la zarzuela* (1647 or 1648), *El verdadero Dios Pan* (1670), and *La vida es sueño* (1673), which contains a battle of personified Virtues and Vices—the topic of the individual sinner's divided will or *bellum intestinum*.[28] Still other *autos,* for example, *La Hidalga del valle* (1640), reflect that Marian devotion which was, of course, one of the most significant medieval contributions to Christian tradition.

The conventional qualities of such plays notwithstanding, the hallmark of most of the finest Calderónian *autos* is not their traditionalism, but rather their merging of traditional themes with topical, occasional allusions to contemporaneous history and current events. Such circumstantial references update and freshen devices grown somewhat hackneyed over centuries of practice; topicality contemporizes both the commonplaces of personification allegory and the Christian doctrine that those commonplaces allegorize.

The *autos* based on the *peregrinatio vitae*[29] typify this blending of convention and contemporization. As a traditional allegory of human existence, the *peregrinatio* originated in metaphors used by the patristic exegetes, who considered the journey of Israel's children to the Promised Land a symbol of man's passage from terrestrial life to the eternal.[30] Pilgrimage allegories were,

27. On the notion of the *peregrinatio vitae,* see especially Juergen H. Hahn, *The Origins of the Baroque Idea of 'Peregrinatio'* (Chapel Hill: University of North Carolina Press, 1973) and Samuel Chew, *The Pilgrimage of Life* (New Haven: Yale University Press, 1962). On the related motif of the quest or progress, see also Fletcher, 151–57.

28. On the theme of the *bellum intestinum,* see also Aurora Egido, *La fábrica de un auto sacramental: "Los encantos de la Culpa"* (Salamanca: Ediciones Universidad de Salamanca, 1982), 117–33.

29. A number of these *autos* are discussed in Ch. 3 of the present study.

30. Cf. Heb. 11:13–16; I Pet. 2:11. See D. W. Robertson's discussion, *A Preface to Chaucer* (Princeton: Princeton University Press, 1962), 351. The conception was significant as well for the Stoics. Marcus Aurelius, for example, writes "[L]ife is a

of course, frequent in the Middle Ages—for example, Degui-leville's *Pèlerinage de la Vie humaine,* Rutebeuf's *Voie de Paradis,* similar *Voies* by Baudouin de Condé, Jehan de la Mote, and Raoul de Houdenc, and, obviously to a limited extent, the *Commedia* and *Piers Plowman.* And in Calderón's corpus as well the hoary metaphor informs a number of the plays.[31]

In *El año santo en Madrid* (1652), for example, Man's nature is defined by the seminal metaphor of the pilgrimage along life's road:

> Aunque la eslavina trueque
> al cortesano vestido,
> no por eso el Hombre deja
> de ser siempre peregrino,
> pues es la vida un camino,
> que al nacer empezamos,
> y al vivir proseguimos,
> y aun no tiene su fin, cuando morimos.   (542)

Although he may exchange his cape for courtly garb, Man nonetheless is still a pilgrim always; for life is a roadway we begin when born and follow while alive; and it does not yet reach its end when we die.

Compelled to follow "las torcidas sendas de este humano labe-rinto" ["the twisted pathways of this human labyrinth"] (540), Man must choose to sojourn in one of two courts, that of the World or that of the Church. The dramatization of this choice materializes the traditional *bellum intestinum,* a theme whose roots in Christian allegorical literature extend to the *Psychomachia.*[32]

---

warfare and a stranger's sojourn." *Meditations,* ed. T. V. Smith, in *From Aristotle to Plotinus* (Chicago: University of Chicago Press, 1934), 241.

31. On this theme in Calderón's *autos,* see Egido, 117–33.

32. On the legacy of the *Psychomachia* in medieval Renaissance Spanish allegory, see especially Louise Fothergill-Payne, "Doble historia de la alegoría (unas observaciones generales sobre el modo alegórico en la literatura del Siglo de Oro," in *Actas*

Even in this early, and admittedly inferior, *auto* we can glimpse Calderón's native power as an allegorist. The play contains numerous allusions to Madrid's celebration of the titular holy year, and Calderón melds topical references, dramatic amplification of the traditional pilgrimage metaphor, and the allegorical theme of the *bellum intestinum*. He thereby achieves a dramatic polysemy that prefigures the dramatic and allegorical intricacy of his mature work.[33]

During the plenitude of his career, Calderón took up the pilgrimage motif with perhaps the greatest theological profundity and allegorical ingenuity. In *A María el corazón* (1664), the personified Vices dance and sing of the delights of worldly pleasure, while the protagonist Pilgrim is locked in struggle with his Thought over the moral path to be chosen in life. The diabolic pair of Culpa and Furor, hidden witnesses to the scene, make explicit the nature of this conflict:

CULPA: Con su Pensamiento anda
      luchando a brazo partido.
FUROR: Oye, que esa es la batalla
      del hombre y su Pensamiento.   (1139)

CULPA: There he goes, fighting tooth
      and nail with his Thought.
FUROR: Listen, that is the battle—hand to
      hand, with all one's might—of
      man and his Thought."

The entire episode, a *psychomachia* in miniature, is set within the dramatic-allegorical context of a pilgrimage to the shrine of Loreto, a journey during which the Vices, in the guise of bandits, ambush and waylay Pilgrim and attempt to divert him from his goal.

---

del Sexto Congreso Internacional de Hispanistas, ed. Alan M. Gordon and Evelyn Rugg (Toronto: Dept. of Spanish and Portuguese, University of Toronto, 1980), 261–64.

33. For more on *El año santo en Madrid,* see below, Ch. 3.

In *A María el corazón* Calderón combines the conventional Christian metaphors of the *peregrinatio vitae* and the *bellum intestinum* with a historically based pilgrimage to a traditional Christian shrine; and with his bandit Vices he weaves into his allegorical design a topical allusion to a vexing contemporary problem, the Spanish plague of *bandolerismo* or banditry.[34]

A somewhat similar scheme informs *Tu prójimo como a ti* (1656?),[35] a late *auto* based on the parable of the Good Samaritan (Luke 10:30–35). Here the victim attacked and robbed by thieves becomes Mankind in general, besieged by the soul's enemies (a bandit Culpa and his diabolic henchmen, World, Devil, and Lasciviousness). Jerusalem becomes the celestial City of God; the priest and the Levite, the priesthood and the ministry of the Old Testament, respectively; the inn to which the Samaritan bears Mankind, the Church; and the Samaritan himself, Christ the Redeemer.

The parable intrinsically suggests parallels to the metaphor of life's pilgrimage—the besetting hazards of the road, encounters with fellow travelers, ambush and rescue—and Calderón strengthens the links between parable and topos by multiplying within the *auto*'s overall scriptural schema pertinent allusions to the pilgrimage metaphor.[36] Furthermore, the connotations of

34. See J. H. Elliott, *Imperial Spain: 1469–1716* (New York: New American Library, 1963), 328, 330, 364.

35. There is a critical edition of this *auto*: Mary Lorene Thomas, ed., "A Critical Edition of Pedro Calderón de la Barca's *Tu prójimo como a ti*" (Diss., University of Michigan, 1984). On this *auto*, see also Donald Thaddeus Dietz, *The Auto Sacramental and the Parable in Spanish Golden Age Literature* (Chapel Hill: University of North Carolina Dept. of Romance Languages, 1973), 68–73.

36. See, for example, "CULPA: Amigos, / al valle, al valle, y venciendo / los intricados caminos / de la humana vida, que es / un confuso laberinto, / todas sus sendas tomad" ["Friends, (let us descend) into the valley, the valley and, traversing the intricate paths of human life, a confused labyrinth, take all its pathways"] (1411); "CULPA: Ya habéis visto . . . / . . . / cómo es el Hombre viador, / cómo es la vida camino" ["You have already seen that Man is a sojourner, and life a roadway"] (1415). The omnipres-

the *auto*'s seminal analogy elicit natural associations with another scriptural metaphor: the two paths between which man must choose his moral life, the broad way that leads to destruction or the narrow way that leads to life and salvation (Matt. 7:13–14).[37] In the *auto,* Man and his Desire, having reached a crossroads, encounter one path covered with thistles and thorns and the other with roses and carnations. Each of the paths leads to a city—Jericho or Jerusalem—which analogically symbolizes, even in geographical or topographical situation, the roadway's moral referent:

> . . . Jerusalén, ciudad
> de Dios . . .
> . . . .
> es, como muchos han dicho,
> aquella primera patria
> de quien desterrado hijo
> ha salido; Jericó
> . . . .
>   es
> el centro donde afligido
> ha de parar; bien lo explican
> el uno y el otro sitio,
> pues uno eminente,
> pues otro sumiso,
> quien va de uno a otro
> va a su precipicio.   (1418)

Jerusalem, city of God, is, as many have said, that first native land from which her son has been exiled. Jericho is the center where the afflicted exile will come to rest. The city sites themselves

---

ence in Calderón's day of the Inquisitorial trial undoubtedly reinforced the motif's suggestiveness and pertinence.

37. On this metaphor, see especially Erwin Panofsky, *Hercules am Scheidewege und andere antike Bildstoffe in der neuren Kunst,* Studien der Bibliotek Warburg, vol. 18 (Leipzig-Berlin: B. G. Teubner, 1930) and Theodore Mommsen, "Petrarch and the Story of the Choice of Hercules," *Medieval and Renaissance Studies,* ed. E. Rice (Ithaca: Cornell University Press, 1959), 175–96.

explain the difference well. Since one is eminently set on high, the other submissively laid low, anyone who goes from the one to the other heads for a certain fall.

The two metaphorized, antagonistic cities of *Tu prójimo* echo Augustine's figurative analogues, which materialize contrastive moral options: spirit vs. flesh, charity vs. cupidity, God vs. world. Jerusalem, "city of God," is in Calderón's *auto* the "first native land" from which man has been exiled. Jericho is the center of affliction where the exile has come to rest, like a stone tumbling from an eminence to a lowly precipice. Desire, not unexpectedly, wants to follow the easier route to Jericho, and Man, after some vacillation, yields to this wish.

In *Tu prójimo* Calderón displays the allusive power of his mature allegorical art. He takes the *auto*'s dramatic nucleus from the biblical parable, but he amplifies his source's figurative possibilities with other, readily applicable biblical allusions—the metaphors of the pilgrimage and the two paths—that suggest additional plot ramifications. He deepens the play's theological resonance by linking the central metaphors to key Augustinian ideas. And he includes topical allusions, references to brigandage, which can be naturally related to the allegorical schema and used to enhance the audience's identification with its problems.

A similar nexus of allusions informs *La nave del mercader* (1674). Once again the traditional pilgrimage metaphor is the nucleus of the allegory. Man describes himself as "stranger" and "pilgrim" on a lonely sojourn to see the world: "Soy / un peregrino extranjero, / que voy a solo ver mundo, / y he visto harto en un momento" ["I am a stranger and a pilgrim who is going to see the world, and I have seen much in but a moment"] (1457). Life is a "confused labyrinth"[38] of "intricate roads" and

---

38. On the topos of life or the world as labyrinth, see Geoffrey Michael Voght's bibliography in "The Mythological *Autos* of Calderón de la Barca" (Diss., University of Michigan, 1974), 347, n. 8 and 350, n. 12.

unknown destiny: "los intricados caminos / de la humana vida, que es / un confuso laberinto" (1445).

Life's mazelike roads, as in *Tu prójimo,* suggest the scriptural metaphor of divergent pathways that materialize humanity's perennial moral dilemma. Man, at a crossroads, hesitates before the road that seems to him nothing but "abrojos, / cambrones, zarzas y espinos" ["rough and craggy brambles"]; he much prefers the "roses, carnations, and lilies" with which the other route tempts him (1449). The Merchant (Christ[39]) hints that appearances are deceptive; the thorny, apparently unwelcoming path may in fact lead to ". . . un ameno sitio, / dulce emulación hermosa / del vergel del paraíso" ["a pleasant site, agreeable, beauteous similitude of the pleasance of Paradise"]; the other, superficially so lovely, ends in the "despeño / de algún fatal precipicio" [the "declivity of some fatal precipice"] (1449). Man debates these alternatives in soliloquy. Initially, he is captivated by the "[m]ás apacible camino" ["more pleasant road"] (1455), which seems to promise the easier journey. The moral and mortal peril this choice entails is mitigated only by the Merchant, whose ship "cargada / de trigo" ["full of wheat"] (1469) (an allusion to the Eucharist), delivers Man from danger.

The seminal metaphor of this *auto* and its title derives from Prov. 31:14: "Facta et quasi navis institoris, / De longe portans panem suum." The scriptural allusion is, however, interwoven with a topical allusion: the highly perilous voyages to the New World, considered here a ". . . nuevo cielo, según / fértil, abundante y rico" [a "new heaven, . . . fertile, abundant, and rich."] A pun is the logical basis for or rationalization of the comparison, since the Empire in another light can also be seen as empyrean: "se deja antever en místico estilo, / con sombras de imperio, a luces de impireo" (1448). In *La nave del mercader* Calderón

39. The basis of the metaphor of Christ as Merchant is scriptural (Matt. 13:44–46).

equates paradise and New World, pilgimage and voyage, Merchant's ship and mercantilist vessel, and he thus analogizes sacral and quotidian or contemporary realms.

The contemporization of theological and literary traditions through occasional allusion, characteristic of Calderón's finest pilgrimage allegories, also informs those *autos* based on the allegorical lawsuit or court of law in which man is brought before divine justice.[40] The Last Judgment promised in the Bible had been an inexhaustible source of inspiration for Western writers throughout the Middle Ages.[41] Numerous medieval *autos* allegorize the Judgment through the metaphor of a tribunal or trial, with all the standard legal personnel and lexicon—defendant, judge, attorneys, etc.—and within the basic juridical schema or sequence of trial, judgment, and sentence. Among Calderón's *autos* the judicial metaphor is the nucleus of a number of such dramas—for example, *El pleito matrimonial* (before 1651), *Lo que va del hombre a Dios* (1652?–57?), *La inmunidad del sagrado* (1664), *Los alimentos del hombre* (1676), and *El indulto general* (1680).

In *Lo que va del hombre a Dios,* the Prince (Christ) constitutes Man his earthly viceroy to govern in his name and to live and

40. For a discussion of this motif in the early *auto,* see Louise Fothergill-Payne, *La alegoría en los autos y farsas anteriores a Calderón* (London: Tamesis, 1977), 57–62.

41. The juridical metaphor informs, for example, the primitive *autos, La justicia contra el pecado de Adán,* the *Aucto de la redención del género humano,* and *Los alimentos del hombre,* as well as *Los acreedores del hombre* of Lope de Vega. In *La farsa sacramental de la residencia del hombre,* for example, Conscience summons Man before the court of divine justice, asking that the Sinner be punished for his original sin and calling as witnesses World, Flesh, and Lucifer. Against their testimony Mercy intervenes as the defendant's advocate, and before the repentant sinner's contrition and confession, Divine Justice pronounces a merciful judgment: it is the Passion that will redeem and save Man, and the Eucharist that represents a reconciliation between Creator and creation. This *auto* (along with other early examples) is included in the *Colección de autos, farsas y coloquios del siglo XVI,* ed. Léo Rouanet (Madrid: Biblioteca Hispánica, 1901), 152–68. Lope's *autos* have been edited by Marcelino Menéndez Pelayo, *Obras,* vols. 2 and 3 (Madrid: Real Academia Española, 1892).

rule in peace. But the Prince also warns of the *residencia* or hearing that awaits Man at the end of his tenure in office:

> . . . advirtiendo
> que cuando más descuidado
> estés, en el trono excelso
> de la majestad vendré,
> no, como hoy, manso cordero,
> sino como león entonces,
> quizá enojado y severo,
> a tomarte residencia
> de todo lo que te entrego.   (276)

> I warn you that when you are most at ease, I shall come in the full majesty of my high throne; not as today's gentle lamb, but rather as a lion, perhaps angered and severe, and I shall demand an accounting of all I have entrusted to your care.

The bulk of the play represents Man's viceroyalty and his malfeasance in office, that is, his surrender to sin, until the Prince calls him to account and brings him to metaphorical trial, with Man's own personified Culpa as prosecutor and Divine Grace as the defense attorney. Found guilty of original sin, Man is thrown into debtors' prison (allegorization of the expulsion from Paradise). It is only the Prince's clemency, that is, the conferral of grace through the sacrament of the Eucharist, that saves and redeems the sinner.

The seminal metaphor of *Lo que va del hombre* is a topical reference to a historical institution: the *residencia,* a formal hearing held at the completion of an incumbent's term of office to determine his liability for any wrongful acts of his administration. Established by the Catholic Monarchs, Ferdinand and Isabella, as a means of extending royal authority over local officials, the *residencia* was later instituted in the New World colonies as well. By employing contemporaneous custom as figure of the Last Judgment ("la alegoría / bosquejo es hoy del más tremendo día" [288], remarks the Prince), Calderón invests his basically traditional allegory with topical appropriateness. The metaphor of the *residencia* also defines precisely the proper relationship between man and Creator: it is a relationship analogous to that of viceroy and monarch, who through his authority maintains his subordinate in office and oversees official accountability. Calderón's metaphorical *residencia* is both more specific than the vaguely defined trials of the early *auto* and more effectively evocative of man's ethical and existential role vis-à-vis God.

The juridical basis of *Los alimentos del hombre* is evident in the metaphorical title, which refers to Adam's *alimentos* or "maintenance allowance," a right of primogeniture for which the son brings suit after his Father disinherits him and expels him from the familial home (i.e., Paradise) as punishment for disobedience. For the hearing to determine Adam's liabilities and rights (a scene similar to numerous trial scenes in the early *auto*), the defendant's Guardian Angel is his advocate and the Devil is the prosecuting attorney. Opposing counsel debate Adam's fate in closely reasoned, and somewhat prolix, legal arguments. The Father, finally moved to clemency by his son's repentance and promise of amendment, hands down a merciful sentence: Adam is to be forgiven, provided that his brother Emmanuel (Christ) pays the "court costs" ("litis expensas") through the Passion and the concomitant institution of the Eucharistic sacrament (1632).

In contrast with the early *Lo que va del hombre,* Calderón's application of the juridical metaphor in *Los alimentos* is incomparably denser in its detailed comparison of legal analogue with man's moral and existential situation. Unfortunately, however, the analogy is often mechanically applied, in sometimes stupefyingly legalistic terms.[42] The *auto*'s juridical scenes in particular are a painstaking, static elaboration of often forced parallels.

42. See, for example, the Angel's presentation of Man's case on pp. 1625–26.

Far more interesting is Adam's *bellum intestinum* or internal conflict, which precedes and prepares his final moral correction and reconciliation with his Father. Adam and his personified Appetite, banished from the family seat, have been reduced to scavenging in the wilderness for sustenance. Adam complains bitterly of his reduced state (in words reminiscent of Segismundo's in Calderón's *La vida es sueño*) until Natural Reason appears to enlighten him. Reason explains to Adam the order inherent in God's creation as well as man's place in that order and his capacity to use free will in choosing between good and evil. When Appetite returns with the fruits of his foraging, Adam, swayed by Reason's arguments, brusquely reproaches Appetite for the interruption and rejects his importunity so he can continue his conversation with Reason: "Vete, villano, de aquí / y persuádete a que puedo / apartar al Apetito / cuando a la Razón me acerco" ["Be off, peasant, and be persuaded that I can dismiss Appetite when Reason's company I choose"] (1623).

The clash among Man, his Appetite, and Reason or, rather, the protagonist's vacillation between the importunity of the one and the cool-headed admonitions of the other, materializes an internal conflict: man's psychic struggle between untrammeled desire and the dictates of rationally guided conduct. Adam's ultimate adherence to Reason takes the allegorical form of a client's acceptance of counsel's legal advice.

What is notable in this scene is the very particular application of the juridical metaphor informing the *auto* as a whole. When Adam accepts the counsel of Reason—projection of an aspect of his own nature—he is actually carrying out an act of self-judgment and self-control, a wholly personal, moral decision effected within an entirely internal forum. The judicial metaphor of *Los alimentos* is the analogue, not merely of the Last Judgment (as in the early *auto*), but also of the process whereby man "justifies" himself, in the traditional meaning of the term.

In Catholic doctrine the terms *justificare* and *justificatio* have manifold meanings. They can refer first of all to the forensic declaration of justice by a tribunal or court, or to external law. However, *justificatio* is also used to refer to a purely interior growth in holiness and to the inner, immanent sanctification of the sinner.[43]

The ultimate interiority of justification in Catholic thought probably inspired the internal "case" that Adam weighs and finally adjudicates in *Los alimentos*. Indeed, the doctrine of justification may be the source of the links Calderón establishes in this *auto* between divine justice, the external law to which man must conform (the basis of the traditional trial metaphor), and Adam's wholly personal and interior "justification."

In *Los alimentos* Calderón has amplified and enriched allegorical tradition (the metaphor of the Last Judgment as lawsuit or trial) by merging it with Catholic doctrine on grace and by laying bare the very workings of man's will, a task the early *auto* scarcely attempted. His trial *auto* thus becomes the allegory of Catholic doctrine on justification in all its varied meanings.

Calderón exhibits his most brilliant fusion of allegorical legacy and contemporaneous doctrine in *La inmunidad del sagrado* (1664). He bases this *auto* on two of Christian allegory's traditional metaphors: that of man's life as judicial trial and that of the Church as a garden, a similitude popular since the Middle Ages.[44] However, with these conventional elements the dramatist blends something new: imagery and dramatic motifs based on the Catholic doctrine of probabilism.

Probabilism in moral theology is a system (developed and

---

43. See the article "Justification" in *The Catholic Encyclopedia,* vol. 6 (New York: The Encyclopedia Press, 1913).

44. See the article "Hortus" in the *Dictionnaire de spiritualité,* vol. 7 (Paris: Beauchesne, 1967).

first promulgated by Spanish Dominicans of the Counter Reformation) that holds that, when solely the lawfulness or unlawfulness of an action is in question, it is permissible for a judge or confessor to follow a solidly probable opinion in favor of clemency and liberty. It is, in effect, a doctrine of reasonable doubt and an argument for clemency in such cases.[45]

In *La inmunidad* it is apparently probabilistic thinking that shapes the judgment passed on Man. As the play opens we learn that Man has been imprisoned in "la cárcel del mundo" ["the prison of the world"] or "la cárcel de la vida" ["the prison of life"] (1116), as punishment for original sin. Fleeing God's justice, he takes refuge in the sanctuary of the Church, described as a garden with seven fountains (the sacraments). Finally captured and brought to trial before the Inquisition, Man faces his personified Culpa as prosecutor, with Divine Grace as defense attorney.

Christ listens to the arguments of opposing counsel, and then remarks:

> La parte allí de la Culpa
> pide castigo y venganza;
> y con piedad y clemencia,

---

45. The accessible bibliography on probabilism, at least in the literary context, is minimal. See the article "Probabilism" in vol. 12 of *The Catholic Encyclopedia,* and Henry Charles Lea, *A History of Auricular Confession and Indulgences in the Latin Church,* vol. 2 (New York: Greenwood, 1968), a reprint of the edition of 1896. Probabilism represented a revolution in moral thinking; it released a flood of treatises in the early seventeenth century, not only in Spain, but in France and England as well. Yet the impact of probabilism on Spanish life and literature has thus far attracted only one large-scale study, Henry W. Sullivan's *Tirso de Molina and the Drama of the Counter Reformation* (Amsterdam: Rodolfi, 1976). The profound infusion of such thinking into the moral stance and allegorical design of those Calderonian *autos* based on the trial metaphor suggests that Calderón's work also represents a virtually unexplored field for investigating this area of seventeenth-century intellectual life. Sullivan himself has made one such application of probabilistic doctrine to the elucidation of a Calderonian *comedia,* "The Problematic of Tragedy in Calderón's *El médico de su honra,*" *Revista canadiense de estudios hispánicos* 5 (1981): 355–72.

pide aquí la de la Gracia;
con que entre Misericordia
y Justicia, en soberana
cuestión dudo, a poder Yo
dudar, escuchando a entrambas.   (1124)

Culpa's part seeks punishment and revenge, that of Grace, pity
and clemency. And so, harking to both sides, and hesitating between Mercy and Justice, I am in doubt (if indeed I could doubt),
in listening to both sides.

That is, recognizing the element of doubt in the case, the uncertainty concerning Man's actual culpability in the Fall, Christ
reasons back and forth between the alternatives of rigor and
mercy. Finally, he acknowledges this to be a case of reasonable
doubt and inclines toward the clement sentence.

This purely verbal display of probabilistic thinking will later
be worked out in the allegorical action of trial and judgment.
Justice, the judge, passes final sentence on Man, choosing, as
had Christ, between severity and clemency:

... me hallo
satisfecha, pues dirá
en su explicación Bernardo
que hallándose a un tiempo Dios
de la Justicia llamado,
y de la Misericordia,
con ambas cumplió, dejando
a la Justicia que muera,
quien fue a muerte condenado;
pero a la Misericordia,
que muera en mejor estado;
y así, atenta a la divina
Nueva Ley de Gracia, fallo,
pues la Justicia es que muera,
y la Gracia a más descanso.   (1130)

I am satisfied; for at one and the same time he is called God of
Justice, and of Mercy, and by both standards he abided: he ren-
dered to Justice the death of one condemned to die, and to Mercy,

death in a better state. And so, heedful of the divine New Law of Grace, I find that Justice demands his death, and Grace, that he die in greater rest.

Christ must eventually offer his own life for Man's in order to expiate the latter's crimes and thus effect his rescue and redemption: he ratifies Justice's merciful sentence with his Passion, which represents the "explication" or fulfillment of the clement Law of Grace (1125).

In *La inmunidad* Calderón adopts the parlance and the very spirit of probabilistic doctrine. Its maxims impart to the *auto*'s referent, the traditional metaphorization of God's judgment on man, heightened theological and allegorical suggestiveness as well as greater topicality, implied reference to a significant current of contemporaneous theological speculation.

Calderón's *auto* brilliantly fuses allegorical tradition and personal invention, Catholic doctrine and topical allusion, sacral referent and quotidian analogue. Tradition and convention doubtless ensured the dramatist his plays' quasi-liturgical status and guaranteed his receipt of royal and municipal patronage as well as a certain dramatic and theological cachet.

But for Calderón the *auto*'s allegory is far more than convention, far more, even, than the opportunity to exhibit his allegorical ingenuity. The *auto sacramental* also offered Calderón a literary forum in which to develop and expound a body of theoretical dicta, subtle, complex, and often profound, concerning allegory itself. The *autos*' personifications incessantly and entertainingly mention the fact that they are participants in allegories, and they explain themselves and their allegories to each other (and, of course, to us). Indeed, one of Calderón's most appealing aspects to anyone interested in personification allegory is the incessant and absolutely unambiguous way in which the dramatist defines the terms with which he works, and the way in which those terms define themselves. More provocatively, the very fact that these allegories in effect define themselves as allegories and, as we shall see, define themselves as modes of definition, constitutes a radical, and radically logocentric, theory of allegory.

Defining allegory is not always so heady a task for Calderón, however. Sometimes his definitions are clear-cut and apparently (only apparently) uninspired. One of the earliest and most famous definitions of the *autos* and their allegory occurs in the *loa* or prologue to *La segunda esposa o triunfar muriendo* (1649?), in the words of a Pastor who is a synecdoche of humanity in general and metaphor for the divine Good Shepherd (a fact not without significance, as we shall see). Pastor's definition of the *autos sacramentales* runs as follows:

> Sermones
> puestos en verso, en idea
> representable, cuestiones
> de la Sacra Teología,
> que no alcanzan mis razones
> a explicar ni comprender.[46]   (427)

The *autos* are "sermons turned into verse, questions of Sacred Theology turned into representable idea, questions that my reason can neither explain nor comprehend."

This definition has usually been taken as a reference to the *auto*'s devout, educative character.[47] And doubtless this is partially true. In the context of Calderón's time, however, this little excursus acquires a much more specific meaning. The *autos* are

---

46. The full implications of Calderón's emphasis on "this day" of dramatic representation, a commonplace in his *autos,* are discussed in Ch. 4 of the present study.

47. See, for example, Parker's discussion, pp. 65–67. On the relationship between sermon and Calderonian *auto,* see also Egido, 91–100.

in this context quite literally "versified sermons," for they incorporate many of the techniques of contemporaneous homiletics.[48]

Those techniques at their most typical aimed, not at the doctrinal exposition or even moralizing admonition one might expect in an oratorical genre, but rather at the emotionally powerful visualization of exemplary deeds.[49] In this the epideictic sermon of the Renaissance differed markedly from the medieval thematic or university variety, which sought to raise questions and test the solutions offered. The preacher of Calderón's day, orator (and dramatist *manqué,* perhaps) strove to awaken in audience members their devotion and desire to emulate sacred heroes or, conversely, their eagerness to avoid censured conduct.[50]

In retelling sacred history, these sacred orators commonly made extensive use of dramatic devices (including dialogue) as well as metaphors strongly reminiscent of the *autos'* dramaturgy.[51] The sermons of Fray Dionisio Vázquez, orator and professor of Scripture at Alcalá, are typical of the new homiletic style. Vázquez constantly exhorts the congregants to "imagine,"

48. On contemporaneous homiletics, see especially Peter Bayley, *French Pulpit Oratory 1598-1650* (Cambridge: Cambridge University Press, 1980); John S. Chamberlin, *Increase and Multiply* (Chapel Hill: University of North Carolina Press, 1976), on the preaching of John Donne; John W. O'Malley, *Praise and Blame in Renaissance Rome* (Durham, NC: Duke University Press, 1979); and Hilary Dansey Smith, *Preaching in the Spanish Golden Age* (Oxford: Oxford University Press, 1978). All contain extensive bibliography.

49. Such so-called epideictic sermons were based on the *ars laudandi et vituperandi,* the oratory of panegyric or of censure. See O'Malley, 39.

50. "[E]pideictic wants as far as possible to present us with works and deeds, and these works and deeds are presented not only for a metaphysical analysis but quite literally for viewing. The epideictic preacher consistently invites [his listeners] to 'look,' to 'gaze upon,' and to 'contemplate.' . . . to describe an action in words. This is what the epideictic preacher tried to do" (O'Malley, pp. 49 and 63).

51. See Egido, 94–95.

to "see" what he evocatively describes; his sermons typically included "visualized" scenes from sacred history.[52]

Often, the contemporaneous preacher in composing his sermon would find his point of departure in just such seminal metaphors or analogies as informed the *auto sacramental*.[53] Fray Alonso de Cabrera, for example, generates a rudimentary allegory from the metaphor of Christ as "caballero aventurero":

> Abrid, cristianos, los ojos de la fe, para ver dos valentísimos justadores que en una fresca ribera hacen campo. . . . Sale a la mira

52. See, for example, the "Sermón de la Resurrección," in Dionisio Vázquez, *Sermones,* ed. Felix G. Olmedo (Madrid: Espasa-Calpe, 1943), 23–25.

53. Such a Christianizing use of metaphor is of course unique neither to the *auto* nor to Renaissance homiletics, but was on the contrary a dominant characteristic of the age. The Renaissance, like the Middle Ages before it, abounded in anthologies or *summae* of similitudes or metaphors destined for use by preachers. St. Anselm was probably the first to compile such a miscellany with his *Liber de similitudinibus* (PL 159, 606–707). The Dominicans ably continued the tradition in their reform of preaching. Their use of *summae similitudinum* in the sacred transformation of oratory culminated in Giovanni di San Gimignano's *Summa de exemplis ac similitudinibus rerum,* a work of enormous popularity and diffusion. See A. Dondaine, "La Vie et les oeuvres de Jean de San Gimignano," *Archivum Fratrum Praedicatorum* 2 (1939): 128–83. In her study of the homiletic tradition in Calderón's age, Hilary Dansey Smith mentions "the traditional method of compiling *conceptos* or *reparos* in the form of concordances or miscellanies, like the medieval anthologies of similes which were still very popular in the Spanish Golden Age" ("Golden Age," p. 87). The *Conceptos esprituales y morales* (1600–1612) and the *Epigramas y hieroglíficos de la vida de Cristo* (1625) of Alonso de Ledesma, and, in England, Robert Cawdry in *A Treasury or Storehouse of Similes* (1600), among many similar works, helped foster the vogue of Christian metaphor. Like many of the *autos sacramentales,* such conceits adapt simple comparisons from everyday life to analogize and illuminate the nature of Christ and sacred history. Cf. the following titles taken from poems in Ledesma, *Conceptos espirituales y morales,* ed. Eduardo Juliá Martínez (Madrid: Consejo Superior de Investigaciones Científicas, 1969): "Al Nacimiento, En metafora de vn galan disfraçado" ["To the Nativity, in the metaphor of a gallant in disguise"] (54–55); "Al Nacimiento, En metafora de vna carcel" ["To the Nativity, in the metaphor of a prison"] (57–58); "Quexas del Demonio â cerca del Nacimiento, En metafora de guerra" ["The Devil's complaints about the Nativity, in the metaphor of warfare"] (58–59); "A la Cruz de Christo, En metafora de fragua" ["To Christ's Cross, in the metaphor of a forge"]

toda la corte celestial y está el mundo todo suspenso, que tenía por invencible al Baptista. . . . Viene Cristo, que es el caballero aventurero, disimulado y desconocido; mas el mantenedor San Juan, como platico y experto en la guerra, luego que vio su gentil postura, el denuedo que mostraba, el aire y gentileza con que venia, que firme y derecho sobre los estribos de la humanidad, reconoce el valor grande que trae encubierto y se apercibe a defenderse. . . . A la primera lanza que corrieron, fuertemente se tuvo y hace rostro y defiende su puesto. . . . Vuelve el divino guerrero a tomar otra lanza y escoge la más recia y gruesa que había en toda la hasteria de la ley de Dios.[54]

Christians, open the eyes of faith to see two incomparable, valient jousters who make camp on a pleasing riverbank. All of the celestial court comes out to watch, and the whole world is astounded, for it had regarded the Baptist as invincible. Christ appears, the knight errant, disguised and unknown; but his president, St. John, being well versed and expert in warfare, recognizes his hidden worth and prepares to defend himself, as soon as he sees his elegant posture, his courage, his bearing and gracefulness, his firm seat in the stirrups of humanity. At the first pass they run, Christ stands firm and defends his position. The divine warrior takes up another lance, choosing the strongest and thickest from all of the weaponry of God's law.

In the lengthy battle description (quoted here only in part) the stirring martial details rather overwhelm the theological. Such a sermon is, in Calderón's terminology, a "representable idea" or dramatic metaphor— an embryonic *auto sacramental,* as a matter of fact.

The use of the concrete, quotidian—and visual or dramatic— as vehicle for considering sacred mystery, basic to epideictic homiletics such as Cabrera's and Vázquez's, echoes Calderón's

---

(135). Doubtless such use of metaphor also received impetus during Calderón's age from the vogue of conceptism (with its interest in metaphor and wit).

54. Fray Alonso de Cabrera, "Sermon de la octaba de la Epifanía," in *Sermones,* ed. Miguel Mir, 3 (Madrid: Bailly-Baillère, 1906), 635.

definition of the *autos* as "idea representable." The interpolated dramatizations, sometimes allegorizations, typical of these Renaissance sermons assimilate the techniques of epideictic homiletics to those of drama, to the *autos sacramentales*. Calderón's *autos* are in this light virtually "sermons in verse," analogous in form as well as objectives to the sacred oratory of the time.[55]

Such use of metaphor, allegory, and sacred scenes was conventional in the pre-Calderonian *auto*,[56] and Calderón thus needed from homiletics no added incentive or model in writing his plays. Nonetheless, his definition of the *auto* as versified sermon implies that the dramatist may have sought and found inspiration in contemporaneous sermons, particularly in their emphasis on sacral and moral exemplarity, in the *ars laudandi et vituperandi*. Calderón insists again and again on the *auto*'s exemplary utility. For example, in *La Torre de Babilonia* (before 1647?) the infamous Tower from Genesis becomes a moral example that metaphorically warns of the fate of all human presumption:

> Siendo figura esa Torre,
> que el viento desvaneció,
> de todos cuantos soberbios
> con osada presunción
> pretenden examinar
> secretos que guarda Dios.

55. An interesting attempt to relate a Counter-Reformation playwright to contemporaneous homiletics is Richard A. Preto-Rodas's "Anchieta and Vieira: Drama as Sermon, Sermon as Drama," *Luso-Brazilian Review* 7 (1970): 96–103. Preto-Rodas's essay is particularly interesting for the present study because both Anchieta and Vieira were Jesuits.

56. On the pre-Calderonian *auto*, see Louise Fothergill-Payne, *La alegoría en los autos y farsas anteriores a Calderón* (London: Tamesis, 1977); Frauke Gewecke, *Thematische Untersuchungen zu dem vor-calderonianischen Auto Sacramental*, Kölner Romanistische Arbeiten ns 42 (Geneva: Droz, 1974); and Barbara E. Kurtz, " 'With Human Aspect': Studies in European Personification Allegory with Special Reference to the Hispanic Contribution" (Diss., University of Chicago, 1983), Ch. 4.

> Oye el cómo, porque sepas
> cuánto Misterio encerró
> de castigo y cuánto ejemplo
> para los que viven hoy.   (887)

That Tower is a figure, dispelled by the wind, of all the prideful who attempt with impudent presumption to probe secrets kept by God. Listen to its tale, so that you may know of the Mystery it contained and the example it sets for the living.

The eponymous protagonist of *El santo rey don Fernando, Segunda Parte* (1671) refers to himself as a cautionary "ejemplo" ["example"]: "Señor, pido perdón; pero / a todos de haberles dado / con mi vida mal ejemplo" ["Lord, I ask your pardon; and not yours alone, but that of all men, for having given them with my life a bad example"] (1318). The educative potential of allegory is likewise invoked in *La humildad coronada de las plantas* (1644), whose allegory is described as an "imaginado ejemplo" [an "imagined example"] (392). In *No hay instante sin milagro* (1672) the history of Mary Magdalene is recounted as a cautionary tale:

> FE: volvamos atrás los siglos,
> a la paridad corriendo
> de lo visible a lo invisible,
> sea el ejemplo primero
> la primera que me dio
> asunto para el ejemplo.   (1344–45)

Let us turn back the centuries, and in passing comparatively from the visible to the invisible, let the first example be the first woman who provided material for an example.

This exemplary history, reifying the invisible, metaphorizes or materializes an abstract moral lesson.

A perceived affinity in devotional, exemplary objectives between *auto* and sermon may have led Calderón to adopt the sermon as partial model for his allegorical dramaturgy, and, as a step or impetus in his increasing theorization of *auto* and allegory, may have helped him to clarify his theoretical conceptualization of the *auto*.

Implicit as well in the dramatist's description of the *auto* as sermon is an emphasis on the genre's rhetoricity and sacramentalism; if the *auto* is public, and popular, ceremonial, its allegory is less aesthetic choice than doctrinal, even cognitive, necessity. For the *auto*'s allegory analogizes the earthly and the transcendent; it combines the appeal of the quotidian and the suasive force of the exemplary. The human intellect, mundane and innately limited, needs quiddities (as Aquinas maintained[57] and Calderón in his wake oftentimes asserts) in order to attain (imperfect) understanding of the intangible and ineffable:

> Y pues lo caduco no
> puede comprender lo eterno,
> y es necesario que para
> venir en conocimiento
> suyo hay un medio visible
> que en el corto caudal nuestro
> del concepto imaginado
> pase a práctico concepto.[58]   (1215)

And since the transitory cannot understand the eternal, it has need for its understanding of a visible medium that within the limited compass of our intellectual ken turns the imagined concept into a practicable conceit.

---

57. See Thomas Aquinas, *In Aristotelis libros De sensu et sensato, De memoria et reminiscentia commentarium:* "Man cannot understand without images (*phantasmata*); the image is a similitude of a corporal thing, but understanding is of universals which are to be abstracted from particulars. . . . And if we wish to remember intelligible notions more easily, we should link them with some kind of phantasms." Quoted by Frances A. Yates, *The Art of Memory* (Chicago: University of Chicago Press, 1966), 70, 71.

58. Cf. the Pauline dictum on the needs of human intellection: "Invisibilia enim ipsius, a creatura mundi, per ea quae facta sunt, intellecta, conspiciuntur" (Rom. 1:20).

That is, the plays' allegory, a "visible medium," translates a conceptual order into a "pretended or representable scene": ". . . [P]ara una fingida / o representable escena / la Retórica nos da / alegórica licencia" ["And for a simulated or representable scene, Rhetoric gives us license for allegory" (1509).[59] More specifically, allegory transcribes "lo eterno," the sacral and the extratemporal, into the visible reality of human stagecraft and the human terms of personifications that "give voice to the inanimate" ["da voz a lo inanimado"] (1189).[60] In Calderón's allegorical art and in his conceptualization of that art, allegory, metaphor, the "práctico concepto," is the principal "tool of our limited resources," the intellect's instrument for attaining analogical understanding of sacred order and sacral concept.

In *La humildad coronada de las plantas,*[61] Cedar (figuration of the Divinity) remarks:

> Y pues hoy en este acto
> introducidos nos vemos,

59. That is, "a conceptual order is given a concrete expression that makes it more directly accessible to human experience, this concrete expression . . . being the dramatic action"; Alexander A. Parker, *The Allegorical Drama of Calderon* (Oxford: Dolphin, 1943), 79. Parker goes on to explain the method as follows: "The 'ideas fantásticas' are . . . transposed into drama by being expressed in terms of something that is a narrative in its own right and therefore directly fitted for the stage—an event or events either recorded in history (e.g. in the Bible), or actually taking place contemporaneously (e.g. the marriage of Philip IV to Mariana of Austria); or a legend (e.g. mythology); or a fictitious narrative illustrating happenings of everyday life (e.g. a quarrel between husband and wife, the production of a play, the purchase of goods in a market, a hunt, etc.), or taken from literary sources (e.g. Gospel parables, themes of *comedias*)" (79–80).

60. Cf. Parker's discussion, 81.

61. On this *auto,* see also Angel San Miguel, "*La humildad coronada de las plantas* de Calderón. Contribución al estudio de sus fuentes," in *Hacia Calderón,* ed. Hans Flasche, Karl-Hermann Körner, and Hans Mattauch (Berlin: Walter de Gruyter, 1979), 117–22, and "*La humildad coronada de las plantas:* Ein aussergewöhnliches 'Auto sacramental' Calderóns?" in Theodor Berchem and Siegfried Sudhof, eds., *Pedro Calderón de la Barca: Vorträge anlässlich der Jahrestagung der Görres-Gesellschaft*

usando, para explicarle [lo insensible]
metafórico el ingenio
de poéticas licencias
y retóricos preceptos.   (392)

And thus today we find ourselves using the metaphorical wit of
poetic license and rhetorical precepts in order to explain the insensible.

"Metaphorical wit," Cedar informs us, is the foundation of or
motive force behind the "poetic licenses" and "rhetorical precepts" that, shaping the *auto*'s allegory, explicate "lo insensible,"
the imperceptible, that which is closed to direct sensory apprehension (in this case the sacral and divine).

For most of the *autos,* a seminal, "representable" metaphor,
analogue of a sacral referent, epitomizes the play's *argumento* or
plot. For example, the story line of *Las órdenes militares* unfolds
"en metáfora de guerra," "in a metaphor of war," Culpa points
out. *El jardín de Falerina* is based on a "metáfora de libro de ca-
ballería" [a "metaphor from the chivalric romances"]; *Tu prójimo como a ti* partially follows "la metáfora del robo" ["the metaphor of thievery"]; *El valle de la zarzuela* develops around a
metaphorical hunt that transmutes into the material terms of
"esta alegórica caza" the Devil's pursuit of the human soul.

The *autos'* central metaphors analogize sacred mystery
through concrete, quotidian *realia;* dramatic expansion of these
metaphors' connotations constitutes the plays' action. That is,
the dramatist elaborates his plot by developing implications inherent in the seminal analogy, which suggests or generates dramatic events.[62]

1978 (Berlin: Erich Schmidt, 1983), 114–23. There is a facsimile edition of this *auto:*
Manuel Sánchez Mariana, ed., *La humildad coronada* (Madrid: Espasa-Calpe, 1980).

  62. Such a technique, elaborating narrative or dramatic action from such seminal,
"generative" metaphors, tends to be a general characteristic of personification allegory. See Kurtz, " 'With Human Aspect,' " 272ff. See also Fothergill-Payne, 22, 23.

If the *autos'* plot lines are metaphorical, so, too, are the dramas' characters. Calderón frequently describes, or has his characters describe, the *autos'* personified figures as similitudes or metaphors, as in *El pastor fido* (1678), where "for the sake of similitude" the characters wear the rustic dress of shepherds: "por similitud los vemos / vestir el villano traje / de pastores . . ." (1588).

Calderón's emphasis on the configurative role of metaphor is not without significance for allegorical theory in general. Some students of allegory maintain that personification is not a metaphor at all, but rather a metonymy that applies the external *habitus* of, say, an angry man to the quality of anger itself; this supposedly metonymic rather than metaphoric basis for personification such scholars use as rationale to deny that personification allegories are allegories at all.[63] That Calderón leaves no doubt as to where he stands on the issue, that he so explicitly defines his personifications as metaphors and his allegories as dramatized metaphors, implicitly challenges modern gainsayers and unambiguously grounds the *autos'* allegory in metaphor.

Allegory is for Calderón quite a bit more as well, more than expanded metaphor, more than "versified sermon." Nowhere is the breadth and depth— and sheer playfulness—of Calderón's allegory more evident than in the fact that he introduces a personified Allegory into one of the plays' prologues (the *loa* to *El sacro Parnaso* of 1659) and gives her a chance at self-introduction and self-definition:

> . . . soy
> (si en términos me defino)
> docta Alegoría, tropo

---

63. Lionel J. Friedman, for example, makes this argument in his review of *Etudes sur le poème allégorique en France au Moyen Age* by Marc-René Jung, *Speculum* 47 (1972): 319. On this point, see also Kurtz, " 'With Human Aspect,' " 50.

retórico, que expresivo,
debajo de una alusión
de otra cosa, significo
las propiedades en lejos,
los accidentes en visos,
pues dando cuerpo al concepto
aun lo no visible animo.[64]

I am learned Allegory, rhetorical trope; significantly, under the allusion of something else, I signify substances in *lejos* [literally, the background distances of a painting], and I signify accidents in *visos* [literally, highlights used to emphasize background objects]. For, by giving body to concept, I animate the invisible.

For the moment I leave *lejos* and *visos* in the original, since their translation and explication is scarcely straightforward, as will be seen. The entire passage is exceedingly difficult; the attempted explanation that follows is tentative.[65]

Lejos and *visos* (along with *sombras,* or shadows, frequently linked in the *autos* with the other terms) are the perspectival devices used in painting to suggest distance and contour: in other words, to create in the two-dimensional picture space the illusion of three-dimensional reality. Personified Allegory's perspectival metaphor implies that the *auto*'s allegorical dramaturgy is visual in the same way that painting is: it translates a transcendent reality into the terms or within the bounds of a

64. Quoted by Parker, *Allegorical Drama,* 79. Valbuena Prat does not include the *loa* in his edition of the *autos.*

65. Most simply and obviously, such perspectival imagery reflects Calderón's long-standing interest in and profound knowledge of the plastic arts. On this interest and knowledge, see Voght, "The Mythological *Auto,*" 33–34, especially his references to relevant bibliography. In addition, see also Manuel Ruiz-Lagos de Castro, *Estética de la pintura en el teatro de Calderón* (Granada: Gráficas del Sur, 1969); Stelio Cro, "Calderón y la pintura," in *Calderón and the Baroque Tradition,* Kurt Levy, Jesús Ara, and Gethin Hughes, eds. (Waterloo: Wilfrid Laurier University Press, 1985), 119–24; and J. Camón Aznar, "Teorías pictóricas de Lope y Calderón," *Velázquez* 1 (1964): 66–72.

more limited (and ultimately illusory, i.e., earthly) domain; it analogizes the sacral and quotidian realms.

More concretely, Allegory's metaphor for allegory asserts that substances (*propiedades*), that is, imperfectly apprehensible sacred mystery, are in allegory "signified" perspectively, that is, as in painterly persepective; in other words, substances are conventionally exhibited or made manifest, as in the *lejos* or background distances of a painting. Such sacral *lejos* are made more clearly perceptible by the *visos* or highlights—by the material accidents of metaphorical *sensibilia*.

This much is typical of Calderón's discussions of *auto* and allegory elsewhere in the plays. However, implicit in Allegory's metaphor may be an even deeper, more suggestive connection between the pictorial and the allegorical. Contemporaneous speculation on painting and perspective conventionally maintained that a picture space is not so much a representation of what the painter sees as a rationalized structuring of perception itself.[66] As logical extension, allegory in a similar fashion may not so much present visually "what is there" as rationalize it, make it accessible to human reason, through its metaphors and their quotidian *realia*.[67]

It is furthermore significant that Allegory's key metaphor

66. See Joel Snyder, "Picturing Vision," in *The Language of Images,* ed. W. J. T. Mitchell (Chicago: University of Chicago Press, 1974), 219–46, esp. 234–46. I am grateful to Prof. Snyder for discussing with me the ideas and texts mentioned in this discussion and Renaissance aesthetic doctrine in general.

67. It should be noted that this speculative connection between Calderón's definition of allegory and contemporaneous aesthetic doctrine is scarcely as farfetched as it may seem at first glance. Peter Bayley points out that metaphors and comparisons drawn from painting and especially perspective were in Calderón's day frequently used in explicating metaphysical problems: "The quasi-scientific observations of natural distortions and reflections were in fact taken as the basis of metaphysical speculations, especially in the debate about substance and accidents so central to such controversy." See Bayley, 142. On further links between Calderón's allegorical theory and the aesthetic speculation of his age, see Ch. 4 of the present study.

links pictorial representation and scholastic terminology of Aristotelian provenance (*propiedades, accidentes*),[68] terminology frequently used at the time in discussing transubstantiation.[69] The probable significance of this conflation is manifold. In the first place, the implied connection suggests that the problems examined in theology, art, and allegory are fundamentally the same. After all, philosophical speculation regarding substance and accidents, and the Eucharist, shares with contemporaneous art theory (and Calderón's allegorical theory) a concern with the limitations of material reality and how those limitations are overcome (in the Eucharist, through perspective, by means of allegory). Furthermore, art and allegory are in this light intrinsically philosophical, theological; they may therefore derive from their mother science an analogical significance and sacredness.

Calderón, interestingly enough, elsewhere describes in similar perspectival metaphors the typological prefiguration of the Eucharist:

> visos son, sombras y lejos
> del prometido Mesías,
> que a nuestros padres y abuelos,
> en vino y pan, han previsto
> el más alto Sacramento.   (1233)

Visos, shadows, and *lejos*[70] of the promised Messiah have foretold to our ancestors, in wine and in bread, the highest Sacrament.

68. This fact, too, may have its importance, since one branch of contemporaneous aesthetic speculation derived its basic premises from neoscholastic doctrine. See ch. 4 of the present study.

69. Donald T. Dietz gives a good brief history of the dogma of transubstantiation in "Liturgical and Allegorical Drama: The Uniqueness of Calderón's *Auto Sacramental,*" in *Calderón de la Barca at the Tercentenary: Comparative Views,* ed. Wendell M. Aycock and Sydney P. Cravens (Lubbock: Texas Tech University Press, 1982), 71–88, especially 72–73.

70. See discussion above for the meanings of the untranslated terms.

The shared perspectival metaphors used to define allegory and Eucharist signalize an analogical link between them, a link that will become basic to Calderón's conception of the *auto sacramental* and its allegory.

In *El nuevo Palacio del Retiro* (1634), the King, allegorical analogue of Christ, undertakes to describe the precise nature of his tenure on the earthly, royal throne: ". . . ocupando iguales / dos lugares a un tiempo" (151), he relates. As divine monarch he "coequally occupies two places at one time"; he is coextensively present in Heaven and, as transubstantiated presence, the species of the Eucharist.

The metaphorized Savior's self-portrait in this *auto* is notable, not as an explanation of Catholic doctrine—nothing new there, after all—but rather for its striking similarity to a definition presented elsewhere in the *autos* in quite a different context:

> La alegoría no es más
> que un espejo que traslada
> lo que es con lo que no es;
> y está toda su elegancia
> en que salga parecida
> tanto la copia en la tabla,
> que el que está mirando a una
> piense que está viendo a entrambas.   (1242)

Allegory is only a mirror which translates what is through what is not; and all its beauty consists in its capacity to bring out so artfully the copy's resemblance to the original that the onlooker will think that he is simultaneously seeing both.

This simultaneous "seeing both," the Calderonian definition of allegory, strikingly resembles Christ's self-definition or, rather, his explanation of his real presence in the Eucharist. Allegory in the *auto,* like the sacrament it celebrates, embodies the coextensive presence of two realities, one quotidian and material, the other transcendent and sacred. Both allegory and

Eucharist supervene or overcome "normal" spatio-temporal relationships; both, by implication and essence, are veils for transcendent, sacral reality. The material species of bread and wine veil the real presence of Christ's body and blood;[71] allegory in the Calderonian *auto* veils the Eucharist itself beneath the material accidents of metaphorized discourse, which makes the sacral reality visible or representable, hence intellectually accessible.

Calderón's analogy of allegory and Eucharist thus has numerous and far-reaching implications. It underscores the *auto*'s ceremonial and liturgical function; it tends by extension to analogize spectator and communicant, who are both, we may conclude, cultic participants in sacred mystery;[72] and it suggests that the *auto*, to at least some extent, partakes of the sacramentalism of the Eucharist it celebrates and allegorizes.

That sacramentalism furthermore charges Allegory's self-definition with compelling significance. Her excursion into ontology, more than the tautology such a self-definition might seem at first thought, is actually at the heart of Calderón's theoretical concerns in the *autos*.

Most obviously, Allegory's explanatory metalepsis simply reflects the didacticism characteristic of the allegorical mode. It is, after all (and as frequently noted), traditional for Christian allegory of the West to foreground its own exegesis, "to indicate," as Northrop Frye pointed out, "how a commentary [on it] should proceed."[73]

71. Cf.: ". . . debajo de un blanco / velo y un terso viril / está ya el Dios de Amor" ["beneath a white veil and a clear monstrance the God of Love is now present"] (380); ". . . el blanco pan, en quien / realmente he de asistir, / siendo su especie el velo / que me haya de cubrir" ["the white bread, in which I shall veritably be present, is in its species the veil that will cover me"] (381).

72. On this point, see also the Afterword to the present study.

73. Northrop Frye, *Anatomy of Criticism* (Princeton: Princeton University Press, 1957), 89–90. See also the related discussion in Jörg O. Fichte, *Expository Voices in Medieval Drama: Essays on the Mode and Function of Dramatic Exposition,* Erlanger Beiträge zur Sprach- und Kunstwissenschaft, vol. 53 (Nuremberg: Hans Carl, 1975).

Allegory's speech, less obviously but more signficantly, implies the parallel-level semiosis (*cuerpo-concepto, propiedades-accidentes,* literal-allegorical) that derives from the most common notion of allegory: that it says one thing and means another. According to this so-called "split-level" model of allegorical discourse,[74] "saying" is the allegorical text's literal level or meaning, "the text's language—its most *literal* aspect;"[75] what that "saying" means is conventionally the allegorical level or meaning, regarded as privileged, abstract, transcendent.

Interestingly, Calderón's own analysis posits just such a parallel-level or split-level model for the *auto.* In the 1677 prologue to the plays the dramatist distinguishes between their *asunto* and their *argumento:*

> . . . siendo siempre uno mismo el asunto, es fuerza caminar a su fin con unos mismos medios, mayormente si se entra en consideración de que estos mismos medios, tantas veces repetidos, siempre van a diferente fin en su argumento.[76]   (42)

74. A number of critics have discussed the nature and problems of the "split-level" model of allegorical discourse. Perhaps most cogent are Morton W. Bloomfield, "Allegory as Interpretation," *New Literary History* 3 (1972): 301–17); Samuel R. Levin, "Allegorical Language," in *Allegory, Myth, and Symbol,* ed. Morton W. Bloomfield (Cambridge: Harvard University Press, 1981), 23–38; and Carolynn Van Dyke, *The Fiction of Truth* (Ithaca: Cornell University Press, 1985), *passim,* but especially pp. 35, 42–44, 203, and 212. Bloomfield points out (pp. 312–13) that "[t]he literal level, in one sense, is a series of noises and/or marks on paper, as is all language. . . . The literal level, in a literal sense, is gibberish. Once the semantic element is introduced, and it must be if these noises are to be more than a foreign language or the chattering of a squirrel, then we have to bring in some meaning immediately. . . . If, then, meaning must be on the literal level . . . the question then arises as to what this meaning must include before conscious interpretation (allegory in the broad sense of the word) begins. When does the area of signification begin?" Van Dyke calls attention to the inadequacy of "the parallel-levels model" (35), demonstrating through analysis of several texts that "[w]ith any allegory, the notion of parallel semiotic levels is indisputably useful as an analytic tool. . . . But such an analysis of components is by no means a description of the compound" (42).

75. Bloomfield, "Allegory as Interpretation," 313.

76. See translation above, 21.

Since the subject matter is always the same [i.e., the Eucharist], it is necessary to fulfill its objectives through the same means; all the more so in view of the fact that these means, so often repeated in the plays, always tend toward a different end in their development within the plot.

A. A. Parker's explanation of this admittedly difficult passage has become classic: "Among [the *autos*] there is consequently identity of *asunto* but variety of *argumentos*. . . . The *asunto* of every *auto* is therefore the Eucharist, but the *argumento* can vary from one to another: it can be any 'historia divina'—historical, legendary, or fictitious—provided that it throws some light on some aspect of the *asunto*."[77]

Nothing radical or surprising here. However, Allegory's meta-allegorical commentary implicitly subverts any simplistic split-level construct. Personified Allegory refers obliquely to external reality, the "real-life" world outside the text, by speaking momentarily in the "real" realm where commentary, explanation, and interpretation occur; at one and the same time, she remains a character and a speaker within the fictionalized world of the text on which she comments.[78] The *autos*' meta-allegorical exegetes such as Allegory (and other, similar self-defining personifications in the plays)[79] thus tend to confound any facile disjunction of textual "levels." (Certainly, the fact that actors, "real" people, are performing the roles and pronouncing the speeches of self-definition would tend to further as well the breakdown of the split-level semiosis.)

In fact, Allegory in metaphorizing allegory transcends as well the typical denotative or deictic function that characterizes typical personification. That is, Allegory, in the very act of self-

<hr/>

77. Parker, *Allegorical Drama*, 59.

78. Donald T. Dietz also disputes the cogency of what he terms Parker's "catchy solution" on different grounds; see Dietz, "Liturgical and Allegorical Drama," 77.

79. José María Díez Borque considers briefly such personifications in *Una fiesta sacramental barroca* (Madrid: Taurus, 1983), 107–9.

definition, implies that allegory consists at least partly in the defining of allegory. In Calderonian allegory (or Allegory), *definiens* and *definiendum*, definition and what that definition defines, are thus one.

Allegory's words ("I signify") thereby subvert any disjunction between saying and meaning, between words and what those words mean. Her statement constitutes what the philosopher J. L. Austin called a "performative utterance" or "illocutionary act": "performance of an act *in* saying something as opposed to performance of an act *of* saying something."[80] Such locutions, characterized by the simultaneity of act and word, verbally signalize the stated action. Allegory's performative utterance, creating signification in the act of defining it, suggests that saying *is* meaning, that is, signifying, conferring significance.[81] Allegory, in "signifying" allegory, "signifies" allegory's radical conjunction of signifier and signified.

And more. If allegory is not deictic, if it does not simply point to a privileged reality outside itself, it becomes on the contrary coextensive with that reality.[82] It becomes, in other words, in the case of the *auto*'s allegory, transcendent. And not merely transcendent, but sacramental. Allegory is numinous and sacral and the *auto* is *sacramental,* Calderón seems to suggest, because it and the Eucharist it celebrates are homologous. And if they are homologies, certain conclusions follow. The radical dis-

80. J. L. Austin, *How to Do Things with Words* (New York: Oxford University Press, 1962), 99. "[A]ll [such utterances]," Austin points out (p. 5), "will have humdrum verbs in the first person singular present indicative active."

81. Cf. Van Dyke, 42: "If a text says one thing it also means that thing: we cannot separate speech from meaning. Thus if it says one thing and means another, it both says and means two things."

82. Cf. Van Dyke, 28: "We must remember that allegory belongs to Derrida's 'epoch of the logos,' in which the distance between signifier and signified is a function of their homology and assumes the existence of a transcendental signified." See also Barbara E. Kurtz, " 'No Word without Mystery': Allegories of Sacred Truth in the *Autos Sacramentales* of Pedro Calderón de la Barca," *Publications of the Modern Language Association* 103 (1988): 262–73.

junction in reality that would ground any disjunct linguistic analysis of sacramental allegory is itself illusory: literature, language, the phenomenal world of which they are a part, are but finite exemplars, reflections, or manifestations of divine essence or divine intentionality, which validates and confers significance upon quotidian reality, including its literature.[83]

The *autos* themselves as dramatic performance likewise transcend any conveniently neat dichotomy of levels or meaning. The dramatic coda of each Calderonian *auto*—the "discovery" of the host and chalice—merges Eucharistic *asunto* into quotidian *argumento,* real into metaphorical, extraliterary into literary—and sacred into profane. The Eucharist exalted in and by the *autos* is no merely literary referent. Rather, the discovery, numinous and sacramental, suggests that both *auto* and Eucharist are for Calderón the conduits of divine intentionality, even divine grace. And both have their origin and their ontological ground in the Logos itself.[84]

It is this sacramental vision that explains, even mandates, the *autos'* use of allegory to analogize and define the sacred: "ajustarnos a hablar / a humano modo es preciso" (54), says Grace in *El año santo en Madrid,* "We must adapt to speaking in the human mode."[85] Indeed, in speaking to man, Christian thinkers believed, God used the "human mode"—spoke in parables and metaphors, by means of humble, ordinary words and things.[86] It is Pastor, allegory of the divine Good Shepherd, who mun-

---

83. See also the Afterword to the present study.

84. For more on the *autos'* implicit logocentrism, see the Afterword to the present study.

85. Cf. as well the following passage from *Sueños hay que verdad son* (1670): ". . . quiere Dios / que para rastrear lo inmenso / de su amor, poder y ciencia, / nos valgamos de los medios / que, a humano modo aplicados, / nos puedan servir de ejemplo" ["In order for us to fathom the immensity of God's love, power, and wisdom, He wants us to make use of those measures that can serve us as example when applied in a human way"] (1215).

86. Cf.: "Thou art a figurative, a metaphorical God." John Donne, *Devotions upon Emergent Occasions* (Ann Arbor: University of Michigan Press, 1965), 124.

danely defines allegory in the *loa* to *La segunda esposa*. And in thus defining allegory, he sacralizes and sacramentalizes its defining.

It is God, Calderón suggests, who legitimates the "human mode" of allegory. The invocation of divine authority to sanction his allegory becomes a hallmark of Calderón's *autos,* perhaps the most salient and significant, as the succeeding chapters will show.

2. Myth and Truth
Auto as Allegoresis

Dígalo el texto
de Pablo: Entre los Gentiles
asienta, que convirtieron
en fábulas las Verdades;
porque como ellos tuvieron
solo lejanas noticias
de la Luz del Evangelio,
viciaron sin ella nuestra
Escritura, atribuyendo
a falsos dioses sus raras
maravillas, y queriendo
que el Pueblo sepa, que no
hay fábula sin misterio,
si alegórica a la Luz
desto se mira, un ingenio,
bien que humilde, ha pretendido
dar esta noticia al Pueblo.
   (*Loa* to *El laberinto del mundo*, 1654?)

Few products of the human imagination have been more perennially alluring, and more productive of scholarly and literary examination, than myth. The legacy of Greco-Roman myth in particular has exercised an unparalleled influence on later expositors, apologists, and creative artists.[1] The gods, god-

1. On this influence, see especially Gilbert Highet, *The Classical Tradition* (London: Oxford University Press, 1949). For the Spanish tradition Highet's work must be used in conjunction with the review article by María Rosa Lida de Malkiel, "La tradición clásica en España, *Nueva revista de filología hispánica* 5 (1951): 183–223.

desses, and heroes of pagan antiquity are the common patrimony of Western art, the "classical tradition" that has informed countless literary and philosophical descendants.

The familiarity of this heritage guarantees its relative intelligibility even for a twentieth-century public no longer perfectly conversant with the narrative particulars of the tales and part of a culture radically out of tune with classicizing ideals. Yet that same familiarity can paradoxically impede our understanding of those artists who use the stories as allusive inspiration for original creations. We think we know who Orpheus was, or what Odysseus was like, even if the details of the primordial myth escape us. Yet the varying and extremely divergent formulations of, say, the Orpheus myth by such writers as the fourteenth-century poet of *Sir Orfeo* and the twentieth-century Cocteau should suggest that our vision of the mythological figure is not the only one possible. Indeed, a reading of Cocteau's *Orpheus,* centered on a subversively obscene eponym, and the Orfeo poet, who writes of a lover-knight imbued with Celtic associations, will come as a distinct shock to anyone coming to the later works fresh from perusing the ancient original.

All of which is to say, quite simply, that the Greco-Roman myths have received highly distinct and highly distinctive reformulations in the centuries since their creation. It is also to suggest that the reworking of the mythological legacy has always been, and must always be, inextricably linked with the issues and problems of interpretation. One man's Orfeo is another's Orphée, and who is to say which treatment is closer to the spirit of the original myth, or whether such an approximation is an artistic desideratum, or what the criteria of aesthetic and philosophical evaluation might be? What authority validates one interpretation against another, privileges one imitation over another?

These are weighty questions indeed, questions that pertain

crucially to the very nature and presuppositions of interpretation. We always read any mythological tale in the light of prevailing philsophical assumptions regarding myth, its ontological and philosophical status; the use of myth in any given age, and the interpretive principles applied to elucidating it, are thus an index to the period's paramount values and biases. Any history of a story's varying reformulations is therefore virtually, although usually implicitly, the history of mythography itself, mythography as the taxonomy of hermeneutics.

The values of our own age, in which anthropological, sociological, and psychological approaches to myth predominate,[2] inevitably leave us poorly prepared to understand the use of myth by a seventeenth-century writer such as Calderón. The playwright inherited and utilized in his *autos* an entire hermeneutic and propaedeutic tradition of incorporating the pagan tales into Christianizing allegoresis and Christian apologetics.[3]

In nine *autos sacramentales* based on Greco-Roman myth,[4] allegorized versions of some of the most famous tales from antiq-

2. G. S. Kirk provides a useful overview and critique of these approaches in *Myth* (Berkeley: Cambridge University Press and University of California Press, 1970).

3. On the relationship between pagan myth and Christian apologetics, see especially Don Cameron Allen, *Mysteriously Meant* (Baltimore: Johns Hopkins University Press, 1970), Ch. 1, "Pagan Myth and Christian Apologetics."

4. Two doctoral dissertations deal with Calderón's mythological *autos*. Geoffrey Michael Voght, "The Mythological Autos of Calderón de la Barca" (Diss., University of Michigan, 1974), considers only *El divino Orfeo* (1663), *Psiquis y Cupido* (1665), and *El laberinto del mundo* (1654?). Sister María Inés Martín Acosta, C.S.J., "The Mythological Autos of Calderón de la Barca" (Diss., Columbia University, 1969), treats the entire corpus, but her analyses are virtually limited to plot summaries of the various plays. See also Jorge Páramo Pomareda, "Consideraciones sobre los 'autos mitológicos' de Calderón de la Barca," *Thesaurus* 12 (1957): 51–80, which also contains some bibliographic data on the earliest studies of Calderón's mythological *autos*, and Ignacio Elizalde, "El papel de Dios verdadero en los autos y comedias mitológicos de Calderón," in Luciano García Lorenzo, ed., *Calderón: Actas del Congreso internacional sobre Calderón y el teatro español del Siglo de Oro* (Madrid: Consejo Superior de Investigaciones Científicas, 1983), 999–1012.

uity, Calderón incorporates the mythological legacy within established conventions of allegorizing, Christianizing exegesis. However, Calderón's achievement in the mythological *autos* far transcends servile obeisance to established usage. In his hands the mythological *auto* becomes the vehicle for a profoundly original, and profoundly illuminating, examination of the complex relation of myth to allegory and of the hermeneutical problems inherent in both. By explicitly thematizing the divine Word as source and guarantor of pagan myth, as well as of language and (illuminated) interpretation, Calderón's plays embody a powerful allegory of the assumed divine origin and sacral significance not only of myth, but also of the *auto* itself. For the dramatist, divine ordination and revealed truth implicitly sacramentalize the *auto* and the human author's hermeneutical and creative endeavors. This conceptualization of the mythological *auto* adumbrates both a metaphysics and a quite powerful allegorical theory, as the following pages will show.[5]

The relationship between myth and allegory or allegorical exegesis has a venerable and ancient lineage;[6] it is a relationship

5. On the implicit logocentrism of this theory, see Ch. 3 and 4 of the present study.

6. The bibliography on the allegorical exegesis of myth is, of course, enormous. For essential background of allegoresis in general, see Henri de Lubac, *Exégèse médiévale*, 2 vols. in 4 (Paris: Aubier, 1959–64); Jean Pépin, *Mythe et allégorie* (Paris: Aubier, 1958); C. Spicq, *Esquisse d'une histoire de l'exégèse latine au moyen âge* (Paris: J. Vrin, 1944). On the allegorical interpretation of myth, see D. C. Allen; Lester K. Born, "Ovid and Allegory," *Speculum* 9 (1934): 362–79; Douglas Bush, *Mythology and the Renaissance Tradition in English Poetry*, rev. ed. (New York: W. W. Norton, 1963); A. M. Cinquemani, "Henry Reynolds' *Mythomystes* and the Continuity of Ancient Modes of Allegoresis in Seventeenth-Century England," *Publications of the Modern Language Association* 85 (1970): 1041–49; Domenico Comparetti, *Vergil in the Middle Ages*, trans. E. F. M. Benecke, repr. 1929 (New York: G. E. Stechert, 1929); J. D. Cooke, "Euhemerism: A Mediaeval Interpretation of Classical Paganism," *Speculum* 2 (1927): 396–410; F. Ghisalberti, "L' 'Ovidius Moralizatus' di Pierre Bersuire," *Studi Romanzi* 23 (1933): 5–136; Anne Bates Hersman, *Studies in Greek Allegorical Interpretation* (Chicago: Blue Sky, 1906); Edgar C. Knowlton, "Notes on Early Allegory,"

so close that one scholar has declared that "myth is allegory; or, perhaps, allegory is myth."[7] Allegory, or at least allegorical interpretation,[8] was born with the attempt by ancient Greek philosophers to explain and rationalize the pantheon. Basic to the endeavor was the belief that the myths embodied profound truths, that they were the symbolic expression of philosophical and theological beliefs or the intuition of scientific explanation formulated in the only terms possible in an age that lacked a precise philosophical and scientific lexicon.[9] The early Stoics in

---

Journal of English and Germanic Philology 29 (1930): 159–81; Frank E. Manuel, *The Eighteenth Century Confronts the Gods* (Cambridge: Harvard University Press, 1959); DeWitt T. Starnes and E. W. Talbert, *Classical Myth and Legend in Renaissance Dictionaries* (Chapel Hill: University of North Carolina Press, 1955); J. Tate, "The Beginnings of Greek Allegory," *The Classical Review* 41 (1927): 214–17, "On the History of Allegorism," *Classical Quarterly* 28 (1934): 105–14, and "Plato and Allegorical Interpretation," *Classical Quarterly* 23 (1929): 142–54 and 24 (1930): 1–10; M. C. Waites, "Some Aspects of the Ancient Allegorical Debate," *Studies in English and Comparative Literature* (Boston: Radcliffe College Monographs no. 15, 1910). Specific material on the fate of the pagan gods and goddesses in the allegorical interpretations of the Middle Ages and Renaissance can be found in D. C. Allen; Bush; O. H. Green, " 'Fingen los poetas': Notes on the Spanish Attitude toward Pagan Mythology," in *Estudios dedicados a Menéndez Pidal* 1 (Madrid: Consejo Superior de Investigaciones Científicas, 1950), 275–88 and *Spain and the Western Tradition* 3 (Madison: University of Wisconsin Press, 1968), 190–202, 414–18, 423–25; Hans Liebschütz, *Fulgentius Metaforalis: Ein Beitrag zur Geschichte der antiken Mythologie im Mittelalter* (Leipzig: B. G. Teubner, 1926); and Edgar Wind, *Pagan Mysteries in the Renaissance* (New Haven: Yale University Press, 1958), especially Ch. 2, "Poetic Theology."

7. D. C. Allen, p. vii.

8. On the notion of allegory as intrinsically interpretative, see Morton W. Bloomfield, "Allegory as Interpretation," *New Literary History* 3 (1972): 301–17.

9. "Allegorical interpretation of the ancient Greek myths began . . . with the philosophers. As speculative thought developed, there grew up also the belief that in mystical and symbolic terms the ancient poets had expressed profound truths which were difficult to define in scientifically exact language. Assuming that the myth-makers were concerned to edify and to instruct, the philosophers found in apparent immoralities and impieties a warning that both in offensive and in inoffensive passages one must look beneath the surface for the true significance of the tales" (Tate, *Plato,* 142).

particular proliferated allegories of Homer and Hesiod, in whom they found, or hoped to find, "the right answers to the problems of the universe."[10] The methodology they employed to uncover those answers was simple: "In carrying out their object they had recourse to etymologies, to plays on words, to the juxtaposition of other passages, to physical allusions, to the symbolism of numbers, to the emphasising [sic] of separate expressions, to inordinate development of metaphor, and interminable inferences from incidental phrases."[11]

The methods and philosophical bases of allegoresis as elaborated by the Greeks were to have a long, exceedingly fruitful development. The Judaic philosophers of Alexandria naturalized Hellenic exegesis as a means of harmonizing Jewish legislation with the much-admired speculative philosophy of the Greeks.[12] Philo (born c. 20 B.C.), the great systematizer and codifier of the methods, felt that the literal sense of Scripture, its statements of fact, need not be taken as literally true: "[T]he sacred words, when taken in their literal sense, are occasionally incredible, and not infrequently trivial, or at any rate inadequate, and therefore must conceal some 'underlying thought,' which patient meditation, aided by God's grace, cannot fail to extract."[13]

Just as the Alexandrian philosophers turned to Stoic allegorism in order to reconcile Mosaic law and Greek philosophy, so too did the Apostolic Fathers adopt the Philonic or Alexandrian exegetical paradigm "in order to make the Old Testament an immediate witness for Christian truth."[14] The tradi-

10. Tate, *Plato*, 2.

11. Frederic W. Farrar, *History of Interpretation* (Grand Rapids, MI: Baker Book House, 1961), 136.

12. On Philo, see Pépin, Ch. 9, section 4 of Première Partie, 190–209.

13. F. H. Colson and G. H. Whitaker in the introduction to their translation of *Philo* in ten volumes (with two supplementary volumes), 1 (Cambridge: Harvard University Press, 1971), xiii.

14. Farrar, 167.

tion of Christianizing apologetics had its birth at the very dawn of the Christian era, as the new faith struggled for political and social standing as well as religious acceptance and diffusion. For example, against the attacks of pagan controversialists such as Celsus (who maintained that the Christian conception of Christ was a purloined amalgam of the myths of Hercules, Bacchus, and Aesculapius, and Christian doctrine a warped version of Platonic idealism), Christian apologists adopted a variety of defensive postures and offensive weapons. Some, such as Justin and Tertullian, maintained that the thought of a few pre-Christians presignified Christian truth in a corrupt form debased by diabolic alteration. Some followed an essentially Euhemeristic interpretation of the pagan pantheon, arguing that the gods were the product of apotheosizing human heroes. Still others claimed an originative divine inspiration for all the basic truths discoverable by the human mind, even those embodied in pagan myth.[15] Justin Martyr, for example, asserted that "the seeds of truth seem to be among all men"[16] who live virtuously in accordance with the dictates of right reason. Apologists compiled a roster of ur-Christians, such as Socrates, Plato, and Hermes Trismegistus, who were presumed to have had glimmerings of Christian truth.

The logical development of these strains of Christian apologetics or polemics was the assimilation of pagan myth to Chris-

---

15. For example, the Christian philosopher Clement of Alexandria (end of second century/beginning of third century) maintained that the Greeks received their philosophy from the inferior angels and from Moses and the prophets:

Before the coming of Christ, philosophy was necessary to the Greeks for righteousness. . . . God is the cause of all good things, but of some before others; hence, first the two Testaments and second, philosophy. Now philosophy was given first to the Greeks until they could be called by God, because philosophy brought the Greeks to Christ as the Law did the Jews. Philosophy, therefore, prepares the way for him who would be perfected in Christ. Quoted by D. C. Allen, 9.

16. Quoted by D. C. Allen, 4.

tian typology.[17] The culmination of this rationalization or Christianization of pagan myth was Augustine. The bishop of Hippo stoutly affirmed the adumbrations of Christian doctrine to be found in the virtuous pagan philosophers and theologians: "From the beginning of mankind, at times covertly and at times openly . . . He continued to prophesy, and before He became incarnate, there were men who believed in Him . . . among the people of Israel . . . and among other peoples."[18] And, of course, Augustine's admiring study of Plato led him to attribute perceived similarities between Platonic philosophy and Christian theology to the illustrious pagan's foreknowledge of revealed truth or his acquisition of some Christian information and thought.[19]

Augustine's attitude toward pagan letters is epitomized in the famous passage of *On Christian Doctrine* (2, 40) where the bishop expounds the notion of the *Spolatio Aegyptiorum.* The passage merits extensive quotation:

> If those who are called philosophers, especially the Platonists, have said things which are indeed true and are well accommodated to our faith, they should not be feared; rather, what they have said should be taken from them as from unjust possessors and converted to our use. Just as the Egyptians had not only idols and grave burdens which the people of Israel detested and avoided, so also they had vases and ornaments of gold and silver and clothing which the Israelites took with them secretly when they fled, as if to put them to a better use. . . . In the same way all the teachings of the pagans contain not only simulated and superstitious imaginings and grave burdens of unnecessary labor . . . but also liberal disciplines more suited to the uses of truth, and some most useful precepts concerning morals. Even some truths concerning the worship of one God are discovered among them. These are, as it were, their gold and silver, which they did not in-

17. On typology, see the discussion and bibliography included in Ch. 3 of the present study.

18. Quoted by D. C. Allen, 18.

19. On this point, see discussion by D. C. Allen, 17–18.

stitute themselves but dug up from certain mines of divine Providence, which is everywhere infused, and perversely. . . . When the Christian separates himself in spirit from their miserable society, he should take this treasure with him for the just use of teaching the gospel. And their clothing, which is made up of those human institutions which are accommodated to human society and necessary to the conduct of life, should be seized and held to be converted to Christian uses.[20]

This passage contains the seeds of principles fundamental to Christian hermeneutics and Christian proselytism.[21] Immanent divine Providence, "everywhere infused," irradiates some of the pagans' teachings, Augustine maintains. With the light of revelation, the Christian can and must discover the truths and precepts contained therein and use them in teaching the gospel.

The Augustinian principles regarding pagan myth became the foundation of most later Christian attitudes toward the mythological legacy. The common denominator of the disparate medieval and Renaissance mythographers was the belief "that pre-Christian poets and philosophers possessed proximate truth,"[22] ethical and/or Christian meanings assumed to lie *sub cortice,* and that such truth could and should be extracted for its moral utility through allegorical, often etymological, exegesis.[23]

20. (Saint) Augustine, *On Christian Doctrine,* trans. D. W. Robertson, Jr. (Indianapolis: Bobbs, 1958), 75.

21. The topos is discussed, for example, in the famous letter to Can Grande della Scala that was presumably written by Dante. See C. S. Latham, *A Translation of Dante's Eleven Letters,* ed. George Rice Carpenter with a preface by Charles Eliot Norton (Boston: Houghton, Mifflin, 1891). On the diffusion of this notion, see Edwin A. Quain, "The Medieval *Accessus ad Auctores,*" *Traditio* 3 (1945): 223–24, and, for the Iberian peninsula, Edward A. Glaser, ed., *Imagen de la vida cristiana,* by Héctor Pinto, *Espirituales españoles,* Ser. B, 1 (Barcelona: Juan Flores, 1967), 59, n. 1234.

22. D. C. Allen, 19.

23. During the Middle Ages in particular allegoresis was the virtually universal approach to myth, as the practical exigencies of education secured a place for pagan literature in the medieval curriculum and likewise demanded their reconciliation or

This theory and method of interpretation had a long vogue, lasting well into the eighteenth century.[24] Although a nascent scientific or empirical spirit is increasingly evident throughout

---

adaptation to Christian doctrine. Such allegorization of pagan myth was throughout the period not only a well-established and universally applied hermeneutical method, but also an implicit assumption about the essential significance, and signification, of myth itself. Apologists saw in the eminent pre-Christian poets and philosophers approximations to Christian truth; others saw a secular but nonetheless valuable form of *philosophia moralis.*

The commentary of the sixth-century mythographer Fulgentius, one of the most influential allegorical interpreters, well exemplifies medieval interpretative beliefs and practices. Fulgentius seeks to disclose the transcendent, universal truths he presumes lie hidden in the Greek tales. Methodologically, he does little that is new; ordinarily, he merely outlines the plot of a particular myth, a plot that is often so condensed as to be virtually incomprehensible as narrative, and simply declares what the various elements of the narrative, or its very words, represent or symbolize, relying heavily on etymology as a source of illumination. He displays little interest in the myths' historical or literary value, which is merely a pretext for moral and philosophical excurses. Such principles and procedures inform innumerable medieval mythographies, such as the *Commentum Super Sex Libros Eneidas Virgilii* of Bernardus Silvestris (fl. 1150), the *Integumenta Ovidii* of John of Garland (mid-twelfth century), the anonymous *Ovide moralisé* (early fourteenth century) and its descendants, and the *Epître d'Othéa* of Christine de Pisan (late fourteenth century). See Bernardus Silvestris, *Commentary on the First Six Books of Virgil's Aeneid,* trans. Earl B. Schreiber and Thomas E. Maresca (Lincoln: University of Nebraska Press, 1979); John Garland, "The Integumenta on the 'Metamorphoses' of Ovid," ed. and trans. Lester Kruger Born (Diss., University of Chicago, 1929); *Ovide moralisé,* ed. C. de Boer et al. (Amsterdam: Verhandelingen Koninklijke Akademie van Wetenschappen, 1915–38); Christine de Pisan, "The Epistle of Othea to Hector," ed. James D. Gordon (Diss., University of Pennsylvania, 1942). The Latin text of *The Mythologies* is available in R. Helm, *Fabii Planciadis Fulgentii opera* (Leipzig: Bibliotheca Teubneriana, 1898), 3–80. More accessible, and universally used, is the translation by Leslie George Whitbread in *Fulgentius the Mythographer* (Columbus: Ohio State University Press, 1971), 39–102. Whitbread provides extensive bibliographies on Fulgentius and his works, as well as on the entire mythographic tradition in general.

24. On the fate of the allegorical interpretation of myth during the eighteenth century, see Manuel, and Arnaldo Momigliano, *Studies in Historiography* (London: Weidenfeld and Nicolson, 1966). Burton Feldman and Robert D. Richardson, eds., provide a valuable anthology of selections and basic bibliography in *The Rise of Modern Mythology, 1680-1860* (Bloomington: Indiana University Press, 1972).

the Renaissance,[25] and despite the attacks and ridicule of detractors such as Rabelais,[26] the etymologizing and symbolic exegesis of the past is still universally observable among Renaissance mythographers.[27]

Numerous Calderonian *autos* can readily be placed within the categories of mythographic interpretation conventional for his time and place. Occasionally, for example, the dramatist's reading of pagan myth is tropological, i.e., concerned with the

25. Yet even Boccaccio, whom Allen (p. 214) calls "the first of the systematic mythographers" of the new spirit, produces in the *Genealogia deorum gentilium* an epitome of medieval allegoresis. In standard medieval fashion, the Italian writer provides summaries of numerous myths and appends to each an allegorical interpretation, which is generally moral or physical. See Giovanni Boccaccio, *Genealogiae deorum gentilium libri,* ed. Vincenzo Romano (Bari: G. Laterza, 1951). On Boccaccio's treatment of mythology, see D. C. Allen, 215–20; C. C. Coulter, "The Genealogy of the Gods," *Vassar Mediaeval Studies,* ed. C. F. Fiske (New Haven: Yale University Press, 1923), 317–41; E. Gilson, "Poésie et vérité dans la *Genealogia* de Boccace," in *Studi sul Boccaccio,* ed. Vittore Branca, 2 (Firenze: Sansoni, 1963–), 253–82; Henri Hauvette, *Boccace* (Paris: A. Colin, 1914); Attilio Hortis, *Studi sulle opere latine del Boccaccio* (Trieste: J. Dase, 1879); Alex Preminger, O. B. Hardison, Jr., and K. Kervante, eds., *Classical and Medieval Literary Criticism* (New York: F. Ungar, 1974); Seznec, *Survival,* 220–24.

26. "Croiez vous en vostre foy qu'onques Homere, escrivent l'*Iliade* et *Odysée,* pensast es allegories lesquelles de luy ont calfreté Plutarche, Heraclides Ponticq, Eustatie, Pharnute, et ce que d'iceulx Politian a desrobé? Si le croiez, vous n'approchez ne de pieds ne de mains à mon opinion, qui decrete icelles aussi peu avoir esté sougées d'Homere que d'Ovide en ses *Metamorphoses* les sacramens de l'Evangile, lesquelz une Frere Lubin, vray croquelarden s'est efforcé demonstrer, si d'aventure il recontroit gens aussi folz que luy, et (comme dicit le proverbe) converces digne du chandron." Quoted by Born, "Ovid and Allegory," 378.

27. This allegorizing spirit or approach is characteristic, for example, of the two best-known Spanish mythographers of Calderón's day. Juan Pérez de Moya in the *Philosophia secreta* (1585) appends to most of the tales he has compiled a *Declaraçion,* which expounds the allegorical sense of the myth as well as its possible historical basis. Baltasar de Vitoria, although much less given than Pérez de Moya to allegorical exegesis, does find in the myths collected in his *Teatro de los dioses de la gentilidad* (1620) statements of ancient philosophy concerning human morality and natural science. On these mythographers, see José María de Cossío, *Fábulas mitológicas en España* (Madrid: Espasa-Calpe, 1952), 65–71.

moral message implicit in or deducible from the ancient tale.[28]
In *Los encantos de la Culpa* (before 1647), the story of Ulysses
and Circe is an allegory of man's inner conflict between appetite
and reason.[29] The Greek hero is a mythological Everyman, "peregrino y navegante" ["a pilgrim and a sailor"] (407), among
the tribulations of life.[30] His vassals or sailors are the human
senses, bewitched and converted into beasts by Circe, or Culpa.
Man's animalization through sensual indulgence is redeemed
and reversed, according to the allegory, by Penitence, who in-
structs Man that the ship of the Church is the only vehicle of escape from Sin, and the Eucharist, the only true food for the
soul.

Calderón's allegorization of the Ulysses-Circe episode converts the myth into a *psychomachia* whose stated purpose is exemplary or cautionary, reflective of the predominantly homiletic conception of the *auto* that the dramatist during this period
had embraced:

> ". . . hoy verás
> todas aquestas viandas
> del viento desvanecidas
> en humo, en polvo y en nada;
> mostrando con este ejemplo
> lo que son glorias humanas,
> pues el manjar solamente
> que es eterno es el del Alma."   (420)

28. On the whole issue of didacticism and morality in Golden Age literature in
general, see Bruno M. Damiani, *Moralidad y didactismo en el Siglo de Oro* (Madrid:
Orígenes, 1987).

29. On this *auto,* see also Aurora Egido, *La fábrica de un auto sacramental: "Los
encantos de la Culpa"* (Salamanca: Ediciones Universidad de Salamanca, 1982), and
Diego Martínez Torrón, "El mito de Circe y *Los encantos de la culpa,"* in García Lorenzo, ed., *Calderón,* 701–12.

30. On the notion of the *peregrinatio vitae,* see especially Juergen H. Hahn, *The
Origins of the Baroque Idea of "Peregrinatio"* (Chapel Hill: University of North Carolina Press, 1973) and Samuel Chew, *The Pilgrimage of Life* (New Haven: Yale University Press, 1962).

Today you will see all these provisions dispelled by the wind and turned into smoke, into dust, into nothingness; and this example shows the nature of human glories, since the only eternal nourishment is that of the soul.[31]

More commonly, it is not a platitudinously tropological but rather a radically typological vision that informs Calderón's treatment of pagan myth, as in most precursory allegorists. In *El verdadero Dios Pan* (1670), for example, the dramatist explicitly allegorizes the shepherd god as a "shadow" or prefiguration of the Good Shepherd of scriptural parable. The fabulous pagan god of "human letters" merely veils "the true God Pan" (1261). Support for this typological interpretation is adduced from complicated etymological analysis. "Pan" in Greek means "everything," we are told, an acceptation which evokes Christ as union of both divine and human: ". . . hay en mí unidas / tan desiguales distancias / como hay de humano a divino, / significándome ambas" ["in me are conjoined highly disproportionate distances, such as that from human to divine, since I signify both"] (1242). Christ is also the Bread of Life,[32] commemorated and hypostatized in the Eucharist, and he is thus associated homonymically with "Pan," since "pan" means "bread" in Spanish (1242).

This complex etymologizing, so farfetched and ill founded to modern eyes, is actually neither whimsical nor factitious. On the contrary, it is grounded in a whole metaphysics of etymology and etymological analysis. In this conception etymology is seen as intrinsically revelatory of hidden, even sacred, meaning: " . . . su apoyo / en las divinas [letras] no falta" ["support for it is not lacking in divine letters"] (1242).[33] Analysis of etymology

31. On the relationship between Calderón's *autos sacramentales* and contemporaneous homiletics, see Ch. 1 of the present study.

32. This interpretation is suggested by Martín Acosta, 172–73.

33. On the traditional use of etymology as an interpretative tool, see especially Ernst Robert Curtius, *European Literature and the Latin Middle Ages,* trans. Willard R. Trask (Princeton: Princeton University Press, 1973), 495–500. For its use by Calderón, see also Páramo Pomareda.

conceived as essentially numinous is thus authoritative; it discloses and validates the typological associations that link myth and revealed truth and legitimize allegorical interpretation of the pagan tales.

The sanctioning of pagan myth as prefigurative, and the use of etymology to confirm the relationship, are the cornerstones of Calderón's allegorizing mythography. It is the Prince (Christ) who in *El divino Orfeo* (1663) expounds the theory of myth that grounds or legitimizes myth's allegorical, Christocentric treatment:

> La Gentilidad . . .
> idolatramente ciega,
> teniendo de las verdades
> lejanas noticias, piensa
> que falsos dioses y ninfas
> atribuya la [*sic*] Inmensas
> Obras de Dios solo . . .   (1847)

Heathendom, idolatrously blind and possessing only vague knowledge of [Christian] truth, attributes to false gods and nymphs the Immense Works performed by God alone.

Myth contains veiled, prophetic allusions to Christianity's eternal truths. The interpreter's task will thus be to "confront Divine and Human Letters" ("en la consonancia amigas / y en la Religión opuestas" ["in their hidden concord friends although antagonists in religion"]) in order to disclose the Christian significance presaged in the myth and to deduce the moral or theological meaning presumed preexistent or innate in the mythological text (1847).

Given the undeniable conventionality of such theories and devices of allegoresis, one might be tempted to dismiss Calderón as a mythographic hack, an unimaginative purveyor of theological platitudes and secondhand allegorizing techniques. But such a dismissal is possible only if one passes over some truly revealing curiosities in the dramatist's mythological and allegorical repertoire. The most obvious, perhaps, is the freedom with which Calderón handles the mythological legacy. In *El verdadero Dios Pan,* for example, he fuses the eponymous god with reminiscences of Endymion, the young shepherd loved by the Moon, and he centers the *auto* on Pan's love for Luna, here the personification of the human soul. Luna, or Moon, is identified variously with Diana and Proserpina. The three analogates—Diana, Moon, Proserpina—are obviously interrelated through their nocturnal associations. Collectively, they figure three possible destinies of the soul, earthly, heavenly, or infernal (1243). Finally, since the shepherd Pan is seen as the type of the scriptural Good Shepherd, elements of the parable are logically and dramatically integrated into the storyline: Pan abandons a flock of ninety-nine sheep to restore to Moon's care one lost lamb.

The latitude that Calderón takes in elaborating, and often completely rewriting, ancient myth increasingly characterizes his mythological *auto.* Indeed, the later, and finest, *autos* in particular are far more than twice-told tales; what confronts us in these plays is no longer Greco-Roman myth but rather Calderonian mythopoeia.

In his last mythological *auto, Andrómeda y Perseo* (1680)[34], for example, Calderón radically rewrites/reinterprets the inherited tale so as to foreground a Christocentric reading. Briefly, the original myth relates that Perseus comes upon the unfortunate Andromeda abandoned and chained to a rock on a lonely seacoast, sacrifice to a monstrous sea serpent. This horrible fate was to be visited upon the girl as punishment for a grievous er-

34. On this *auto,* see also Hans Flasche, "Antiker Mythos in christlicher Umprägung: Andromeda und Perseus bei Calderón," *Romanistisches Jahrbuch* 16 (1965): 290–317, and Sebastián Neumeister, "Calderón y el mito clásico: *Andrómeda y Perseo,* auto sacramental y fiesta de corte," in García Lorenzo, ed., *Calderón,* 713–21.

ror committed by her mother, the beautiful but vain and foolish Queen Cassiopeia: Cassiopeia had arrogantly boasted that her beauty was matchless, surpassing even the loveliness of the Nereids, daughters of the sea god. To castigate this vainglory and brazen impertinence, Jupiter decreed the sacrifice of the princess to a sea monster. Perseus, coming upon the girl by chance, is instantly captivated by her beauty. He waits with her for the monster, whom he slays and beheads. After this triumphant victory, the king and queen give him Andromeda's hand in marriage.

The story of Perseus was told in antiquity by both Ovid and Apollodorus, and during the Spanish Renaissance by Pérez de Moya.[35] Christian allegorizers of the Middle Ages and Renaissance variously interpreted the hero. Occasionally he was allegorized as St. George,[36] occasionally as a national hero to be exalted through analogy to the pagan hero.[37] Occasionally, he was conceived as a type of Christ. Boccaccio, for example, interprets Perseus's slaying of Medusa as an allegory of Christ's triumph over the princes of the world. In his treatment of the myth, he focusses on the hero's triumph over the Gorgon rather than on the central love interest. To be sure, Perseus's conquest of the monster offered more fertile ground for Christological analogizing than Perseus's relationship with the princess. Precedent for a specifically Christological reading of the Perseus-Andromeda episode is not lacking.[38] However, no treatment is as extensive or as thoughtful as Calderón's allegorization. The dramatist virtually rewrites the tale; he conflates the Medusa and

35. On the Perseus myth and its literary and allegorical manifestations, see Edwin Sidney Hartland, *The Legend of Perseus* (London: D. Nuff, 1894–96).

36. See Seznec, 213.

37. Perseus was allegorized as Henry of Navarre by Nicolas Renouard in his *Les Metamorphoses d'Ovide traduittes en Prose Francoise* . . . , published in Paris in 1614. See D. C. Allen, 196.

38. It appears, for example, in Christine de Pisan's *Epître d'Othéa.*

Andromeda episodes (separate incidents in the ancient versions) and alters freely the inherited material so as to highlight the Christological typology. In his reading Perseus becomes Christ, and Andromeda, Human Nature, an interpretation the dramatist derives from a highly complex, and highly artificial, etymological interpretation of the princess's name. Perseus's rescue of the supposedly doomed princess becomes the story of the Savior's redemption of mankind.

Christian accommodation necessarily entails substantial revision of the mythological tale. While the Perseus-Andromeda episode does offer some vague parallels to the salvation history of humanity—and hence some basis for a Christological reading—numerous details resist facile, or even ingenious, analogizing and must be considerably transformed in order to yield Christian undermeanings. For example, Cassiopeia's sin of pride and arrogance, motive force behind the myth's chain of events, virtually disappears in the *auto*. Andromeda, as Human Nature, must take on the theologically crucial role of committing the "original" and originary sin. The princess's error echoes Cassiopeia's sin in the original myth:

> Peregrina
> es en todo mi belleza.
> ¿Qué (Humana Naturaleza)
> te falta para divina?
> Los cielos no hicieron, no,
> cosa en todos sus modelos
> más hermosa, ni aun los cielos
> son tan bellos como yo.   (1695)

My beauty is most singular. What, Human Nature, do you lack to be divine? The heavens have made nothing more beautiful; nor are the heavens themselves as beautiful as I.

Like Cassiopeia, Andromeda displays an arrogantly prideful assurance that her beauty is virtually divine; despite the uneasy warnings of her own personified Free Will (a character naturally absent from the myth), the princess sees in herself "el más perfecto ejemplar / que vio el sol . . ." ["the most perfect exemplar seen by the sun"] (1696).

However, Andromeda's moral failings go far beyond pride and presumption; she is guilty as well of the far more grievous and theologically relevant sin of disobedience to divine mandate. The Devil, jealous of the "deidad humana" ["human deity"] (1700) who reigns over her father's (obviously edenic) garden, is outraged because the princess "aspira a ocupar el solio / que perdí . . ." "aspires to occupy the throne that I lost" (1700)—an obvious allusion to Lucifer's fall. To assist him in revenge, he calls upon Medusa, who takes on the dual allegorical identity of sin and death: ". . . horrorosa / imagen de la culpa y de la muerte, / que en piedra o bruto al racional convierte" ["hideous image of sin and of death, image that converts rational beings into stone or brute"] (1699). Medusa readily agrees to help; her own grievous ugliness makes her jealous of the preferment Andromeda enjoys. It is Medusa who suggests the plot that will bring the downfall of the hated princess: the Gorgon will fatally poison a "forbidden tree" in the royal garden, and the princess's Free Will, tempted by the tree's fateful apples, will fall victim to the Devil.

Calderón's handling of this crucial scene is significant for understanding his entire approach to myth throughout the *autos sacramentales*. In addition to modifying the nature and causes of Andromeda's plight, obviously fused here with the Christian gnosis of Genesis, Calderón introduces the Gorgon into that predicament, giving prominence to a figure that does not appear in the Andromeda episode of Perseus's adventures. In the Perseus story, in fact, the hero slays the monster before he even encounters the princess, and the two events are narratively and thematically unconnected. Yet Calderón could scarcely pass up the opportunity to conflate them in his Christian allegorization. In the iconographic tradition that developed around Perseus throughout the Middle Ages and Renaissance,[39] the Medusa adventure was the most significant of the hero's career and it was, furthermore, the most suggestive of Christological parallels: the Gorgon's horrific appearance and destructive animus, as well as the famous snaky hair, made the monster readily assimilable to Christian demonology, so that Perseus's conquest becomes an obvious analogue of Christ's victory over sin and death.

Her diabolic associations notwithstanding, Calderón's Gorgon is not the Devil but, rather, the Devil's henchman.[40] In the *auto* the Devil himself does allegorize an analogous figure from the myth: Phineus, Andromeda's disappointed suitor, who loses her to the heroic Perseus. The Devil offers a complex etymological rationale for the correspondence, in a pun naturally difficult to convey in English:

> por empresa he de llevar
> en el escudo del rostro
> esculpido Finis-Ero,

39. See Seznec, *passim*.

40. Calderón's Devil is almost invariably accompanied in the *autos sacramentales* by such henchmen or alter egos. As Parker points out, the Devil "is always paired with a companion or accomplice who is given such names as Guilt or Sin, Darkness, Night. And this new character is a dramatic counterpart to another who appears as a companion of Human Nature, and who is called Innocence, Grace, or Light. Guilt is the negation of Innocence, Sin the negation of Grace, Darkness the negation of Light." Parker convincingly argues that this pairing avoids a theologically heterodox conception of the Devil and his influence, since Calderón faced several difficulties in dramatizing this figure: "how to present the Devil as evil, ... how to avoid presenting him as a personified Principle of Evil, as an antithetical counterpart to the Principle of Good, and ... how to connect the evil in Original Sin with the Devil's malice." See A. A. Parker, "The Devil in the Drama of Calderón," in *Critical Essays on the Theatre of Calderón,* ed. Bruce W. Wardropper (New York: New York University Press, 1965), 3–23.

pues de sus dichas y gozos
he de ser fin, cuya letra
nombre me ha de dar famoso
de Fineo, pues Fineo
y Finis-Ero es lo propio.   (1699–1700)

For device I shall bear sculptured on my shield "Finis-Ero,"
since to her [Andromeda's] pleasures and happiness I shall write
finis, the spelling of which will give me the name *Fineo,* for Fineo,
and *Finis-Ero* are one and the same.

Despite the nominal justification of the analogy, the demonic
Phineus is not really comparable to his mythological eponym.
In the myth the frustrated lover is a wholly subordinate, unde-
veloped, and shadowy personage whose very insubstantiality
serves to throw into greater relief the god-like Perseus. In the
auto Phineus is a central figure and, as the Devil, principal in
the fall of mankind. The theological or sacred register completely subsumes the mythological in this portion of the play, as
Phineus alludes to the traditional story of Lucifer's fall ("Al
mismo Dios le presenté batalla" ["On God himself I waged
war"] [1699]) and to his jealousy of the favored Human Nature,
who supplanted him in divine favor.

The demonic temptation and moral fall of Human Nature
transform Andromeda into a type of Eve as well as personification of mankind; this transformation, as well as the account of
the princess's perdition, distances the *auto* still further from the
myth. Perseus comes to warn Andromeda against eating the
forbidden fruit and to hint of some sea-born peril that may en-
sue if she disobeys: if she does not refrain from eating the garden's fruits, one of which is poisoned, she will surely die (1703).

Calderón abandons both the spirit and the chronology of the
myth as he diverges from retelling the mythological tale in order to restate the scriptural account of man's fall. Perseus-
Christ does not come upon Andromeda by chance, as in the

myth; rather, he seeks her out to warn her of impending moral danger (taking on thereby some of the attributes of the Father, Yahweh of Genesis). Andromeda's expulsion from her father's garden and her abandonment on the rocky coast become the penalty for disobedience rather than a chastisement of her mother's, or her own, pride. The punishment of the princess is thus no longer the capricious visitation upon an innocent that the myth related; it is on the contrary the manifestation of divine justice at its most exigent, formidable, and righteous.

In the *auto*'s climactic passage the dramatist gives tighter, more rational dramatic and moral causality to the account of Andromeda's fate by emphasizing the action's scriptural and theological referent. He so freely alters the inherited myth, in fact, that at times the mythological narrative virtually disappears, submerged in a relatively straightforward retelling of sacred history.

Perseus's rescue of Andromeda parallels the mythological account, but with telling differences. In the first place, the liberation of the princess is merged with Perseus's defeat of Medusa, as the christic figure thus allegorically conquers sin and death. In the second place, whereas the mythological Perseus emerged unscathed from his battle against the sea monster, his allegorical analogue must pay with his life, promising Human Nature that she will yet become his wife when he returns to earth "in another form":

> Y así, pues muriendo puedo
> vencer, triunfar y morir,
> prevente para las bodas,
> que yo bajaré por ti
> en otra forma a la Tierra.   (1712)

And since in dying I can vanquish, triumph, and still die, prepare for your wedding; for I shall descend to earth for you, in another form.

At the close of the play Perseus returns, bathed in an aura of universal rejoicing and typological resonances ("Viva el divino Perseo, / viva el segundo David" ["Long live divine Perseus, long live the second David"] [1712]). The wedding banquet of Andromeda and Perseus becomes the celebration of the Eucharist, as the triumphant hero promises his bride to remain with her always under the species of the consecrated wine and bread: "aquestas especies (frutos / de la espiga y de la vid, / siendo mi Carne y mi Sangre) / son en las que he de vivir / contigo. . . ." ["In these species (fruits of the wheat shaft and the vine, my Body and my Blood), I shall live with you"] (1712–13).

What is most intriguing in Calderón's version of the Perseus myth is his considerable editorial revision of the tale. The dramatist is not simply glossing the story, not merely analogizing its narrative and characters to their presumably sacred prototypes. Rather, he is rewriting the myth so extensively, and with such a thoroughgoing Christocentric interpretation, that he is virtually writing Calderonian typology, giving interpretative testimony to the sacred truth he allegorically expounds.

The veritable evangelical or apostolic role that Calderón implicitly assumes for himself in *Andrómeda y Perseo* is even more prominently on display in his handling of the fable of Cupid and Psyche. The dramatist wrote two *autos* based on the tale, one for Toledo (1640?) and the other for Madrid (1665).[41] A comparison of the plays with the Apuleian original reveals how radically Calderón reformulated and allegorized the pagan original. A comparison of the two *autos* further attests the increasing abstraction and increasingly complex theological weight with which the dramatist approached myth in his career's later stages.

The fable of Psyche and Cupid derives from the second-century *Metamorphoses,* or *The Golden Ass,* by the Roman writer

41. Calderón also wrote a secular *comedia* on the same theme, *Ni Amor se libra de amor,* first staged in 1662.

Lucius Apuleius, where it appears as an interpolated tale. This story of the princess and her love for the God of love himself was perennially one of the most popular myths (although it does not appear in the older mythographies and was not printed in Europe until 1469.)[42] It was, in addition, one of the mythological stories most persistently and thoroughly subjected to symbolic readings. For example, Plotinus interprets the pair as, respectively, the soul and God.[43] For Fulgentius, Psyche represents the spirit and Cupid, cupidity (*cupiditas*), sent by Venus to eliminate her rival.[44] For Boccaccio, the marriage of Cupid and Psyche symbolizes the love between God and the human soul.[45] Pico della Mirandola interprets the tale, or more specifically the trials Psyche must suffer in order to regain Eros's love, as an allegory of the stages in mystical initiation.[46] Although details of interpretation may differ, the general tendency of exegesis was to see in the tale the story of the soul's journey toward its God.

In his allegory of the myth Calderón makes a number of ma-

42. A Spanish translation by Diego López de Cortegana was first published in 1513. See Alexander Scobie, *Aspects of the Ancient Romance and its Heritage, Beiträge zur klassischen Philologie,* no. 30 (Meisenheim am Glan: Anton Hain, 1969), 93–95, and "The Dating of the Earliest Printed European Translation of Apuleius's *Metamorphoses,*" in *More Essays on the Ancient Romance and its Heritage, Beiträge zur klassischen Philologie,* no. 46 (Meisenheim am Glan: Anton Hain, 1973), 47–52; also Theodore S. Beardsley, Jr., *Hispano-Classical Translations Printed between 1482 and 1699* (Pittsburgh: Duquesne University Press, 1970). On the literary and allegorical fate of the Apuleian fable, see Elizabeth Haight, *Apuleius and His Influence* (New York: Longmans, Green, 1927) and Antoine Latour, *Psyché en Espagne* (Paris: Charpentier, 1879). Specific material on the Christian interpretation of the fable can be found in Voght, "The Mythological *Autos,*" 243.

43. In *Enneads* VI, ix, 9: "That the Good is Yonder, appears by the love which is the soul's natural companion . . . , so that both in pictures and in fables Eros and the Psyche make a pair." Quoted by Wind, *Pagan Mysteries,* 62.

44. But "greed is taken with the spirit and links itself to her, as it were, in marriage"; Whitbread (Fulgentius), 89. Psyche's subsequent ordeals symbolize the soul's purgation from sin.

45. See Voght, 162.

46. See Wind, 145.

terial changes that substantively alter the Apuleian original and differ as well from other allegorical treatments of the tale. Most significantly, the dramatist eliminates the series of tasks imposed on the girl by the vengeful Venus; he concentrates entirely upon the relationship among the protagonists in order to allegorize the dialectic of faith and doubt as it relates to the doctrine of transubstantiation.

The *auto* of 1640 presents World as an Emperor whose three daughters are Idolatry, Synagogue, and Faith. Through this nexus of familial relationships Calderón allegorizes the traditional Christian conception of history as the succession of three eras.[47] In this vision, the first era of human history was that of natural law, corresponding to the dominance of paganism. The second or Judaic period was that of the Mosaic or written law, under which mankind (or the progenitors of the Judeo-Christian tradition) came under the rule of explicit divine directives. It is the third age that represents "[e]l cumplimiento feliz / de aquella gran promisión" ["the happy fulfillment of the great promise" (368): it is the era of the New Covenant, or Law of Grace, an epoch that began with the coming of Christ.[48] This historical schema Calderón merges with the family history of World. The oldest of the monarch's three daughters, Idolatry, is married to Paganism, ". . . que ciegamente / tres mil dioses adora" ["who blindly adores three thousand gods"] (347). The second has wed Judaism (347). Faith (or Psyche), the youngest daughter, is as yet unmarried, though for some time she has been the object of fervent courtship by Apostasy.

The introduction of Apostasy, who has no counterpart in the original, constitutes the first, and major, change that Calderón makes in Apuleius's fable; the entanglements of love and jeal-

---

47. The Pauline exposition of the succession occurs in Rom. 2:14–15, 2:17–29, and 3:21–31.

48. See Voght's explanation of this passage, pp. 169–70.

ousy that arise from the developing love triangle motivate most of the *auto*'s action. Faith believes she has been promised "al Dios verdadero, que asiste en el Mundo, / sacramentado, después que murió" ["to the true God, who is present in the World in sacramental form since his death"] (348). This belief Faith faithfully maintains. Even though she has never seen her promised spouse, even though he has been slain by Judaism, she hopefully and lovingly waits for him to return to her "disfrazado y encubierto" ["disguised and concealed"] (a "disguise" that objectifies the material species of the sacramental bread and wine) and she rejects out of hand Apostasy's contention that he, not her husband, is the promised "Dios de amor" ["God of Love"].

Faith flees Apostasy's importunity and his efforts to persuade her that her love for the unknown god is ill founded. The disappointed suitor attempts to detain her, but Cupid, identifying himself as deity, suddenly appears to defend the girl. Apostasy turns irresolute in the face of a possibly divine rival; nevertheless, he hesitates to believe the unknown newcomer because Cupid's face is veiled and Apostasy cannot trust what he cannot see. The god's response is significant: "Sin verlo, lo has de creer / con oírlo" ["Without seeing him, in hearing him alone, you must believe him"] (349).

The principle that Cupid enunciates is a fundamental tenet of Catholic belief: faith is transmitted by word, the Word of God. In placing this cardinal concern of Christian faith at the center of Apostasy's amorous problems, Calderón universalizes the *auto*'s themes. The myth is no longer merely the tale of Psyche's struggles with faith and doubt; it embraces as well the historical reality of the varying reactions to the coming of the Messiah and the rise of Christianity.

The conflicts that Calderón delineates in this portion of the *auto* (conflicts that naturally have no counterpart in the original tale) materialize a particular historical moment—the beginning of the Christian era, when a new faith was supplanting the old and struggling against those who would repudiate it—and a specific religious problem—the temptations and challenges that doubt poses to faith. Faith's rival suitors, Apostasy and Christ-Cupid, incarnate the alternatives available to mankind in the era of the New Covenant and to the individual of any age striving for belief but troubled by religious uncertainty. Through the allegory of Psyche's romantic dilemma, Calderón merges the psychological conflicts inherent in religious faith with a synoptic representation of *Heilsgeschichte*.

The remainder of *Psiquis y Cupido* develops the conflicts adumbrated in the opening scenes. Paganism, Judaism, and Apostasy attempt to discover the true identity of Faith's suitor. Of the three, Apostasy comes closest to tearing away the veil that conceals the god's face, but at the last moment he finds himself unable to move his arm.

In this one slight action Calderón allegorizes or translates into dramatic terms apostasy's (and Apostasy's) intellectual failure of faith:

> Yo confieso solo un Dios.
> La Idolatría atrás dejo,
> y le confieso Humanado
> en un puro Virgen Pecho.
> . . . .
> pero que tú seas, te niego,
> el Dios que adoro; pues no
> estás detrás de ese velo
> en Cuerpo y Alma. . . .   (351)

I confess that there is one God alone. Idolatry I here abandon, and I acknowledge that God has taken on Human form in a pure Virgin breast. But that you [Cupid] are the God I adore, I deny; for you are not, in both body and soul, behind that veil.

Apostasy comes closer than either Paganism or Judaism to recognizing Christian truth, but he fails at the last moment to disclose the identity of the one true god he believes in and seeks. That he will fail we know from his very name; it is the nature of his failure that is of interest. Paradoxically, Apostasy fails to uncover the hidden god because he wants to, because he seeks to verify empirically something he should accept as an article of faith, and he doubts the dogma of transubstantiation, doubts the existence of the true presence of Christ's body and blood in the sacramental bread and wine (". . . no / estás detrás de ese velo / en Cuerpo y Alma . . .").

Apostasy's deficiency of faith is to be contrasted with the perfected belief that Faith-Psyche learns in the course of the *auto*. Exiled by her father, World, who believes himself dishonored because his daughter has an unknown lover, Faith must confront the ultimate challenge to her confidence in her lover. Cupid comes to her in darkness, identifies himself as the god of Love, promises his love and constancy, and asks in return only that she believe in his transubstantiated presence without seeing him face to face:

> tendrás para Vianda
> un Pan y Vino, en quien
> mil distintos manjares
> cifrados verás. . . .
> . . . .
> . . . pero aunque
> te sepa a Pan y Vino,
> ni Pan ni Vino es.
> De todo este agasajo
> no quiero que me des
> más gracias, Psiquis mía,
> que el no quererme ver
> cara a cara, creyendo
> que en Alma y Cuerpo esté,
> detrás de un velo blanco,
> cuya cándida tez
> encubre en sus especies
> mi Amor y mi Poder.   (356)

For nourishment you will have Bread and Wine, in which you will find a thousand different dishes enciphered. But although it may taste like Bread and Wine to you, it is neither. For all these gifts, Psyche, I want no more thanks than this: do not seek to see me face to face; simply believe that I am here, in Soul and in Body, behind a white veil, whose snowy surface conceals beneath its species my Love and my Power.

This scene's turn of events deviates crucially from the original fable. Apuleius's Psyche does not know the identity of her husband, and so his imposition of secrecy becomes a test of the girl's trust in the love and goodness of the spouse she never sees but who treats her with kindness and devotion. Calderón's Cupid, on the other hand, tells Faith who he is while forbidding her to seek sensory verification of his identity; the test of faith in this case is a challenge to Faith's belief in the word of God. This change is dramatically effective, since it heightens Psyche's psychological conflict. It is theologically justifiable as well, since the test of Faith becomes a test of the only kind of knowledge the true Christian believer can have, i.e., knowledge founded only upon the word of God rather than on rational, empirical grounds. When at the *auto*'s climax Faith lights a candle in order to see the sleeping Cupid, her action is not merely disobedience to Cupid-Christ's command but also the misguided attempt to substitute for faith the false light of reason.

Faith recognizes and repents of her error, and Cupid returns to pardon her and offer her the sacrament: "y para que nunca dudes / cuánto puede mi palabra, / este es mi Cuerpo y mi Sangre, / y que Yo lo diga basta" ["and so that you may never doubt the value of my word, this is my Body and my Blood, and that I say it is enough"] (362). Once again, it is the word of God on which Faith is exhorted to found her belief and the Eucharistic transubstantiation that makes manifest to her and to mankind in general the efficacy of that word.

In *Psiquis y Cupido* Calderón departs considerably from the plot line of the Apuleian fable. In particular, developing a love triangle among Cupid-Christ, Faith-Psyche, and Apostasy augments the possibility of dramatic conflict and permits the assimilation of individual religious dilemma and *Heilsgeschichte* in one allegorical action, an action centered on the problematic of faith and doubt.

Calderón's second treatment of the Cupid-Psyche myth was written for Madrid and presented for the first time in 1665. In comparison with its predecessor, the 1665 *auto* departs even more radically from the Apuleian original.

The *auto* opens with a contrastive dialogue between Hate and Love. Hate, dressed as the Devil and mounted on a black horse reminiscent of Rev. 6:5,[49] declares his intention to overturn the order of the universe and challenge the very power of God:

> . . . entera
> vuelta al Universo doy,
> no sin apoyo en la osada
> apóstata emulación
> con que a Dios compito. . . .   (367)

"I am turning the Universe upside down, not without precedent in the bold, apostate rivalry with which I compete with God."

Love, speaking as a "contrario eco" ["contrary echo"] (367), calms the sea's turbulent waters (symbolic of the tribulations of man's life)[50] and swears to "temper with my harmony the shock caused by your horror" (". . . suavizar de tu horror / el susto con mi armonía" [368]).

49. This interpretation is also made by Franz Lorinser, *Don Pedro Calderón de la Barca, Geistliche Festspiele* 5 (Regensburg: G. J. Manz, 1856–72), 303, n. 3, and Voght, "The Mythological *Autos*," 247, n. 24.

50. On the sea as symbol of life's tribulations, see especially Hugo Rahner, *Greek Myths and Christian Mystery,* trans. Brian Battershaw (London: Burns and Oates, 1963), 307, 317–18, and 349–53, and Voght, 140–41, n. 53, and 250–51, n. 28.

This *auto*'s figure of Hate conflates Satan and the apostate personification of the earlier play; Love, in his turn, is both the mythological god Cupid and the Christian Savior. The conjunctive referents of the two personifications essentially reprise equivalent roles in the 1640 *auto*. However, the differences are substantial and revealing. In the first place, Love and Hate are unambiguously presented in the 1665 *auto* as antagonists locked in inevitable competition. Love indeed makes the conflict explicit: "yo el Amor, y el Odio tú, / forzosa es la oposición" ["since I am Love, and you Hate, our opposition is inevitable"] (368).

The opposition or antithesis between Cupid and Apostasy is nowhere near as absolute nor as clearly delineated in Calderón's first version of the myth. In the second place, Love and Hate are constantly associated throughout the 1665 *auto* with images of celestial light and nocturnal darkness, respectively. The connotations of this antithesis do far more than reflect and accentuate the two figures' opposition; the allusive imagery also implies that Love and Hate incarnate immanent cosmic principles of antagonism. The equations of Satan-darkness on the one hand and Christ-light on the other suggest a theological conception dangerously close to Manicheism.[51] Even if we do not wholly accept the controversial supposition of Calderón's latent or imperfectly sublimated Manicheism, it is undeniable that the metaphysical connotations the playwright associates with the antagonists confers upon the *auto* a cosmic resonance not to be found in the earlier play or, naturally, in the original fable. All the natural forces of the universe are implicated in the developing conflict between Love and Hate, in the ongoing drama of sacred history.

When the *auto* opens, Hate is reading in "la fábula de Psiquis" ["the fable of Psyche"] (368) of a supreme monarch and

---

51. On Calderón's possible Manicheism, see discussion in Ch. 1, of the present study.

his three daughters, the youngest of whom the king threw into the sea "por envidia de las dos" ["because of the envy of the other two"] (368). This story Hate interprets allegorically: the oldest daughter, married to Paganism, corresponds to Natural Law; the second, married to Judaism, to Written Law. The youngest, yet unmarried, is the Law of Grace, Third Age (Psyche), who lives in hope of a royal husband, ". . . cuyo honor / a la majestad exceda / de una y otra . . ." ["whose honor may exceed the majesty of the other two"] (369). Hate fears the accession to temporal power of a "new Law," a "third age," successor to the natural and written laws or ages of the world. It is to prevent this marriage that Hate devotes his boundless malignity. He ideates, or imagines, the dramatic representation of an ". . . alegoría / de poética ficción" ["allegory of poetical fiction"] (369), and, confounding fiction and reality, hopes to see Third Age thrown into a symbolic sea of tribulations ["es la tribulación / y zozobra de la vida / del mar significación"] before she finds her theologically significant marriage to a divine monarch.[52]

The subsequent fortunes of Psyche-Third Age deviate more and more from the Apuleian fable. In particular, the account of the girl's abandonment by her father has no real counterpart in the original. In the fable, Apollo's oracle commands Psyche's father to leave his daughter on a high hill, bride to a fierce and powerful serpent. In the *auto,* World acts for more rational and pragmatic reasons: ". . . empieza aquí / la sinrazón (¡ay de mí!) / que es tal vez razón de Estado" ["here begins the unreason which is perhaps a reason of State"] (373). He finds it politically

---

52. The full theological and allegorical ramifications of Hate's coauthorial intervention in Apuleius's fable are discussed in the Afterword of the present study; see also Barbara E. Kurtz, " 'No Word Without Mystery': Allegories of Sacred Truth in the *Autos Sacramentales* of Pedro Calderón de la Barca," *Publications of the Modern Language Association* 103 (1988): 262–73.

expedient to sacrifice one daughter to avoid incurring the enmity of her jealous sisters. This dynastic consideration Calderón likens to the theological and political struggles of the early Christian era (375).

Psyche-Third Age's misfortunes and her status "without estate," without the standing of a married woman, mirror the political and social insecurity of the early Christians before the rise of the Church as both religious and temporal power.[53] Love's loving protection and rescue of Third Age analogize Christ's establishment of the New Jerusalem for the faithful in his Church; indeed, the god constructs for his bride a palace resembling that of Rev. 21. Psyche-Third Age does not merely personify the human soul or individual Christian; she also synecdochally symbolizes the Church as the corporate entity embracing the souls of all the faithful.[54] By developing World's dynastic problems and Psyche's familial conflicts as metaphor for the circumstances of early Christianity, Calderón integrates a synopsis of Church history into his allegorization of Apuleius.

As in the earlier *auto*, Psyche's temptation and disobedience of Cupid's mandate are treated in the 1665 play as allegory of the problematic of faith and doubt concerning transubstantiation.[55] Here, however, more clearly than in the first *auto*, Psyche's psychic struggles are treated as the *psychomachia* or inner conflicts of the individual soul: ". . . como un individuo / parti-

53. See Voght's discussion, pp. 193–94: "The mythological story is shown to contain in veiled form the history of the rise of Christianity in relation to the cosmic forces at play in the universe" (194).

54. Voght points out (p. 201) that the institution of the Church made possible for the first time the systematic promotion of the law of Grace.

55. AMOR: de embozo a tus umbrales
me hallarás, porque así
siempre he de estar contigo,
y no quiero de ti
más de creer que es obra
de Amor, sin inquirir

cular que habrá en ella / que lo quiera examinar" ["as a private individual, there will be much in experience that I wish to examine"] (384).

Psyche-Third Age simultaneously figures the early Christian era (or age of the first promulgation of the Law of Grace) and the human soul (or mankind generically conceived).[56] The microcosmic *psychomachia* of the individual Christian's salvation history is thus depicted within the macrocosmic context of Church history.[57] Moreover, the Christian periodization relates theologically and allegorically to the competition between Satan and Christ for the human soul. The individual's *psychomachia* is thereby assimilated to the sacred history it recapitulates and to the drama of cosmic conflict, the clash of the immanent principles of Love and Hate, that it reflects and in which it participates. The analogy of sacred and individual histories involves far more than a conceptistic "poetic of corre-

---

si debajo de un blanco
velo y un terso viril
está ya el Dios de Amor.   (380)

You will find me in disguise on your threshold, and in that form I shall always be with you. And from you I desire nothing more than that you believe that my presence is the work of Love, and not inquire whether the God of Love is present beneath a white veil and a clear monstrance.

56. In this interpretation I agree with Lorinser and Voght (202): "Edad III . . . represents collectively the Christian era and its symbolic body, the Church as a group of believers; while on the individual level she symbolizes a human being living in the Christian Age or in the Church."

57. The notion of man as microcosm is specifically evoked in the *loa*: ". . . el Hombre / también es mundo pequeño . . ." ["man as well is a little world"] (364). Calderón's integration of microcosmic and macrocosmic aspects of Christian *Heilsgeschichte* resembles the structure of his allegorical progenitor, Prudentius's *Psychomachia.* As Macklin Smith points out in his examination of the *Psychomachia,* the text presents "a contrast of opposing visions, and this contrast places the microcosmic personification allegory in the perspective of macrocosmic struggle. The warfare in everyman's soul implies the war of the Church against the forces of Satan." M. Smith, *Prudentius' Psychomachia* (Princeton: Princeton University Press, 1976), 6.

spondence":[58] the play of analogies suggests rather that the individual's moral and psychological struggles are implicated in sacred history, that the patterns of *Heilsgeschichte* are reproduced or typologically fulfilled in the Christian's quotidian experiences,[59] that both individual *psychomachia* and sacred history are theophanic reflections of cosmic order. The individual's *bellum intestinum,* sacred history, and the cosmos itself are analogates whose referent is the Revelation. All strands of allegorical action converge on the Eucharist, which guarantees the salvation of the individual believer, confirms the establishment of the Law of Grace in the Church, and conveys the grace of divine intentionality.

In comparison with the *auto* of 1640, the later play exhibits a notable increase in abstraction. It is suggestive in this regard that World's three daughters are here designated simply as Edad I, Edad II, and Edad III; the mythological equivalence between *auto* and fable is severely attenuated so that the Christian analogues may be more strongly highlighted. Very little of the Apuleian fable remains in the 1665 *auto*—mostly a pattern of relationships, which itself is altered so as to reflect more exactly the story's theological referent. The *auto* of 1665 is a symbolic logic of Christian theology, founded on the analogy of soul, sacred history, cosmos, and godhead, a logic that Calderón discloses and kerygmatically proclaims.

58. The phrase is Joseph A. Mazzeo's. He has extensively studied the importance and universality of philosophic and literary notions of analogy in such studies as "Metaphysical Poetry and the Poetic of Correspondence," *Journal of the History of Ideas* 14 (1953): 221–34, *Renaissance and Seventeenth-Century Studies* (New York: Columbia University Press, 1964), and "Universal Analogy and the Culture of the Renaissance," *Journal of the History of Ideas* 15 (1954): 299–304. On the notion of universal analogy, see also Judson Boyce Allen, *The Ethical Poetic of the Later Middle Ages* (Toronto: University of Toronto Press, 1982).

59. The full ramifications of the typological correspondence between Christian *Heilsgeschichte* and individual experience are discussed in Ch. 3 of the present study.

Calderón's treatment of myth in the *auto sacramentales*—his use of etymological analysis, typological readings, and, of course, the overarching allegorization that shapes the plays—is frequently conventional, sanctioned by centuries of Christianizing hermeneutical practice. Yet the dramatist's license in handling the canons of mythography and allegoresis is extraordinary. Calderón edits with a free hand, conflates different myths or mythological figures, omits numerous details not readily assimilable to sacred history, adds characters and material of his own invention, and, in general, alters the tales with imaginative independence from sources and even, on occasion, from theological exactitude.

This imaginative and theological revisionism is somewhat surprising in view of the truth value that Calderón, like many earlier allegorizers, accords to pagan myth. He constantly asserts the traditional belief that pagan myth adumbrates or even prefigures Christian truth. Such a typological conception of myth would seem to be radically at odds with extensive editorial freedom. What happens to the intimations of sacred truth in myth if the allegorizer embellishes the tales with incidents and characters of his own invention, alters the mythological originals with a fine disregard for their letter, if not for the underlying spirit? Or we can pose the question from a slightly different perspective: If the pagan myths embody sacred truth, why do they require radical revision in order to yield their Christian signficance?

The conventional answer, both for traditional Christian hermeneutics and for Calderón as allegorizing interpreter, is that sacred truths are embodied in pagan myth in a veiled form that necessitates exegesis for its proper elucidation and communication. In *El divino Jasón* (before 1634?), for example, Jason (Christ) explains to the Argonauts (the disciples) the meaning of their enterprise. The quest for the Golden Fleece symbolizes

Christ's pursuit of the human soul through the institution of the Church. This legend is a shadow or veil that one must penetrate or interpret in order to attain the true Christian significance:

> ... mas vosotros
> podéis atender ahora
> a lo oculto y misterioso
> y al alma desta figura,
> que no la penetran todos,
> porque entre sombras confusas
> la verdad que yo conozco
> está escondida. ...   (63)

But you can attend now to the hidden and mysterious soul of this figure—a spirit few can penetrate; for the truth I know is hidden amidst confused shadows.

This is all well and good, we might say. But what, if anything, guarantees that this interpretation will be a valid, or *the* valid one, doctrinally sound and theologically efficacious, and not, as might be feared, capricious, factitious, or even fraudulent?

The warranty of allegoresis is, of course, a central concern in any hermeneutics, and most particularly in a Christian allegoresis that claims to reveal (presumably) divinely ordained truth and to have theoretical cogency mundanely conceived. Conveniently enough for this problematic and for Calderón's theory of allegory, the centrality and corroborative basis of Christianizing interpretation are illustrated in *El sacro Parnaso* (1659).[60] Here, indeed, the dramatist allegorizes an entire philosophy of theologically grounded mythographic and allegorical interpretation.

---

60. On this *auto,* see also Hans Flasche, "Elementos teológicos constitutivos en el auto sacramental *El sacro Parnaso,*" in Luciano García Lorenzo, ed., *Calderón,* 37–47, and Alan Soons, "Calderón's Augustinian *Auto: El Sacro Parnaso,*" in *What's Past Is Prologue: A Collection of Essays in Honour of L. J. Woodward,* ed. Salvador Bacarisse,

The *auto* opens with a call to all mortals to attend an unspecified competition; we later learn that it is a writing contest among various Church Fathers. The personifications Judaism and Paganism hear the summons but cannot fully understand it. Judaism finds it ". . . ajeno a mis ciencias" ["alien to my learning"] (777); Paganism finds that it is couched in a language of which he is ignorant. Each, however, captures something of the message: Judaism grasps only that the summons has been issued by the "apostate" Paul; Paganism, that it pertains in some half-understood way to a deity unknown to his pantheon. Both perceive that the musical summons emanates from a distant mountain, the Parnassus of the title (figuration of both the mythological place and the New Jerusalem of Scripture), and each attempts to interpret his perception. Judaism guesses that the mount is part, or at least an image, of Paradise; Paganism conjectures that it is the site of the Elysian Fields.

At this juncture, Faith appears and tells the two that both have erred in their interpretations, although both have made worthy efforts. She suggests to the puzzled pair that each has founded an edifice of falsehoods on a portion of religious truth. To demonstrate the errors, Faith has Judaism read the description of creation in Genesis and Paganism read a similar description in Ovid's *Metamorphoses*. The similarity of the two passages Faith adduces as proof of the partial foreshadowing of revealed truth in the beliefs and texts of the pre-Christian religions. Ultimately, she invites Paganism and Judaism to go to the sacred mount after they have bathed in the Castalian fountain (figure, we later learn, of the baptismal font).

This opening scene of *El sacro Parnaso* not only allegorizes the relationship of Paganism and Judaism to Christian revelation; it also figures the role of interpretation in religious faith

Bernard Bentley, Mercedes Clarasó, and Douglas Clifford (Edinburgh: Scottish Academic, 1984), 124–31.

and understanding (and, indeed, the role of faith in interpretation). The pre-Christian religions, it is suggested in the corresponding personifications, captured or foreshadowed part of Christian truth; both personifications, however, ultimately fail to interpret properly the half-glimpsed message because each, like all interpreters, makes his suppositions in the light, and within the constraints, of his own theology and religious understanding. The pre-Christian religions thus failed because they were not illuminated by the true faith, the faith that, confirmed by the divine grace conferred in baptism, guarantees perfected understanding and grounds valid interpretation. Correct interpretation becomes virtually equivalent to salvation, and Christian witness equivalent to correct interpretation.

Calderón has, furthermore, left us (in allegorized form, naturally) an explicit statement concerning the ontological status of editorial license in Christocentric interpretation. In the prologue to *El laberinto del mundo* (1654?), allegorization of the myth of Theseus, Faith states:

> Dígalo el texto
> de Pablo: Entre los Gentiles
> asienta, que convirtieron
> en fábulas las Verdades;
> porque como ellos tuvieron
> solo lejanas noticias
> de la Luz del Evangelio,
> viciaron sin ella nuestra
> Escritura, atribuyendo
> a falsos dioses sus raras
> maravillas, y queriendo
> que el Pueblo sepa, que no
> hay fábula sin misterio,
> si alegórica a la Luz
> desto se mira, un ingenio,
> bien que humilde, ha pretendido
> dar esta noticia al Pueblo.   (1558)

Paul's text[61] asserts that the Gentiles converted truth into fables; since they possessed only vague notice of the light of the Gospel, they corrupted our Scripture, attributing its rare marvels to false gods. Desiring the people to know that there is no fable without mystery, if that fable is examined allegorically in the light of that mystery, a wit, though humble, has attempted to convey this news to the People.

This declaration (typical of many scattered throughout the *autos* and their prologues) does not merely define in terms of Christian typology the relation between myth and revealed truth; it conceptualizes as well the way Calderón evidently viewed his own role as writer of allegorized myth. Especially noteworthy is his express denial, through Faith's words, that he was the actual author of the mythological *autos;* rather, he presents himself as the editor or transmitter of their truths. This vision of the playwright's limited "authorial" role would seem to imply, by logical extension, that the sacramental plays themselves are interpretative in nature rather than fundamentally creative. The dramatist's own mythological inventions or interpolations can thus be seen as explicative or illustrative gloss.

It is likewise suggestive that Calderón in this passage implicitly claims for himself a function analogous to that of the writers of the Gospels. His humble "ingenio" (wit) conveys or transmits the "news" of myth's hidden philosophy; that is, he bears the tidings of divine mystery, serves as veritable apostolic witness to sacred truth. It should be recalled in this regard that Scripture, although the word of a "human witness to divine revelation,"[62] is ultimately, in Christian thinking, "God's witness to himself," or "revelation itself mediated through human words."[63] This mediative function of Scripture resembles the

61. The text referred to is most probably Rom. 1:14–25. See Voght, "The Mythological *Autos*," 46, n. 40.

62. Donald B. Bloesch, "The Primacy of Scripture," in *The Authoritative Word,* ed. Donald K. McKim (Grand Rapids, MI: Wm. B. Eerdmans, 1983), 118.

63. Bloesch, 117 and 118.

"human mode" of allegorical discourse that Calderón constantly asserts is the medium of the *autos'* explication of Eucharistic doctrine.[64] In both Gospel and allegorical *auto* it is divine authority, Calderón suggests, that sanctions and sacralizes personal testimony to sacred mystery and sacred truth, God alone who speaks through the human author who writes of that truth. Explicative gloss, illuminated by the true faith that legitimizes interpretation, participates in the numinous significance inherent to kerygma, in the proclamation of salvation in Christ and the recapitulation of sacred history. The allegorizer as author is thus implicated in the divine ordination of typology as typic subfulfillment of apostolic witness, ministry, and proselytism.

The notion of allegory as interpretative and mediative kerygma, fundamental to Calderón's interrelation of allegory, myth, and truth, is profoundly examined and developed in what is perhaps the most brilliant of the mythological *autos, El divino Orfeo* (1663).[65] The Orpheus *auto* is an allegory of divine

64. For example, "ajustarnos a hablar / a humano modo es preciso" (54), says Grace in *El año santo en Madrid.*

65. Calderón wrote two *autos sacramentales* based on the Orpheus myth, one of them the 1663 play (first published in 1677), the other undated but probably earlier. On the chronology and merits of the two *autos,* see Voght, "The Mythological *Autos,*" 108–9, n. 4; also Donald Dietz, "Toward Understanding Calderón's Evolution as an *Auto* Dramatist," in *Studies in Honor of Ruth Lee Kennedy,* ed. Vern G. Williamsen and A. F. Michael Atlee (Chapel Hill, NC: Estudios de Hispanófila, 1977), 51–55. On this *auto,* see also Kenneth Dale Buelow, "A Semi-Critical and Annotated Edition of *El Divino Orfeo, Segunda Parte,* by Pedro Calderón de la Barca" (Diss., University of Wisconsin, Madison, 1976); Kathleen Dolan, "Eurydice and the Imagery of Redemption: Calderón's *Auto del divino Orfeo," Proceedings of the Pacific Northwest Council on Foreign Languages* 26 (1975): 196–98; Pedro R. León, "Sobre el manuscrito autógrafo de *El divino Orfeo,* 1663, de Calderón," *Revista canadiense de estudios hispánicos* 5 (1981): 321–37, and *"El divino Orfeo* ca. 1634: Paradoja teológico-poética," in Luciano García Lorenzo, ed., *Calderón,* 687–99, and "Un manuscrito de la Loa para *El divino Orfeo,* 1663, de Calderón," *Revista canadiense de estudios hispánicos* 9 (1985): 228–50; José María de Osma, "Apostilla al tema de la creación en el auto *El divino*

creation, Christ's salvation of the human soul, and, ultimately, the divine origin and numinous significance of allegory, allegorical interpretation, and language themselves.

The *auto* opens with disclosure on the first cart of "una nave negra, y negras sus flámulas, banderolas, y jarcias, y gallardetes" ["a black ship, with black pennants, banderoles, rigging, and streamers"] (1840). From this infernal ship emerges the Devil, or Prince of Darkness. His verbal self-portrait designates him as "Corsario," "Ladrón," or "Pirata de los Mares" ["corsair," "thief," or "pirate of the seas"] (1840)—epithets that derive from a number of biblical passages[66] and that here receive concrete elaboration. This diabolical "pirate" is accompanied by Envy, who as double or projection exteriorizes one aspect of the Devil (his envy of man) and who materializes a tenet of Christian theology: the notion that "by the envy of the devil, death came into the world" (Wisd. 2:24). The Prince and his Envy hear a voice, ". . . voz que ahora dulcemente grave / quiera unir lo imperioso y lo süave" ["a voice that, sweetly grave, conjoins the imperious and the mild"] (1840). The Prince explains the significance of this music:

> . . . debajo de métrica armonía
> todo ha de estar, constando en cierto modo
> de número, medida y regla todo,
> tanto que disonaría
> si faltara una sílaba.   (1840)

Everything subsists in metrical harmony, for everything consists to a certain extent of number, measure, and rule, so much so that the loss of a single syllable would mean dissonance.

Orfeo de Calderón de la Barca," *Hispania* 34 (1951): 165–71; Alice M. Pollin, " 'Cithara Iesu': La apoteosis de la música en 'El divino Orfeo' de Calderón," in *Homenaje a Casalduero,* ed. Rizel Pincus Sigele and Gonzalo Sobejano (Madrid: Gredos, 1972), 419–31; Carol Janet Ripandelli, "The Tropological Model of the Fall in *El divino Orfeo* and *El mágico prodigioso* by Calderón de la Barca" (Diss., Florida State University, 1979); and Voght, "The Mythological *Autos,*" 51–151.

66. For example, John 10:1–21.

The celestial or Orphic music in its "metrical harmony" materializes the harmony or concord immanent in the cosmos.[67]

At this moment the second cart opens to disclose a celestial globe and a tableau formed by Orpheus-Christ, the seven days, and Human Nature. What follows is an allegory of Creation told in accordance with Genesis, as Orpheus through vocal invocation effects the realization and ordering of the universe.[68] Orpheus-Christ completes his creative labor by fashioning Human Nature:

> Vive, pues, vive y anima,
> ya que para que nos una
> un lazo de Amor y sea
> süave nuestra coyunda,
> mi Voz te inspira. . . .   (1842)

67. On the notion of universal order or harmony as a correlative of musical harmony, see especially Leo Spitzer, "Classical and Christian Ideas of World Harmony," *Traditio* 2 (1944): 409–64 and 3 (1945): 307–64, republished in book form, ed. Anna Granville Hatcher (Baltimore: Johns Hopkins University Press, 1963). Voght supplies some additional bibliography on the theme, 119–20, n. 24.

68. ORFEO: ¡Ah de ese informe embrión!
               ¡Ah de esa masa confusa
               a quien llamará el Poeta
               caos y nada la Escritura!
       TODOS: ¿Quién será quien nos busca?
       ORFEO: Quien de la nada hacer el todo gusta.   (1840)

       ORFEO: Ahoy, formless embryo!
               Ahoy, confused mass,
               called by the Poet "chaos,"
               and by Scripture, "nothing."
         ALL: Who is it that seeks us?
       ORFEO: He who pleases to make everything out of nothing.

As Voght points out (p. 56): "Calderón's portrayal of Creation by the power of a voice the source of which is not visible to the world is in accord with an ancient patristic tradition, based primarily on John 1:1–18, which views the 'Word' as the manifestation of the Omnipotent which directly effected the formation of the universe. . . . Calderón equates the 'voz,' which creates everything in his two plays, with the 'Verbum' of John 1." See as well Voght's commentary and bibliography, 115–16, n. 17.

Live, live and take heart, for my voice inspires you so that we
may be united in soft bonds by the ties of Love.

Envy and the Prince of Darkness, having witnessed this
scene, are appropriately envious of the sovereign rank conferred upon Human Nature, and they conspire against her and
her preeminent status. The Prince's "magical voice" conjures
the aid of Lethe, mythological river of Hades and allegorical
conflation of Death and man's original sin:

> ¡Oh tú, río del Olvido,
> pues que mi voz te conjura,
> para que también mi voz
> por la oposición perjura
> de Dios, prodigios intente,
> . . . .
> la yerta cerviz, levanta,
> . . . .
> mi mágica voz escucha.   (1843)

Oh, river of Oblivion, raise up your head, since my voice conjures you; so that my voice as well can perform prodigies in perju-
rious opposition to God. Attend to my magical voice.

This "magical voice," infernal and destructive, contrasts
with the divine and creative voice of Orpheus; and the product
of Lethe's diabolic conjuration is set against the Orphic voice's
creation of the luminous universe.

After the initial scene of infernal obscurity, after the allegorization of Creation contrasted with the diabolic labors, the scene
shifts to the festive jubilation of the Days, who sing and dance
to a psalm that translates into literal music, into a scenic element, the metaphorical and philosophical music that informs
the *auto*'s very conception: "Al Señor confesemos / Que con una
voz sola / Es el principio y fin / De tantas bellas obras" ["Let us
confess to the Lord that with a single voice He is the beginning
and the end of so many beauteous works"] (1844). This psalm

attests to a centuries-old strain of Christian thought: the tradition, traceable to Augustine, that finds in the temple of the universe an exemplar of the supreme power and goodness of the greatest Artificer.

The rejoicing of the Days, materialization of the universal harmony that it also literally stages, culminates in the unitive and sacramental symbolism of a wedding, that of Orpheus-Christ and Eurydice-Human Nature.[69] However, the Prince and Envy, ever the diabolic conspirators and troublemakers, insinuate themselves into this joyous nuptial scene. Their temptation of the "Divina Belleza" ["Divine Beauty"] follows the equivalent scene in Genesis centered on Eve's enticement by the forbidden fruit: "Come y como Dios serás" ["Eat, and you will be like God"] (1849).

The crafty artifice of the Prince and Envy thus effects the fall of mankind. As a consequence of this primordial sin, death and time enter the world (in accordance with Paul). The Pauline assertion is dramatized in the *auto* through the Days' allegorical action: as each Day passes across the stage, Envy, dressed all in black, steps into his pathway to hurry him along, "de suerte que siempre haya noche entre uno y otro DIA" ["so that there is always night between one and the other days"] (1849).

Envy, multivalent image of the Devil's essential nature, the diabolical servant of Genesis, and the sin of man, becomes in addition the symbol of night, "imagen de mi inobediencia" ["image of my disobedience"] (1849) (in the words of Nature). And the Days' "rebelado motín" ["rebellious mutiny"] (1850) allegorizes the natural disorder caused by human sin.

69. On the tradition of nuptial imagery used to symbolize the soul's union with God, see the bibliography included by Voght, 137, n. 47. An important source of this imagery for the Christian allegorical tradition, a source not mentioned by Voght, is Hugh of St. Victor's *Soliloquium de arrha animae.* See Hugh of St. Victor, *Soliloquy on the Earnest Money of the Soul,* trans. Kevin Herbert (Milwaukee: Marquette University Press, 1956).

Nature in a faint falls into the arms of the Prince of Darkness; her swoon signifies the moral fall of mankind. Ultimately, however, Eurydice-Human Nature is redeemed by Christ: the musician carves in the wood of his literal harp a symbol of Christ's cross, contrastive and antidotal remedy for the edenic tree associated with original sin. The Orphic descent to Hades, the rescue of Eurydice, becomes in Calderón's allegory Christ's Passion, the self-sacrifice that redeemed man's original sin: "Padre mío, Padre mío, / ¿por qué me desamparaste?" (1853), "Father, Father, why hast thou forsaken me?" cries Orfeo, echoing the words of Christ on the cross. At the climax of the *auto* and its theological infrastructure, Calderón drops entirely the plot's mythological thread in order to adhere to the eternal redemptive drama of the Passion, commemorated in the Eucharist and allegorized in the *auto sacramental.*

The play ends with the appearance of a golden ship (traditional image of the Church),[70] which bears the Eucharistic sacrament. This ship counterbalances the diabolical ship of the *auto*'s opening, just as the Eucharist combats the infernal corsair who piloted it. Through such emblematic staging Calderón symbolizes the perennial fall of man and his ultimate hope and redemption.

A bare plot summary can give only an imperfect idea of Calderón's allegory in *El divino Orfeo*. His technique is grounded in a masterly conflation of mythological tale, Christian history

70. On this symbol, see Jean Daniélou, "The Ship of the Church," in *Primitive Church Symbols,* trans. Donald Attwater (London: Burns and Oates, 1964), 58–70; Pierre David, "Notes sur deux motifs introduits par Gil Vicente dans l'Auto da Embarçao da Gloria," *Bulletin des Etudes portugaises,* Nouvelle série (1945), 190; Gabriel Llompart, "La nave de la iglesia y su derrotero en la iconografía de los siglos XVI y XVII," in *Gesammelte Aufsätze zur Kulturgeschichte Spaniens,* ed. Johannes Vincke *et al., Spanische Forschungen der Görresgesellschaft* 25 (Münster: Aschendorff, 1970): 309–35; Alfred Maury, *Essai sur les légendes pieuses du Moyen Age* (Paris: Librairie Philosophique de Ladrange, 1843), 103.

and doctrine, and classical philosophical thought. The very use
of Orpheus as a type of Christ is, of course, the most prominent
example of the technique; however, this typology was well established in Christian iconography, and Calderón's use of this
allegorical tradition is nothing new.[71] What is striking is the
philosophical and theological depth with which the dramatist
enriches the conventional analogy. For example, the key passage in which the Prince explains the Orphic music is clearly
Christian in conception (Augustine, for example, uses similar
language in many passages). But Calderón emphasizes the Pythagorean and Platonic substructure of that conception:

> . . . debajo de métrica armonía
> todo ha de estar, constando en cierto modo
> de número medida y regla todo,
> tanto que disonaría
> si faltara una sílaba.[72]   (1840)

Pythagoras, in postulating that "all things are numbers,"
had discussed the relation of number and music. His theory
influenced Plato's cosmogony as expounded in the *Timaeus:*
"[W]hen all things were in disorder, God created in each thing
in relation to itself, and in all things in relation to each other,
all the measures and harmonies which they could possibly

71. On the classical and medieval treatment of Orpheus, see Maurice Bower, "Orpheus and Euridice," *The Classical Quarterly,* n.s. 2 (1952): 113–26; John Block Friedman, *Orpheus in the Middle Ages* (Cambridge: Harvard University Press, 1970); Klaus
Heitman, "Orpheus im Mittelalter," *Archiv für Kulturgeschichte* 45 (1963): 253–94,
and "Typen der Deformierung antiker Mythen im Mittelalter: Am Beispiel der Orpheussage," *Romanistisches Jahrbuch* 14 (1963): 45–77; M. O. Lee, "Orpheus and Euridice: Myth, Legend and Folklore," *Classica et Medievalia* 26 (1965): 198–215; John
Warden, ed., *Orpheus* (Toronto: University of Toronto Press, 1982); Pablo Cabañas,
El mito de Orfeo en la literatura española (Madrid: Consejo Superior de Investigaciones Científicas, Instituto Miguel de Cervantes de Filología Hispánica, 1948). Orpheus as prophet or type of Christ is discussed by early apologists such as Pseudo-
Justin and Clement. See Páramo Pomareda, 68–70, and Voght, 70–71.

72. See translation above, p. 103.

receive."[73] Through the medium of Augustine's Neoplatonism this cosmogonic conception was incorporated into Christianity and came, finally, to shape this Calderonian passage: the universe is harmonious music, the "métrica armonía . . . [que] todas las cosas junta" (1840) in a symphony of all creation.[74]

In Calderón's Pythagorean and Platonic reformulation of the scriptural account of creation we may glimpse another facet of Orpheus's complex symbolism, another reason for his selection as the type or figure of Christ. Orpheus is the musician, appropriate composer of such a harmonious and harmonic universe. He is also the "voz que atractiva mueve a ir en su busca" ["voice which through force of attraction stirs movement in its pursuit"]—the words of the *auto*'s persistent refrain. Most obviously, this definition of Orpheus (involving a pun on the Spanish *voz*, both "voice" and "word") analogizes the mythological figure to the incarnated Word or "Verbum" of Scripture, an echo of the "In principio erat Verbum" of the Fourth Gospel. Orpheus-Christ furthermore describes himself as "[q]uien de la nada hacer el todo gusta" ["he who pleases to make everything out of nothing"]. He is, besides the incarnated Word, the executant word of the Father who, by ordaining *Fiat lux,* that is, by pronouncing a word or words, effected the work of creation.[75]

This executant *voz* recalls the *primum mobile* (more exactly, *primus motor*) of Greek philosophy, the prime mover that har-

73. Plato, *The Collected Dialogues,* ed. Edith Hamilton and Huntington Cairns (Princeton: Princeton University Press, 1969), 1195.

74. Voght (58–59) cites a scriptural text (Wisd. 11: 21b) as another possible source for the idea of the cosmos as a harmonic system.

75. As Voght points out (68), the identification of Christ with the godhead, and the belief that it was the Son who created the world, can be traced to patristic tradition. On the idea of the Logos as creator of the world, see Voght's bibliography, 115–16, n. 17.

monizes the cosmos and mobilizes all creation through its motive attraction. The philosophical conception of Christ as prime
mover, as motive love that sets the universe in motion, is naturally assimilated to the allegorical presentation of Orpheus the
lover and husband, in a complex integration of philosophy,
myth, and theology. Orpheus-Christ is thus "voz" in all its tri-
partite meaning: the "voice" of the mythological musician, the
incarnated "Word," and the Father's words "Fiat lux," which
made the universe an exemplar of divine power and a theoph-
any of divine grace.

The punning on the conception of Orpheus as word and
voice, a synonymy of meanings that implicitly analogizes sacral
"Verbum" and human language, suggests as logical consequence that language itself is likewise innately performative
and sacral. The punning that informs the *auto* is also a synecdoche for a broader, theologically richer idea of harmony or consonance central to the play's allegory: the consonance inherent
in music informs the entire structure of the harmonious and
harmonic universe as well as the *auto sacramental* that harmo-
nizes or conflates Christian, mythological, and philosophical
conceptions of the godhead. Music is defined in *El divino Orfeo*
as "a consonance . . . so well executed in the perfect Construc-
tion of the Instrument of the World that, as certain consequence, God is its Musician":

> . . . una consonancia, y que esta
> está tan ejecutada
> en la Fábrica perfecta
> del Instrumento del Mundo,
> que en segura consecuencia,
> es Dios su Músico. . . .   (1847–48)

This passage allegorizes the so-called argument from design,
that is, the argument that "the orderly teleology of non-con-
scious agents in the universe entails the existence of an intelli-

gent universal Orderer."[76] The allegorization of a seminal philosophical/theological argument within the context of pagan myth signalizes and incorporates the very harmonization of human and divine letters that the *auto* explicitly proclaims as both the purpose and the method of its allegory.

The consonance inherent in music and the universe is said to characterize as well the harmonization of "Divine and Human Letters" perceived in the sacral patterns of typological prefiguration (pagan Orpheus) and fulfillment (Christian Savior). Of both musical harmonics on the one hand and harmonized Scripture and pagan literature on the other, it is God who is the Composer or Supreme Artificer. Implicit in Calderón's allegory of the Orphic "voz" is not only a vision of language as numinous because it derives ultimately, radically from the originary Word but also a linguistic-theological conception of God as originative authority for the allegorical interpretation or harmonization of pagan myth and Christian truth. Divine authority itself is the immanent guarantee of "validity in interpretation" grounded in illuminated understanding, understanding grounded in the true faith.

A brilliant epitome of this harmonization of theological, mythographic, and linguistic speculation is itself allegorized in the prologue to *El divino Orfeo*. This tour de force of allegorical discourse and linguistic-metaphysical speculation consists of a competition between "Divinas y Humanas Letras" (1835) to determine which possesses the greatest excellence. Five ladies and

76. Anthony Flew, "Aquinas," *A Dictionary of Philosophy* (New York: St. Martin's, 1979); see also "argument from (or to) design." The earliest complete articulation of this teleological argument was made by Plato in the *Timaeus* 29E–30A, where he represents the Demiurge as a craftsman. The specifically Christian formulation of the argument was given by Thomas Aquinas as the fifth of the Five Ways or proofs of the existence of God (*Summa Theologica,* Q.2, Art.3). See Frederick Ferré, "Design Argument," *Dictionary of the History of Ideas,* ed. Philip P. Wiener (New York: Scribner's, 1968), 670–77.

five courtiers come on stage in turn, each displaying a letter of the alphabet and proclaiming the preeminence of that letter as antonomasia of one of Christ's attributes. The letters and associated words are E (*Eucharistía,* Eucharist), A (*Amor,* Love), I (*Juicio de Dios,* God's Judgment), C (*Caridad,* Charity), T (*Temor,* Fear), H (*Honra,* Honor), S (*Sabiduría,* Wisdom), A (*Aumento de la Gracia,* Increase in grace), I (*Inefable Grandeza,* Ineffable grandeur), and R (*Redención,* Redemption). All participants ultimately acknowledge the victory of "R," because the universal redemption comprehends all the preceding attributes: "La Redención, en quien cifra / Dios todas las dichas vuestras" ["The Redemption, in which God enciphers all your virtues"] (1837). As Music intones a celebratory song, the "letters" execute two dance figures, the first of which spells out *EU-CHARISTIA* and the second, *CITHARA IESU.*[77] The anagram is explained as a figuration of the subject matter of the play to follow: the story of Orpheus seen as an allegory of Christ's Universal Redemption of mankind. A consequence of this analogy is the metonymic and typological equation of the Orphic cither and the cross of Christ's Passion.[78]

The prologue to *El divino Orfeo* is most obviously an explanation or proclamation of the *auto*'s allegory. However, it also synoptically allegorizes Calderón's conception of myth, language, and allegory as they relate to revealed truth. The victory conceded to R, Redemption, establishes Christ's redemption of mankind as his preeminent attribute; so much is evident. More intriguing is the initial disorder of the letters summoned on

---

77. Voght (126, n. 34) points out that "[t]he use of this anagram . . . in connection with Orpheus as a type for Christ does not originate with Calderón. It is found in *Imago primi seculi Societatis Jesu a provincia Flandro-Belgica eiusdem Societatis repraesentata* (Antwerp, 1640), 463."

78. On Orpheus's instrument as symbol of the Cross, see the *Dictionnaire d'archéologie chrétienne et de liturgie,* eds. Fernand Cabrol and Henri Leclercq, vol. 13, Part Two (Paris: Librairie Letouzey, 1936), col. 2735–54.

stage by Music; they arrange themselves to spell out *EUCHA-RISTIA* at the musical prompting of Divine Pleasure. The letters' formation of a dance figure materializes divine creation seen as the production of universal harmony out of chaos. More significantly, their formation of a semantically meaningful word suggests the primacy of the Word in creation, its ability to confer not only meaning but also the power to signify, to manifest divine presence and purpose in the cosmos. That the word they form is "Eucharist" further suggests that the numinous significance of creation or divine creative power is itself inherent in human language: *nomina* seen as equivalent to *noumena*.[79] As the dancers anagrammatize the word "Eucharistía" to form the words "Cithara Iesu" they materialize as well both the sacramental occasion and the subject matter of the *auto,* of the "Human and Divine Letters" (myth and Scripture) used as basis of the play's argument. The *auto*'s subject, the Eucharist, is numinously immanent in the allegory, which thereby acquires not merely the divine authorization of the Eucharist it celebrates but also something of the theme's sacramental character. The analogy of allegory and sacrament is implicit in the very nature of the "victory" in this logomachy. "R," the victor, is notably described as a cipher or code: God, we are told, "enciphered" all the attributes of the Savior in the Redemption, which is the synoptic "good news" sent to mankind "encoded" in the Eucharist, concealed in the material species of the sacra-

---

79. Maureen Quilligan has brilliantly discussed the intrinsic relationship between allegory and what she terms the "suprarealist attitude toward language": "Allegories are not only always texts, . . . they are always fundamentally about language and the ways in which language itself can reveal to man his highest spiritual purpose within the cosmos. As such, allegory always presupposes at least a potential sacralizing power in language, and it is possible to write and to read allegory intelligently only in those cultural contexts which grant to language a significance beyond that belonging to a merely arbitrary system of signs." See Quilligan, *The Language of Allegory:* (Ithaca: Cornell University Press, 1979), 156.

mental bread and wine.[80] This encoding of divine mystery is breathtakingly similar to the operations of allegory itself, which analogizes sacred truth under the veil of human letters. Not for nothing is the *auto* denominated *sacramental*—it is the kerygmatic incorporation and representation of sacred truth.

The logomachy of this *loa* can stand as a miniature of Calderón's entire approach to myth in the *autos sacramentales*. The dramatist everywhere anagrammatizes the individual components of the original tales, shifting and altering them so as to create virtually new stories. Yet the transpositional possibilities must have been there (as in etymology), immanent and divinely ordained, or the allegorist could not have discovered them: "este Anagrama [contiene] / las Letras de ambos Sentidos" ["this anagram," one character explains, "contains the Letters of both Senses"] (1838). In *El divino Orfeo* and its prologue, allegory is the transformation of an original and originative reality, a transformation that discloses and kerygmatically proclaims a heretofore unsuspected but always latent, and sacred, significance. This transformation or interpretation is the work of the illuminated imagination of the human expositor. But it is God who is the Supreme Composer or Artificer, and it is sacred history, or the providential revelation of divine will, that ultimately configures all allegorical treatments of sacred truth.

Calderón's conception of language and truth, like Augustine's, is powerfully and essentially logocentric. The implicit logocentrism that grounds and validates language, myth, and

---

80. In the *loa* to *El Santo Rey don Fernando, Segunda Parte,* the Eucharist is similarly described as a cipher: ". . . aquel Alto Sacramento, / en quien el Padre cifró / el Poder, la Ciencia el Hijo / y el Espíritu el Amor" ["that High Sacrament, in which the Father enciphered Power, the Son Wisdom, and the Holy Spirit Love"] (1290).

allegory is itself explicitly formulated by Truth in *El laberinto del mundo* (1654?). Discoursing on the nature of "truth," the personification first explains to Falsehood the use of etymology as an interpretative tool:

> Si llegas
> a interpretar nuestros nombres,
> para que dos luces tengan
> dentro de una Alegoría
> Divinas y Humanas Letras   (1561–62)

Our names are to be interpreted so that Divine and Human Letters possess two lights within one Allegory.

Etymological interpretation, she implies, discloses the meaning of both divine and human letters, of both scriptural and mythological truth (ultimately, of course, the same), and the result of such interpretation is allegory. By extension, we may conclude, the allegorist is interpreter; divine truth, immanent in the text he explicates, irradiates all that he does, all that he writes. That it is Truth who explicates the allegorized disquisition on truth allegorizes the immanence in allegory of the divinely warranted truth that the personification incarnates.[81] "No hay palabra sin misterio," Culpa declares in *Las órdenes militares* (1662); "Ni misterio sin prodigio," responds Innocence. There is no word without mystery, or mystery without miracle. Lucifer alludes to these principles in *Las espigas de Ruth* (1663): "Apenas, Discordia, en toda / la sacra página encuentro / la voz Semilla, que no / esté brotando Misterios" ["Scarcely, Discord, do I find the word 'seed' in the sacred page that it is not prodigious of Mysteries"] (1089). In other words, if the word itself is intrinsically mysterious in the theological sense, innately numinous or

---

81. Etymological interpretation depends upon a conception of language itself as intrinsically numinous, charged with innate divine significance as a product of a divine Creator. This conception was standard during the Renaissance, and it was frequently echoed by Calderón.

sacramental, then etymology—even the apparently illusory or fictitious or capricious etymologizing characteristic of much allegorical exegesis—will inevitably elicit truth. And just as inevitably, the human expositor will serve as witness to that truth. The use of etymology as the basic tool of mythographic interpretation must thus reflect a conception of myth itself as similarly numinous and of mythographic interpretation as implicated in the testimony to revelation.

Truth goes on to explain how it is that the "human letters" of myth and the "divine letters" of sacred truth can find simultaneous expression in allegory. "It is Concept that engenders Truth," she says, "Mind that conceives it, Idea that gives it nourishment, Language that gives it birth":

> ... a la Verdad también
> el Concepto es quien la engendra,
> la Mente quien la concibe,
> la Idea quien la alimenta,
> . . . .
> es quien la pare la lengua.   (1562)

In this view it is the concept (understood here platonically as the abstract or universal created by God and explicated by revealed theology)[82] that is originative; the authorial mind receives it, "incubates" its full development (following the anatomical analogy used here), and finally expresses it in language. The au-

---

82. A. A. Parker provides a useful discussion of Calderón's conception of the "concept": ". . . the imagination presents the reflecting mind with the picture it requires in order to understand an idea, and with the diagram it requires in order to communicate it by means of illustration or analogy. Thus the mind transforms the concept with which theology furnishes it into a mental picture which fixes it (*concepto imaginado*), and then, in order to communicate the concept to other minds, it makes use of this mental picture which, through the technical resources of the stage, is turned into a dramatic picture and endowed with movement (*práctico concepto*)." See Alexander A. Parker, *The Allegorical Drama of Calderón* (Oxford: Dolphin, 1943), 75.

thor's role is thus subordinate and contingent, mediative rather than wholly creative, always and fundamentally interpretative rather than originative.[83] The concept—unitary, originary, sacral—is the true numinous and generative telos.

The notion of the contingency or hierarchy of authorship, explicit in this passage and implicit in many of the *autos,* is crucial to the whole question of the truth value and its authorization in the Calderonian *auto sacramental.* When Calderón alludes to, or has his characters allude to, the source of the tales he allegorizes, he is always vaguely referring to the "fábulas" of the pagans. Are these "originals" of the tales to be taken as the seminal, prototypical, and presumably oral or popular versions promulgated in pagan religious doctrine and ritual? Or as the first known literary manifestations of this source material by pagan, but secular, writers who took up and elaborated the myths in narrative or dramatic form? Or as subsequent versions by more or less contemporary authors, versions to be considered "original" because they served as Calderón's inspiration or source for his allegorized adaptations? Given Calderón's oft-expressed attribution of pagan myth to divine inspiration (in

---

83. Cf. the comments of Rosemond Tuve in her consideration of divinizing or moralizing commentaries on profane literature:

> This offer of meanings which "one may understand" is a common element in the poetical theory of these early interpreters; their phrasings prove that they do not claim that the author really meant this and that the images at bottom really signify that. . . . [T]his (often) represents a willingness to talk about imported meanings just because they are usually thought profitable.
>
> [There was] a belief that the images can truly carry, though they were not intended to, the imposed significance, and that if we assume this experimentally and read on, we may learn something new about the subject onto which we have artificially grafted the image.

Rosemond Tuve, *Allegorical Imagery* (Princeton: Princeton University Press, 1966), 236. On the medieval conception of the poet as interpreter of "God's book," see Giuseppe Mazzotta, *Dante, Poet of the Desert* (Princeton: Princeton University Press, 1979) 267–68, and Marcia L. Colish, *The Mirror of Language,* rev. ed. (Lincoln: University of Nebraska Press, 1983), 253.

the Christian sense), he presumably regarded God as the supreme and originary author of the myths, which in this vision analogously acquire something of the status and warranty of Christian parable.[84] The human authors who rework the myths participate in the sacred truth value of the originals: the secular authors of antiquity are secondary participants; the modern writers who use pagan authors as source material, tertiary; the modern writers drawing on the work of chronologically proximate precursors, quaternary. The pipeline of divine ordination is not disrupted or diluted by such intermediary nodal points; on the contrary, such mediation confirms the transcendence and universality of sacred truth.

The originary connection of immanent, sacral truth to authorial endeavor shapes Calderón's theorization of the mythological *auto sacramental*. For Calderón, it is God who is the source of the truth "everywhere infused" that informs the human letters of myth as well as the divine literature of Scripture. The dramatist of the allegorical *auto sacramental* is the mystagogue, the illumined expositor and transmitter of revealed truth, that Augustine maintains the ideal (Christian) interpreter must be. In the playwright's view the *auto* is dramatized allegoresis, kerygmatic revelation, a divinely warranted procla-

---

84. Cf. David L. Jeffrey's discussion of Augustine and Dante: "This very Augustinian notion of the human writer as a scribe and translator is the characteristic posture of a great number of medieval writers, not just Dante, and the use of the book-scribe metaphors alerts the medieval reader to such a writer's view of himself as a kind of student, and his work as text with a context, with reference for meaning to another text. That is, the Book of Memory which Dante studies has as its Author God himself, to whose writing in history the poet responds, as a scribe. For Dante, in the *Inferno* (XV, 88–90), the poetic tradition extending from Homer to himself bears a kind of collective witness, as an anthology of scribal translations, to God's continuous narrative presence in the reality of temporal human experience." David L. Jeffrey, "Introduction" ("The Self and the Book: Reference and Recognition in Medieval Thought"), in *By Things Seen,* ed. David L. Jeffrey (Ottawa: University of Ottawa Press, 1979), 10.

mation of the complex and subtle homologies that bind and irradiate myth, truth, allegory, and interpretation as theophanic
testimony to providence and sacred truth.

The *auto*'s precise role in such transmission, its status as kerygma or quasi-sacred proclamation, is the subject of the next
chapter.

3. History and Time
Auto as Kerygma

La Alegoría y la Historia
tan una de otra se enlazan.
   (*La protestación de la fe*, 1656)

In *A María el corazón* (1664), Furor (the Devil's alter ego) remarks, "... a luz de alegoría ... / a lugares / ni a tiempos nos obliga / la precisión ..." ["in the light of allegory we are obliged to precision in neither place nor time"] (1137). The personification is attempting to rationalize the coexistence in the same "historia" of personages from various periods of the Christian era. "[S]iendo fingidas / ideas, como somos / de alguna fantasía," Furor explains. That is, we, as personified figures, are ideas, the allegorized products of human fantasy, which, in employing rhetorical tropes, enables the spectator to overcome the everyday bounds of space and time and thus grasp their underlying meaning:

> ... y así
> porque nos facilitan
> los retóricos tropos
> el que el oyente mida
> los instantes a horas,
> las horas luego a días,
> y los días a años.   (1137)

Rhetorical tropes enable the hearer to measure hours as instants, days as hours, and years as days.

Statements such as Furor's recur throughout Calderón's *autos,* invariably in similar contexts. Allegory, we are constantly reminded, permits the supersession of normal spatio-temporal relationships, the juxtaposition of, say, Adam, Moses, and Christ in the same dramatic space and the same allegorized time. Human imagination can range freely through history, conjoining people and events on the basis of their significance rather than historical, or quotidian, accuracy. This imaginative freedom discovers unity and recognizes connections independent of mere chronology or geography, or even dramatic verisimilitude ordinarily conceived.

Such a treatment of time is actually a perennial feature of Christian allegory, which, as D. W. Robertson pointed out, is radically anachronistic; it tends to reduce time and history "to a kind of continuous present," so that personages from the Old Testament, the New Testament, and one's own age can inhabit, and interact within, the same narrative or drama.[1]

A. A. Parker has made similar observations about Calderón's handling of allegory in the *autos sacramentales.* He suggests that it is "the conceptual nature of the *autos*" that permitted Calderón "to embrace all times and places in one dramatic action." Ultimately it is the freedom of human imagination itself that enables allegory's dramatic and rhetorical license: "[Calderón's drama] is a 'representación fantástica', and therefore possesses all the freedom with which the imagination breaks down the barriers of ordinary experience."[2]

1. D. W. Robertson, Jr., *A Preface to Chaucer* (Princeton: Princeton University Press, 1962), 301: "There is a sense in which the spiritual understanding of Christian allegory produces a similar effect [similar to the simultaneity of God's vision of the past, present, and future], so that temporal sequence acquires something of the nature of an illusion."

2. Alexander A. Parker, *The Allegorical Drama of Calderón* (Oxford: Dolphin, 1943), 76. On Calderón's conception of time, see also Leslie J. Woodward, "La dramatización del tiempo en el auto *Los alimentos del hombre,*" in *Hacia Calderón, Cuarto*

True enough. However, Calderón's conception of history and time, and his allegorization of both in his *autos,* are more complex than Parker's explanation implies. In fact, the Calderonian *autos* frequently enunciate a very special, intimate relation of history, time, and allegory. In Calderón's view, it is a relationship grounded in homology, in the essential christocentricism of both history and time, and in typological correspondences infinitely deployed throughout history. Furthermore, Calderón's historical *autos* confound traditional theoretical distinctions between typology and allegory and posit an unprecedented, unparalleled vision of the sacral, sacramental analogy of temporality, sacred history, and (most provocatively), dramatic performance itself.

In focussing intense dramatic attention on history, Calderón often merely echoes centuries of Christian speculation and Catholic doctrine. This theory and doctrine suggest that Christianity veritably begins *with* history and that Christian theology begins *as* history.[3]

Coloquio Anglogermano, Wolfenbüttel 1975, ed. Hans Flasche, Karl-Hermann Körner, and Hans Mattauch (Berlin: Walter de Gruyter, 1979), 123–28, and Anthony J. Cascardi, "Calderón's Encyclopaedic Rhetoric," *Neophilologus* 16 (1982): 57.

3. On the relationship between Christianity and history, and Christian views of history and historiography, see especially C. A. Patrides, *The Phoenix and the Ladder* (Berkeley: University of California Press, 1964). See also Paul Ricoeur, "Toward a Hermeneutic of the Idea of Revelation," *Harvard Theological Review* 70 (1977): 1–37; Jean Daniélou, "The Conception of History in the Christian Tradition," *Journal of Religion* 30 (1950): 171–79, "The Problem of Symbolism," *Thought* 25 (1950): 423–40, and *The Lord of History,* trans. Nigel Abercrombie (London: Longmans, Green, 1958); Hans Urs von Balthasar, *A Theology of History* (New York: Sheed and Ward, 1963); D. Rudolf Bultmann, *History and Eschatology* (Edinburgh: Edinburgh University Press, 1975); L. G. Patterson, *God and History in Early Christian Thought* (London: Adam and Charles Black, 1967); T. Preiss, "The Christian Philosophy of History," *Journal of Religion* 30 (1950): 157–70; Antonio Quacquarelli, *La concezione della storia nella società dei primi secoli dopo Cristo* (Bari: Adriatica, 1968); and Eric Charles Rust, *The Christian Understanding of History* (London: Lutterworth, 1947).

It was Augustine who laid down the lines of the traditional conception in *The City of God*. Here the bishop attempts a theological interpretation of world history. He rejects categorically the pagan "theory of cycles, which are alleged to effect the inevitable repetition of things and events at periodic intervals."[4] Against this vision, he finds as "the only possibility left which is agreeable to true religion"[5] the acceptance of a determinate beginning to history in creation and the unicity of historical progress through time.[6]

This vision of history and time was to become the standard Christian position, the "theological commonplace"[7] of most Christian thought. In this view, time is linear, and history is the arena of unique, unrepeatable, and unrepeated events.

4. (Saint) Augustine, *Concerning the City of God against the Pagans,* trans. David Knowles (Middlesex, England: Penguin Books, 1972), Book 12, Ch. 21, p. 498.

5. Augustine, 501.

6. Cf. Augustine, 498–99:

It is intolerable for devout ears to hear the opinion expressed that after passing through this life with all its great calamities (if indeed it is to be called life, when it is really a death, a death so grievous that for love of this death we shrink from the death which frees us from it), that after all these heavy and fearful ills have at last been expiated and ended by true religion and wisdom and we have arrived at the sight of God and reached our bliss in the contemplation of immaterial light through participation in his changeless immortality, which we long to attain, with burning desire—that we reach this bliss only to be compelled to abandon it, to be cast down from that eternity, that truth, that felicity, to be involved again in hellish mortality, in shameful stupidity, in detestable miseries, where God is lost, where truth is hated, where happiness is sought in unclean wickedness; and to hear that this is to happen again and again, as it has happened before, endlessly, at periodic intervals, as the ages pass in succession; and to hear that the reason for this is so that God may be able to know his own works by means of those finite cycles with their continual departure and return, bringing with them our false felicities and genuine miseries, which come in alternation, but are everlasting in this incessant round. For this theory assumes that God can neither rest from his creative activity, nor grasp within his knowledge an infinity of things.

Who could give a hearing to such a notion? Who could believe it, or tolerate it?

7. The phrase is John McIntyre's, in *The Christian Doctrine of History* (Edinburgh: Oliver and Boyd, 1957), 3.

However, the unicity and linearity of time and history are subtended by the patterns and recurrences that any percipient observer can find in historical events. History, or at least its interpretation, always depends upon some notion of causality, and the notion of causality in its turn implies closure, an ultimate, originary significance, which confers meaning and organizes those connections of men and events that permit interpretation.[8] For the Christian, and especially the Christian theologian, this originary and configurative significance is found in the revelation: "In the Christian view the Incarnation transformed history not in the sense that it transcended time but in the sense that it redeemed time and invested history with purpose. The Incarnation became history's axis by entering history and centering history on God."[9] It is the revelation that dis-

8. "[H]istorical interpretation must always move backward from the finally understood meaning . . . back through the connections of men and events which developed and constituted that meaning. . . . Fixing an anchor in the onwardness of time allows certain things (persons, groups, thoughts, actions) to take on intelligible meaning because they can be described as evolving, tending, causing, contributing to, exhibiting, exemplifying, resisting, denying, or irrelevant to the closure that anchors time and meaning." Nancy F. Partner, "Making up Lost Time: Writing on the Writing of History," rev. art., *Speculum* 61 (1986), 109. Partner goes on to point out the general similarity of historical interpretation to the methods and presuppositions of Christocentric exegesis: "This indispensable pattern [of historical analysis] is not unlike the formal structure of biblical exegesis as developed by the Christian exegetes, for whom the closure of Incarnation and Passion revealed the truth so long hidden in the open-ended narrative struggle of Jewish Scripture." Cf. Stephen A. Barney, *Allegories of History, Allegories of Love* (Hamden, CT: Archon Books, 1979), 33: "[I]t is the formal resemblance of a fiction to its interpretation, its frame or antitype, that forges the link [basic to typological allegory]. We feel that we are taught most authoritatively when a typological relation is established between a fiction and the Ur-form of that fiction, the most important text in the genre. Hence typology works most powerfully, as typology, when it brings a traditional genre into relation with the Bible, or the Virgilian texts, or Greek myths, or folk tales."

9. Holly Wallace Boucher, "Metonymy in Typology and Allegory, with a Consideration of Dante's *Comedy*," in *Allegory, Myth, and Symbol*, ed. Morton W. Bloomfield (Cambridge: Harvard University Press, 1981), 134.

closes the sacral significance of all individual events "as interrelated and mutually illuminating,"[10] and universal history as the story of the cosmos as "one great drama whose beginning is God's creation of the world, whose climax is Christ's Incarnation and Passion, and whose expected conclusion will be Christ's second coming and Last Judgment."

The latter words are Erich Auerbach's.[11] It is he who has perhaps most cogently discussed the Christian conception of history and time. According to this so-called figural vision, "every occurrence, in all its everyday reality, is simultaneously a part in a world-historical context through which each part is related to every other, and thus is likewise to be regarded as being of all times or above all time."[12]

This analogical reading of history, historical events, and historical personages is also known, of course, as typology: "the broad study, or any particular presentation, of the quasi-symbolic relations which one event may appear to bear to another—especially, but not exclusively, when these relations are the analogical ones existing between events which are taken to be one another's 'prefiguration' and 'fulfillment.' "[13] More specifically, typology refers, in a Christian context, to "the science of history's relations to its fulfilment in Christ."[14] In practice,

10. Boucher, 133.

11. Erich Auerbach, *Mimesis,* trans. Willard R. Trask (Princeton: Princeton University Press, 1953), 158. Cf. Barbara K. Lewalski, "Typology and Poetry: A Consideration of Herbert, Vaughan, and Marvell," in *Illustrious Evidence,* Earl Miner, ed. (Berkeley: University of California Press, 1975), 42.

12. Auerbach, *Mimesis,* 156.

13. A. C. Charity, *Events and Their Afterlife* (Cambridge: Cambridge University Press, 1966), 1.

14. Henri de Lubac, quoted by Charity, 1. It was probably Paul who first used the Greek word *typos* to describe "the prefiguring of the future in prior history"; Leonhard Goppelt, *Typos,* trans. Donald H. Madvig (Grand Rapids, MI: William B. Eerdmans, 1982), 4. For example, the fortunes of Israel are seen as *typoi* of those of the Church. Cf. I Cor. 10:11 ("Haec autem omnia in figura contingebant illis: scripta

the typological exegesis of Scripture was based on the discovery in the persons and events of the Old Testament prefigurations of Christ and of occurrences in the New Testament.[15]

The centrality of divine ordination for typological relationships and exegesis entailed a distinction, fundamental although not always carefully maintained, between typology and allegory[16]:

The general term "allegory" was commonly understood to involve the use of fictions or contrived sequences of signs which are not true or real in themselves but refer or point to underlying spiri-

---

sunt autem ad correptionem nostram, in quos fines saeculorum devenerunt") and Rom. 5:14 ("Sed regnavit mors ab Adam usque ad Moysen etiam in eos qui non peccaverunt in similitudinem praevaricationis Adae, qui est forma futuri"). By the time of Barnabas, Hermas, and Justin, "this usage had become firmly established" (Goppelt, 5). It was Thomas Aquinas who definitively formulated and established the "classical" elaboration of typology for Catholic hermeneutics (*Summa Theologica* 1q1, a.10). Thomas distinguishes in Scripture a twofold meaning: the literal sense, present in the words themselves and derived from explication of the words' literal or figurative meaning; and the typological sense, variously termed the *sensus realis, spiritualis, typicus,* or *mysticus,* "which is based on the literal sense, in that the persons, things, and institutions that are spoken about are also divinely appointed prototypes of things in the future" (Goppelt, 7, n. 26). The typological conception of Scripture thus depends upon a reciprocity of significance between Old and New Testaments: "The prototype receives its full meaning from the antitype, but it has this meaning only in its own existence. This existence, however, has meaning only insofar as it prefigures the antitype" (Goppelt, 17).

15. On typology, see, for example, Charity; R. P. C. Hanson, *Allegory and Event* (Richmond, VA: John Knox, 1959); Rudolf Bultmann, "Ursprung und Sinn der Typologie als hermeneutischer Methode," *Theologische Literaturzeitung* 75–76 (1950–51): 205–12; J. S. Preus, *From Shadow to Promise* (Cambridge: Harvard University Press, 1969); "Typological Interpretation of the Old Testament," trans. John Bright, in *Essays on Old Testament Hermeneutics,* ed. Claus Westermann, English trans. ed. James Luther Mays (Richmond, VA: John Knox, 1963), 17–39; Hartmut Hoefer, *Typologie im Mittelalter* (Göttingen: A. Künmerle, 1971); Goppelt; Erich Auerbach, "Figura," in *Scenes from the Drama of European Literature* (New York: Meridian Books, 1959); Elizabeth Salter, "Medieval Poetry and the Figural View of Reality," *Proceedings of the British Academy* 54 (1968): 73–92; and the essays included in Earl Miner, ed., *Literary Uses of Typology* (Princeton: Princeton University Press, 1977).

16. See discussion below for fuller consideration of the complex relationship between allegory and typology.

tual truths. The typological process by contrast is a pattern of signification in which type and antitype, as historically real entities with independent meaning and validity, form patterns of prefiguration, recapitulation, and fulfillment by reason of God's providential control of history.[17]

Calderón wrote a number of *autos,* based on Old Testament themes, that explicitly discuss the existence and operations of typology in this traditional sense. *Primero y segundo Isaac* (1658), for example, presents Isaac as the prefiguration of Christ[18] and Rebecca as the type of the Virgin Mother as well as the Church.[19] Their wedding feast becomes "la concordia / de Cristo y la Iglesia" ["the concord of Christ and Church"] (818). As dramatic representation, the nuptials entail the discovery of the Eucharistic host and chalice, which sacramentalize "the second Isaac" and thus confirm and fulfill the prophetic typology of the Messiah's forebear.[20]

Old Testament *autos* such as *Isaac* essentially rework biblical narrative so as to highlight its typological significance. These plays are "representational," in the special sense of the term pro-

17. Lewalski, "Typology and Poetry," 42. Cf. Goppelt, 13: "Allegorical interpretation . . . is not concerned with the truthfulness or factuality of the things described. For typological interpretation, however, the reality of the things described is indispensable." On the distinction of typology and allegory, see also Charity, 58, 171 n. 199, and 203–7.

18. "Cordero Sacrificado / vio en *Primero Isaac* el Mundo, / y hoy en el *Isaac Segundo* / ve figura y figurado" ["The world saw in the Sacrificial Lamb the First Isaac, and today in the Second Isaac, World sees both the figure and the figured meaning"] (820).

19. On this *auto,* see also Angel L. Cilveti, "Dramatización de la alegoría bíblica en *Primero y Segundo Isaac* de Calderón," in *Critical Perspectives on Calderón de la Barca,* Frederick A. de Armas, David M. Gitlitz, and José A. Madrigal, eds. (Lincoln, NE: Society of Spanish and Spanish-American Studies, 1981), 39–52.

20. Cf. as well *La Torre de Babilonia* (before 1647?), *Sueños hay que verdad son* (1670), *El viático cordero* (1665), *La serpiente de metal* (1676), *¿Quién hallará mujer fuerte?* (1672), *La piel de Gedeón* (1650), *Las espigas de Ruth* (1663), *El arca de Dios cautiva* (1673), *La primer flor del Carmelo* (1648?), *El árbol de mejor fruto* (1677), *Mística y real Babilonia* (1662), *La cena de Baltasar* (1632?).

posed by Parker: they retell scriptural history or recast it in dramatic form.[21] In such *autos* the playwright's approach to typology is thus relatively straightforward, and relatively imitative.[22]

To see these plays as primarily representational is not, however, to belittle their literary worth or theological power as reworkings of scriptural source material. Large portions of the Bible, particularly the synoptic gospels, are at least partially narrative, and one school of modern theological thought finds in biblical narrative *as narrative* "the proper locus for significant theological reflection."[23] If Christian theology is partly history-telling, hence story-telling,[24] the retelling of that history becomes kerygmatic rather than merely recapitulative or mimetic.[25]

Kerygma is, we may recall, "the proclamation of the kingdom of God and of the 'gospel of God, which he had promised beforehand through his prophets in the Holy Scriptures' (Rom.

21. Parker, *The Allegorical Drama,* 160ff.

22. Scholars familiar with Dante and Dante scholarship will note in Calderón's treatment of history, time, typology, and allegory a strong resemblance to the Italian poet's conception of the issues. For a brilliant examination of the problems in Dante, see especially Giuseppe Mazzotta, *Dante, Poet of the Desert* (Princeton: Princeton University Press, 1979).

23. Michael Goldberg, *Theology and Narrative* (Nashville: Parthenon, 1981), 267, n. 19.

24. On this point, see in general Hans W. Frei, *The Eclipse of Biblical Narrative* (New Haven: Yale University Press, 1974), especially the "Introduction," 1–16.

25. On the kerygmatic function of history-telling, see H. Richard Niebuhr, *The Meaning of Revelation* (New York: Macmillan, 1941), 32:

> The preaching of the early Christian church was not an argument for the existence of God nor an admonition to follow the dictates of some common human conscience, unhistorical and super-social in character. It was primarily a simple recital of the great events connected with the historical appearance of Jesus Christ and a confession of what had happened to the community of disciples. Whatever it was that the church meant to say, whatever was revealed or manifested to it could be indicated only in connection with an historical person and events in the life of the community. The confession referred to history and was consciously made in history.

1.2)."[26] The relationship of kerygma to history is intimate, inherent. In the first place, the Christian preacher who publicly proclaimed the life and teachings of Christ "thought of himself as the divinely authorized announcer, or herald, of very important news after the manner of John the Baptist";[27] that is, as contemporary witness to Christian truth, as the continuator in the present of prophetic, apostolic witness.[28] In the second place, Christ's life and meaning subsumed both the message of universal history and the preacher's celebratory testimony. And that typological paradigm implicates both universal history and contemporary witness in sacred history.[29]

Calderón appears to acknowledge explicitly just such a kerygmatic role for his *auto*. Indeed, the kerygmatic function of the *autos'* history-telling is proclaimed by History herself in the *loa* or prologue to *El verdadero Dios Pan* (1670):

> Ya que el contento de hoy
> es tan general contento
> que al que no está loco hubo
> quien dijo que no está cuerdo,
> ¿quién duda que a mí me toque,
> más que a otro algún festejo,
> el júbilo y la alegría
> de sus aplausos, pues siendo

26. "Kerygma," *New Catholic Encyclopedia,* 8 (New York: McGraw-Hill, 1967): 167–69.

27. "Kerygma," *NCE* 8: 168.

28. On the conception of witness in the Christian tradition, see articles "Witness," *New Catholic Encyclopedia,* 14 (New York: McGraw-Hill, 1967), 980–81, and "Witness," *The New International Dictionary of New Testament Theology,* ed. Colin Brown, trans., with additions and revisions, from the German *Theologisches Begriffslexikon zum Neuen Testament,* ed. Lothar Coenen *et al.,* 3 (Grand Rapids, MI: Regency Reference Library, 1978): 1038–51, which contains extensive bibliography. Kerygma and witness are fundamentally connected: "The thought is that to be touched by the testimony of Jesus Christ places one in the service of witness. It obliges one to pass it on . . ." ("Witness," *The New International Dictionary,* 3: 1046).

29. See "Kerygma," *NCE,* 8: 168.

la Historia en común, es fuerza
que también haya de serlo
en particular, con que,
humana y divina a un tiempo,
en la parte de divina
me están llamando a su obsequio,
en el Sacrificio que hoy
ofrece la Tierra al Cielo,
ya la Epístola de Pablo,
ya de Juan el Evangelio.   (1237)

Since today's joy is so general that anyone not mad would be
called a fool, who can doubt that to me, more than in the case of
any other festivity, befalls the happiness and jubilation of the day.
For, since I am collective or universal History, perforce I am private history as well. So that, human and divine at one and the same
time, I am, as divine, summoned by the Epistle of Paul and the
Gospel of John to pay homage to them, in the Sacrifice which today Earth offers to Heaven.

The kerygmatic import of Calderón's *autos* would thus appear to reside in the plays' constantly repeated, devotional retelling of universal history: man's creation, temptation, and fall,
and his redemption through the Sacrifice proclaimed by Paul
and John and commemorated in the Eucharist, which constitutes both the *auto*'s occasion and, as the "discovery" of the host
and chalice at the play's conclusion, its dramatic coda as well.

The precise theological and ontological status of such recapitulation of sacred history, the question whether secular literature can truly be kerygma in the technical sense, is nowhere
made clear in Calderón's *autos*. Nor was it necessary for the dramatist to confront, at least in the case of the Old Testament
autos, some of the thornier issues raised by the modern, allegorized dramatization of sacred mystery—the kerygma of
scriptural narrative in a sense ensures the theological legitimacy
of re-creations of that narrative. However, the relationship between "historia divina" and "historia humana" (to use History's

terminology), between sacred history and *auto,* between typology and allegory, is altogether more problematic, and more thoroughly scrutinized, in those *autos* based on events of Calderón's own time.[30]

The so-called topical or circumstantial *autos*[31] are often (and sometimes rightfully) considered Calderón's weakest.[32] It may indeed seem hard to make an enthusiastic case for the aesthetic or theological value of plays that allegorize Christianity's central mysteries through sometimes stupefyingly banal analogies drawn from secular history and even current events. For example, the historical metaphor that informs *El nuevo palacio del Retiro* (1634) is the remodeling in 1633 of the Buen Retiro palace in Madrid.[33] The *auto* allegorizes the royal palace in elaborate (and, it must be admitted, bizarre) sacral analogues: the Retiro is simultaneously a postfiguration of Noah's ark (". . . en aqueste edificio, / de que fue figura aquel" ["this building, of which that previous one was figure"] (139), figure of the

30. On the relation of contemporaneous history and allegory in Calderón's *autos,* see also Stephen Rupp, "Allegory and Diplomacy in Calderón's *El lirio y la azucena,*" *Bulletin of the Comediantes* 41 (1989): 107–25.

31. The circumstantial or topical *autos* may be defined as those in which the dramatist allegorizes events and personages of secular, usually contemporaneous, history in order to analogize Christian *Heilsgeschichte.* This definition of the circumstantial *auto* differs slightly from the conception of the "autos de circunstancias" that Angel Valbuena Prat follows in his edition of the *autos.* Although he does not define the term, he includes in this group primarily plays based upon analogies drawn from events of the dramatist's own time. On these circumstantial *autos,* see also Sebastián Neumeister, "Las bodas de España: Alegoría y política en el auto sacramental," in *Hacia Calderón: Quinto Coloquio Anglogermano, Oxford 1978,* ed. Hans Flasche and Robert D. F. Pring-Mill (Wiesbaden: Franz Steiner Verlag GMBH, 1982), 30–41.

32. Cf. the comment by Valbuena Prat in his edition of the *autos:* "Es donde predominan las obras flojas e inactuales" ["It is where weak works predominate"] (35).

33. On the palace, see Jonathan Brown and John H. Elliott, *A Palace for a King* (New Haven: Yale University Press), 1980. Rupp also discusses a similar allegorical treatment of the Buen Retiro in *El lirio y la azucena.*

Church, and prophecy of the New Jerusalem of Revelation. The regal court and various royal councillors also have their counterparts: King Philip IV is the divine Son of Justice or Christ; his Queen, Elizabeth of Bourbon, is the Law of Grace; the royal favorite, the Count-Duke of Olivares, is Mankind; Paul presides over the Supreme Council, Matthew the Council of the Indies, Peter the Council of War, Andrew the Inquisition; and so forth.[34] The sacramental bread becomes the prize offered to the winners of a royal joust that was a historically verifiable part of the palace's inaugural festivities.

In *El nuevo palacio* Calderón must stretch the topical analogy virtually to the breaking point of credibility, even aesthetic taste and theological validity, in order to include the Eucharistic allusion that was, after all, the *autos'* dramatic pretext and theological keystone. Obviously, and regrettably, the topical referent of such an allegory served a memorialist—and politically opportunistic—function for a genre that was, throughout Calderón's career, increasingly linked with and dependent upon royal and municipal patronage.[35] An *auto* of this type is little more than decorative typology, "a forced and perhaps even playful adaptation of the [typological] method."[36]

However, the topical metaphors or analogies of the circumstantial *autos* are often far more than mere historical pretext, more, even, than appeal to contemporary interests, knowledge,

34. J. H. Elliott discusses the organization of the conciliar system of this period, *Imperial Spain 1469-1716* (New York: New American Library, 1963), especially 167–78.

35. See J. E. Varey, "Calderón's *Auto Sacramental, La vida es sueño,* in performance," *Iberoromania* 14 (1981): 75–86: "The plays . . . became in a sense less popular, the emphasis being placed more and more on the performances before the Court, the Councils and the Municipality."

36. The phrase and the category are those of Robert Hollander, "Typology and Secular Literature: Some Medieval Problems and Examples," in Earl Miner, ed., *Literary Uses of Typology,* 7–8.

and tastes. For it is here, in the allegorization of secular event, that Calderón most daringly posits an analogical, indeed typological, relationship of contemporary occasion and sacred history.[37]

Obviously, it is one thing to retell scriptural history so as to underscore canonized figural interpretation, as the dramatist does in the so-called biblical *autos*. It is quite another to extend the typological paradigm to the all-too-human personages and all-too-mundane events of one's own time, as Calderón does in the circumstantial *autos*. In these plays contemporaneous events analogize prototypes in sacred history; and the allegorical *auto* itself is posited as contemporized witness to sacred truth. Calderón suggests, in fact, that topical referent can be typological fulfillment, that secular event and profane allegory can and do participate in the sacral patterns of typology.[38] History veritably *is* allegory, allegory virtually *is* history.

Calderón's typological reading of contemporaneous event informs even the early, relatively simple (and relatively simplistic) *La segunda esposa y triunfar muriendo* (1648–1649?), which commemorates the 1648 marriage of King Philip IV and Mariana of Austria.[39] Following the advice of Matrimony, who urges him to remarry after the death of his first wife (Synagogue, or the unfortunate Elizabeth also allegorized in *El nuevo palacio*), the King (Christ) selects Ana (Grace or Church) as his consort. This temporal succession of consorts is linked metaphorically to the chronological succession of pre-Christian and Christian

37. Margaret Rich Greer acutely analyzes the interplay of secular history, specifically, the power of the monarch, and Calderón's secular theater in "Art and Power in the Spectacle Plays of Calderón de la Barca," *Publications of the Modern Language Association* 104 (1989): 329–39.

38. Cf. Mazzotta's view of the "providentiality of the temporal order" in the *Divine Comedy* (316).

39. On this *auto,* see the critical edition and introduction by José María Díez Borque, *Una fiesta sacramental barroca* (Madrid: Taurus, 1983). See also Neumeister.

eras. But it also analogizes stages in the individual Christian's salvation history. Man, invited to the royal nuptials but waylaid by Sin and Death, is saved only by the timely intercession of the King and Baptism, ". . . el primero ministro / de cuantos para su Esposa / tiene el Rey en su servicio" ["the first minister of all those the King has in his service for his Queen"] (437). The sacrament of Baptism confers upon Man a second life, a temporary, partial victory over his diabolical enemies. It is only the King's self-sacrifice for Man's sake that effects the final conquest: ". . . cuando el triunfar muriendo / la Vida a la Muerte quito, / la vida al Hombre restauro" ["by triumphing in death, I snatch Life from Death, and I restore Life to Man"] (443). The perpetual commemoration of this act, this Passion, in the Eucharist ensures man's ultimate triumph over both Death and time: ". . . el morir aquí una vez, / es a vivir para siempre" ["to die here a single time is to live forever"] (447).

In the midst of these theological details the *auto*'s circumstantial pretext—the royal wedding of 1648—tends to disappear. There is no precise equivalent in contemporary history that can be readily analogized to the Passion, although Calderón does try, equating the assault of Sin and Death with Philip's real-life enemies (442). It must be admitted that in this early play the dramatist has yet to achieve complete mastery of his allegorical tools; the topical referent is a weak, farfetched basis for the Christological and Eucharistic analogies. Nevertheless, *La segunda esposa* does contain some signs of Calderón's more mature technique. The repeated, typological supersession of temporal versimilitude, characteristic of the later *autos,* is at least suggested in this play. For example, in his own death the King finds the conflation of three distinct temporal moments: the Passion, the foundation of the Church, and the safe passage of the historical Spanish Queen to her new homeland. The strictures of exact chronology have broken down into a temporal anachrony, into the "continuous present" of allegorical representation.

More interesting than this conflation of historical moments is the *auto*'s implicit analogy of Christological and circumstantial registers. Contemporaneous event becomes more than expedient metaphor, as though it were imbued with a sacral significance of its own.

The vision of contemporaneous history as potentially, analogically sacred, and of occasional metaphor as charged with a significance beyond mere topicality, become the hallmark of Calderón's typological historicism in the later *autos*. "[L]a Alegoría y la Historia / tan una de otra se enlazan" (743), we are told in *La protestación de la fe* (1656), "History and Allegory are so intertwined. . . ." Allegory does not simply exploit historical event as metaphor for the sacred. Rather, ". . . iguales corren / los dos paralelos líneas / de las dos luces que hacen / lo real y la alegoría", ["As equal lines the two parallels of the two lights cast by the real and the allegorical run in tandem"] (738). The real (understood here as sacred history) and the allegorical (understood as the secular event that analogizes and metaphorizes that history) are interdependent because analogical, because they are grounded in the same transcendent significance.

The interdependence of human and sacred history, of allegorical and real, grounds the allegory of *El año santo de Roma*, written to commemorate the celebration in Rome of the 1650 Holy Year. Like many Calderonian *autos,* the central metaphor of *El año santo* derives from the traditional Christian conception of life as sojourn or pilgrimage.[40] The opening instrumental summons all "pilgrims" (i.e., all mankind) to Rome in order to achieve beatitude:

> Venid, venid, peregrinos,
> venid, venid que este año

40. On the metaphor of the *peregrinatio vitae*, see especially Juergen H. Hahn, *The Origins of the Baroque Idea of "Peregrinatio"* (Chapel Hill: University of North Carolina Press, 1973) and Samuel Chew, *The Pilgrimage of Life* (New Haven: Yale University Press, 1962). On the motif in Calderón, see Aurora Egido, *La fábrica de un*

la Puerta se abre que estuvo cerrada
por tantas edades, por siglos tan largos;
y pues que la Vida es jornada de todos,
dichosos aquellos que peregrinando
merecen que el año reparta con ellos
la acción de piadoso, el renombre de *Santo*.   (491–92)

Come, come, pilgrims, come, come, for this year the Door is opened that was closed through so many ages, for such lengthy centuries. And since Life is a journey for us all, fortunate are those who, because of their pilgrimage, deserve to share in the year's pious activity and holy renown.

Man, the archetypal "pilgrim," appears on stage and defines his existential task as the choice between two divergent paths, the broad way that leads to destruction and the narrow way that leads to life and salvation (492).[41]

Throughout the *auto* Calderón plays constantly with the temporal motif suggested by the play's circumstantial referent. He counterpoises several temporal registers: the centuries of Church history, the holy year, the life of man, eternity. The holy year of the title becomes a synecdoche that relates human existence to the temporal continuum of sacred history and the universe; the synecdochal analogy underscores the fugacity of man's life measured against a universal scale. That scale, time itself, is a seamless whole which manifests divine presence and creative power:

Todas las horas de quien
están los días compuestos,
los días de quien tejidas
están la [sic] semanas, siendo

---

auto sacramental: "Los encantos de la Culpa" (Salamanca: Ediciones Universidad de Salamanca, 1982), 117–33.

41. Matt. 7:13–14: "Intrate per angustam portam: quia lata porta, et spatiosa via est, quae ducit ad perditionem, et multi sunt qui intrant per eam. Quam angusta porta, et arcta via est, quae ducit ad vitam: et pauci sunt qui inveniunt eam!"

eslabones de los meses,
como de los años ellos
y los años de los siglos,
unidas partes del tiempo,
todas las bendijo Dios.[42]   (495)

All the hours that form the days, all the weeks woven of the
days, all the weeks interlinked in the months themselves entwined
in the years merged into centuries—all these conjoined segments
of time, all were blessed by God.

More interesting than this temporal telescoping of history is
the treatment of the *auto*'s own time span or duration in actual
dramatic performance. The play itself, it is suggested, telescopes eternity and man's salvation history into the temporal
register or within the temporal limitations of representation:
". . . a dos luces, / en dos sentidos tenemos / lo que fue, y es, y ha
de ser, / reducido a un argumento" ["In two lights, in two
senses, we have what was, what is, and what is to be reduced
to one argument (or plot)"] (496). Calderón thus integrates the
play's own time scale as performance into a holistic temporal
vision.

The idea that the *auto*'s performance time illustrates or reflects eternity is a bold one. For, it is suggested, the *auto*'s presentation of time is analogous to the divine vision of temporality: "unidas partes del tiempo, / todas las bendijo Dios." In the
divine vision, as in the *auto*'s peculiar temporal foreshortening,
time is indivisible, and all of its parts are homologous, conjoined and interrelated, not by chronology, but rather by analogically theophanic significance.

Within this allegorical foreshortening of universal history,

42. Cf. *loa* to *El Santo Rey don Fernando,* Segunda Parte: "Aunque desde el primer
día / en que Dios la Luz formó, / sucesivos unos de otros, / todos son días de Dios"
(1290), "Since the first day when God made light, the days, succeeding one after the
other, are all the days of God."

contemporaneous allusion acquires special meaning. Just as the holy year microcosmically or synecdochally reflects eternity, allegory telescopes sacred history. *Sub specie aeternitatis,* from the temporal perspective of God, allegory and the holy year are analogues, isomorphically structured. Allegory is thus the perfect vehicle for representing temporality itself as sacral exemplarism.

El año santo en Madrid (1652) proposes a similar microcosmic-macrocosmic conception of history and time in terms of a related topical analogue: the favors and indulgences associated with the 1650 Holy Year in Rome that in 1651 were extended to the Court of Spain. In comparison with *El año santo de Roma,* the 1652 *auto* more explicitly integrates the topical register into the cosmic/allegorical vision of history. In the first place, Madrid, as site of the holy year's commemorative celebrations, is described as the "hieroglyph of eternity": "jeroglífico es el sitio / de la duración del tiempo" (557). Furthermore, the *auto* refers again and again to the "hoy" or "today," that is, the present time of dramatic representation. Performance is one particular moment in universal time and one special manifestation of sacred truth: ". . . hoy no es asunto mío / lo particular; y así, / . . . / . . . has de ver que hoy / a lo general aspiro . . ." (540), Divine Grace explicitly states; ["my theme for the day is not the particular or private; and so you will see that today I aspire to the general"].

The "today" of dramatic performance (represented in real or quotidian time), the holy year, and universal history are, according to *El año santo,* syndecdochally related in time. Moreover, the *auto*'s temporal registers are analogically related in significance—they are correlative symbols of humanity's salvation history:

> . . . ya el daño
> de aquel duelo tuyo, y mío,
> en que te vio victorioso

el Arbol del Paraíso,
reparó feliz el Año
Santo de aquel concedido
Plenísimo Jubileo
de la gran Muerte de Cristo,
cuya sagrada memoria
renovaron al principio
a siglo entero los años,
y después a medio siglo.   (541)

The harm caused by your contest, and mine [Grace declares to Sin], a contest in which you emerged victorious, through your strategem with the Tree of Eden, was felicitously remedied by the Holy Year of the Jubilee held in commemoration of Christ's death, the sacred remembrance of which was at first commemorated every one hundred years, and afterward every fifty.

The allegorical *auto* is thus virtual analogate of sacred history.

Calderón exploits this historical, temporal synchrony or anachrony with perhaps the greatest explicitness in *La vacante general* (1647?). Here the dramatist allegorizes contemporaneous circumstance—the competitive examinations for canonries held in 1649 in the cathedral of Madrid—as the provision of prebends left vacant when the Law of Grace superseded the Old or Written Law.

It is John the Baptist who issues the call to examination:

Este altivo, este eminente
poblado monte soberbio,
. . . .
sea público teatro
de nuestro pregón, haciendo
notorio al mundo este edicto,
pues como profeta puedo
anticipar sus noticias,
hasta que se llegue el tiempo,
que el sol que hoy anuncio pueda
señalar. . . .   (473)

Let this eminent and superb wooded mount be a public theater for our proclamation, which issues this edict to the world; as prophet I can anticipate or foretell its news, until such time as indicated by the sun which today I announce.

John's edict sets the *auto*'s historical and temporal registers: contemporaneous event (the examinations) and sacred history (the supersession of the Old Law as well as John's role as prophet, as the type or foreshadowing of Christ). Church further proclaims John's significance not only as prophet, but also as witness who testifies to or incarnates divine revelation:

> Porque siendo, como he dicho,
> su cargo y su ministerio,
> solo anunciar al Mesías,
> y ya tan cerca le vemos
> en Juan, pues aunque él no es Luz,
> testimonio es de Luz. . . .   (475)

As I have said, his charge and his ministry is to announce the Messiah, whom we already see so close at hand in John, since John, although he is not light, is testimony to light.[43]

The notion of testimony or witness suggested here, of resonant theological connotations, will be basic to the play's allegory. Emmanuel is witness to God, a revelation of providence. And the *auto*'s topical register—the contemporaneous occasion—becomes another instance of such witness, as Emmanuel states: "La Materia de este día, / . . . / es la de los Sacramentos." ["The subject for today is the sacraments"] (483). That is, the *auto*'s metaphorical basis, its contemporaneous analogue, is one

---

43. The verses are a paraphrase and translation of John 1:7–8: "Hic venit in testimonium / Ut testimonium perhiberet de lumine, / Ut omnes crederent per illum. / Non erat ille lux, / Sed ut testimonium perhiberet de lumine." The conception of testimony or witness is especially significant and developed in Johannine literature. See article "Witness," *The New International Dictionary of New Testament Theology,* especially 1042–46.

more revelation of or witness to immanent divine presence in history.

The typic vision of secular history, the belief that even national history can participate in the typological patterns of *Heilsgeschichte,* informs Calderón's circumstantial *autos* and gives them their theological and allegorical power. In this vision, "[h]istory had not ceased to produce types with the close of the Apostolic Age and with the last, Apocalyptic book of the New Testament;"[44] rather, subsequent events likewise generate new types to serve as testimony of the revelation. Such is the message of *El cubo de la Almudena* (1651), where Castile's war of reconquest against the Moors (especially during the age of the Cid) is a type of the timeless, perennial struggles of the Church militant against heresy and apostasy.[45]

The secularization of typology is indeed explicitly set forth as doctrine in the *auto*'s preludial *loa*. Here Church, in attempting to convince Heresy of the dogma of transubstantiation, invites her to turn for illumination to the annals of Spanish history: "revuelve al tiempo pasado / los anales, y las series, / y verás" ["turn over the annals and the events of the past, and you will see"] (563). Holland, Portugal, and Aragon appear in turn to proclaim the real presence in the Eucharist of Christ's body and blood. At the prologue's end Castile, truest defender of the faith, comes on stage to demand that Heresy "humble herself before the faith of Spain" ("dobla la cerviz proterva / a la Fe de España ..." [565]). Faith, bearing the Inquisitorial standard, seizes Heresy, chains her, and forces her to bear witness "this day" to the triumph of the Eucharist.

44. Anthony Raspa, *The Emotive Image* (Fort Worth: Texas Christian University Press, 1983), 132.

45. On this *auto,* see also Geoffrey M. Voght, "Calderón's *El cubo de la Almudena* and Comedy in the *Autos Sacramentales,*" in *Critical Perspectives on Calderón de la Barca,* Frederick A. de Armas, David M. Gitlitz, and José A. Madrigal, eds., 141–60.

At various times the Catholic Netherlands, Portugal, and the Crown of Aragon had all been the site of rebellion against Castilian dominance and of heretical desertion from the Catholic fold. Their ultimate submission to Castilian hegemony and their proclamation of Catholic truth in this *loa* implies none too subtly that the Castilian monarchy's expansionist international policies are a contemporary witness to divine presence in history and to the Eucharist which that history celebrates.

Calderón's jingoistic apologia undeniably makes for grim reading in the twentieth century. It can thus be exceedingly difficult to see through the religious and nationalistic chauvinism to the comprehensiveness of the dramatist's allegory. Nevertheless, potent that conception is. Faith, reminding Heresy (and the audience) of the *auto*'s circumstantial pretext, suggests that contemporaneous event, like national history, like *Heilsgeschichte,* can be a witness to the "continuous revelation [in history] of God's power and providence."[46] Furthermore, the *auto*'s dramatic performance, staged "this day" in celebration of historical occasion, is one further link in the chain of sacralized events. This succession has indeed culminated in the Eucharistic *auto* that commemorates and exalts sacred history as well as national history conceived as sacral.

The conception of *auto* as kerygmatic, as contemporary witness to sacred truth and as analogate or synecdoche of sacred history, is nowhere more powerfully developed than in *Las órdenes militares* (1662). This circumstantial *auto* allegorizes the measures necessary for admittance to one of Spain's prestigious military orders. Here Christ is a knight who, for acceptance in the orders, must undergo examination of his lineage. The investigation entails the scrutiny, and ultimately the triumphal affirmation, of his genealogy, that is, the Immaculate Conception of his mother.

46. Steven N. Zwicker, "Politics and Panegyric: The Figural Mode from Marvell to Pope," in Miner, ed., *Literary Uses of Typology,* 116.

As the play opens, Culpa (polysemous personification of sin or guilt and the Devil's alter ego)[47] appears on stage, book in hand. Perusing biblical allusions to the promised Messiah, Culpa is puzzled and apprehensive; none of this can she understand. To resolve her uncertainty, she decides to submit Christ's lineage and alleged Messianic role to the test of what she terms a "representable metaphor":

> . . . tengo
> procurando apurar este
> místico sentido (puesto,
> que sola la conjetura
> es concedida a mi ingenio)
> de reducir a un dictamen,
> a un discurso, a un pensamiento
> la experiencia para ver
> si en representable objeto
> de metafórica frase
> tantas confusiones venzo.   (1019)

I must try, by probing this mystical sense, to convert experience to surmise, to reasoning, to thought, so that I can see whether I can resolve this confusion in the representable object of a metaphorical phrase.

Culpa hypothesizes a set of metaphorized circumstances. She imagines that the world is a monarch, and the unknown youth a soldier of fortune who comes to the Court of the World to solicit recognition for his deeds. She then plans to inquire into the soldier's military record and petition through a metaphorical *audiencia* or trial:

> Supongamos, pues, que el mundo
> es un monarca supremo,
> . . . .
>   supuesto
> que bienes del mundo son

---

47. On this figure and its meaning, see Ch. 1, of the present study.

las coronas, y los cetros.
Supongamos que este joven
es, pues no le conocemos,
. . . .
un soldado de fortuna.
Y para que desde luego
la idea empiece, supongamos
que a pretender por sus hechos
viene a la Corte del Mundo. . . .
Cautelaré mis astucias,
investigando, inquiriendo,
ya que no puedo en las luces,
en las sombras, sus intentos;
pues es forzoso rastrear
de los informes del mesmo
nombre, y Patria, ¿en qué ocasiones
ha Militado, qué puestos
ha ocupado, qué papeles
trae, y qué pide por premio?   (1019)

Let us suppose, then, that the world is a supreme monarch, since
crowns and scepters are worldly goods. Let us suppose, since we do
not know him, that this youth is a soldier of fortune. And so that
the idea may begin, let us suppose that he comes to the Court of the
World to solicit recognition of his deeds. I shall take wise precau-
tion, investigating and inquiring into his designs by shadow, since
I cannot by light. For it is incumbent to find out from his references
his name, on what occasions he has fought, what posts he has held,
what papers he bears, what reward he seeks.

In other words, Culpa veritably ideates the *auto* itself as a
means of testing her suppositions regarding the Messiah's lineage. Through dramatic expansion of the metaphorized situation, she hopes to achieve analogical, anticipatory knowledge of
what is closed to her direct apprehension, that is, the unknown
Savior of Scripture.[48]

48. In Calderón's view, derived ultimately from Thomas Aquinas, the Devil's
knowledge is only conjectural or speculative with respect to the future. On the nature of the Devil's knowledge, and the Thomistic origin of the conception, see Ch. 3

Culpa's role in this *auto* is intriguing. She is no mere character; rather, she is both demiurge ("Yo soy aquella primera / voz . . ." ["I am that first voice"]) and even quasi-author or dramatist.[49] However, in the allegory, as in sacred history, Culpa has a rival or antagonist—John the Baptist (Lucero), who within the allegory, as in history, provides testimony to and prophecy of divine providence:

> LUC: Soy un soldado,
> que en el Militante gremio
> de las campañas del mundo
> a merced sirve del sueldo
> de un valiente Capitán,
> de quien a darte luz vengo.
> . . . .
> No lo [luz] soy yo, pero
> testimonio de luz sí.   (1021)

I am a soldier, who in the military service of the world's campaigns serves by the grace of pay from a valiant Captain, of whom

---

("Conocimiento diabólico") of Angel L. Cilveti, *El demonio en el teatro de Calderón* (Javea, Valencia: Albatros, 1977). Cf. Parker's discussion of this plot device: "[The Devil] is presented either as devising a new scheme to effect the moral destruction of mankind, and examining beforehand in his imagination the chances of success it is likely to have; or else as following the events in human history, piecing them together, endeavouring to ascertain what each one is leading to and into what plan providence is fitting it: he will seize on one and try to foresee its future course, working it out in his imagination in a way that may enable him to make it serve his own ends" (Parker, *Allegorical Drama*, 90–91).

49. The vision of the *autos'* allegory as materializing or dramatizing imaginative activity, particularly that of the Devil or one of his alter egos, recurs again and again throughout Calderón's *autos*. The dramatist repeatedly presents the Devil or one of his doubles as a kind of dramatist who invents the allegory of the play's action as a mental representation of his plans for bringing about Man's fall. For some of the literary, theological, and philosophical implications of the Devil's "authorial" role in Calderón's *autos,* see Parker (*Allegorical Drama*, 90–94), Angel L. Cilveti, and Barbara E. Kurtz, " 'With Human Aspect': Studies in European Personification Allegory with Special Reference to the Hispanic Contribution" (Diss., University of Chicago, 1983), Ch. 5, and " 'No Word without Mystery': Allegories of Sacred Truth in the *Autos Sacramentales* of Calderón de la Barca," *Publications of the*

I come to give you light. I am not myself light, but testimony to light I am.

John's figural role in the *auto* as type or foreshadowing of Christ contravenes Culpa's ontological and theological stature as diabolical demiurge. John's prophetic voice, intervening in the allegory, likewise overturns his adversary's authorial authority and invalidates her allegory:

> LUC (*Cantando*): Como el Pueblo es voz de Dios
> y Juan la voz de Dios sea,
> bien viene, que en voz del Pueblo
> cante Juan, y el Mundo atienda.
> . . . .
> que Juan Gracia se interpreta,
> y siendo voz de la Gracia
> es bien la Culpa la sienta.
> Adelantar pretendió
> en alegórica idea
> los siglos, mas como áspid
> murió a su ponzoña mesma.   (1036)

LUCERO (Singing): Since the People are the voice of God, and John the voice of God, may John sing, and the World attend. For John is to be interpreted as Grace, as, since he is the voice of Grace, it is meet that Culpa hear it. In an allegorical idea she [Culpa] attempted to set the centuries ahead, but like a viper she died of her own poison.

Culpa's allegory dissolves into the historical witness of John's prophetic, typic supervention in history; it dissolves as well into the contemporaneity of the Eucharistic supervention in the *auto*'s performance. This dissolution converts the play into something more than or other than fiction—into sacral synecdoche of *Heilsgeschichte,* into history rather than allegory: "Mi representable objeto / se va haciendo realidad" ["My representable object is turning into reality"] (1025), Culpa acknowledges;

Modern Language Association 103 (1988): 262–71, as well as Ch. 4 of the present study.

". . . fuera, a correr sin velos, / Historia, y no Alegoría" ["unveiled, it would be History, and not Allegory"] (1019).

And isn't that, after all, what a dramatic performance is? One facet of contemporaneous history, one aspect of reality, and not merely "representable object"? In a Christian and particularly a Eucharistic context, the *auto sacramental*—a genre and a performance so intimately connected with Corpus Christi—participates in the sacral significance of all of history, all reality, even. The ultimate significance of Calderón's constant insistence on the "today" of performance doubtless lies here. Contemporaneous circumstance is for him no mere pretext: *auto sacramental* is not simply dramatic representation. Rather, they are both the very weft of human history, and as history, event—and *auto*—function as testimony, as witness. Through allegory Calderón converts circumstantial pretext into history, and *auto* into kerygma.

The analogizing of secular and sacred history, basic to Calderón's historical *auto,* manifests a very particular conception of history and time, a holistic, organicist vision wherein "any one manifestation of event-in-the-world may be taken as a relatum illustrative of the entire world order, and vice versa."[50] Such a conversion of secular history into quasi-sacred myth in fact characterizes much Renaissance allegory—for example, Spenser's mythologizing of Elizabethan England in the *Faerie Queene* or Boccaccio's allegorization in the *Sixth Eclogue* of certain contemporaneous political events.[51] Indeed, for many Christian allegorists of the Renaissance, the holistic analogy of sacred mystery and contemporaneous event transcends sacred and secular realities to embrace the *minor mundus,* man him-

50. Stephen G. Nichols, *Romanesque Signs* (New Haven: Yale University Press, 1983), 12.

51. In this regard, see comments by Michael Murrin, *The Veil of Allegory* (Chicago: University of Chicago Press, 1969), 109.

self.[52] The personal experiences of the individual likewise manifest and witness sacred truth,[53] and they can thus be assimilated to the providential scheme of "recapitulations and fulfillments operating throughout history."[54]

The personal as well as historical dimension of typology was actually nothing new; the medieval schema of exegesis had, after all, included the individual application of Scripture as the third or tropological level of meaning. If the Church is the mystical body of Christ, the extension of typic postfiguration to the individual Christian is not only legitimized, but even mandated. Most often in Calderón's age, dominated by a "theocentric world view of Thomistic and Aristotelian antecedents,"[55] the individualization of typology involved divinizing the monarch and sacralizing nationhood and national goals. In fact, numerous historians and literary writers of the Middle Ages and Renaissance explicitly invoked typology as they found in contemporary rulers models of christomimesis.[56]

52. On the notion of man as microcosm, see especially Rudolf Allers, "Microcosmos, from Anaximandros to Paracelsus," *Traditio* 2 (1944): 319–407; Leonard Barkan, *Nature's Work of Art* (New Haven: Yale University Press, 1975); and Francisco Rico, *El pequeño mundo del hombre* (Madrid: Castalia, 1970).

53. The individual soul's participation in the transcendental analogies of sacred history is fundamentally Augustinian: since the soul's three powers are analogous to the Trinity, Augustine maintained, that analogy can serve as the basis for knowledge of transcendental reality. See Augustine (Saint), *The Trinity,* Book 9, Ch. 12 (vii): "Thus, in that realm of eternal truth from which all things temporal were made, we behold with our mind's eye the pattern upon which our being is ordered, and which rules all to which we give effect with truth and reason, in ourselves or in the outer world. Thence we conceive a truthful knowledge of things." In *Augustine: Later Works,* ed. John Burnaby (Philadelphia: Westminster, 1955), 65.

54. Lewalski, "Typological Symbolism and the 'Progress of the Soul' in Seventeenth-Century Literature," in Miner, ed., *Literary Uses of Typology,* 82.

55. Otis H. Green, *Spain and the Western Tradition* 4 (Madison: University of Wisconsin Press, 1968): 4.

56. On christomimesis, see especially Ernst H. Kantorowicz, *The King's Two Bodies* (Princeton: Princeton University Press, 1957). See also Zwicker, "Politics and Panegyric," and *Dryden's Political Poetry* (Providence: Brown University Press, 1972); Paul J. Korshin, "The Development of Abstracted Typology in England,

For an age in which kingship was sacrally symbolic, contemporizing and individualizing sacred history and typology was especially significant for both theology and literature.[57] The monarchy, and the ruler as its human embodiment, were considered part of the "great chain of being" that links and orders all spheres of existence.[58] Central to the symbolism of this "chain" was the notion of primacy, the idea that every class of beings, both sentient and inanimate, contains a primate, a particular representative exalted above all others: the eagle among birds, for example, among animals the lion, and among men, naturally, the king or emperor.[59] The chain of being metaphorizes cosmic hierarchy and harmony, for "[the primacies] are all part of a greater whole and . . . a reference to two or three implies both the rest of them and the ordered universe, in the background."[60]

Just such a secular typology and analogical theocentrism in-

1650–1820," in Miner, ed., *Literary Uses of Typology*, 147–203; Francis Oakley, "Jacobean Political Theology: The Absolute and Ordinary Powers of the King," *Journal of the History of Ideas* 29 (1968): 323–46; Gian Roberto Sarolli, "Dante e la teologia politica: simbolismo cristologico e cristomimetico," in *Prolegomena alla 'Divina Commedia'* (Florence: Olschki, 1971), 248–88; Nichols, *passim*. On related notions in Calderón, see D. González de la Riva, "Cristocentrismo en los autos sacramentales de Calderón, por Gabriel de Sotiello," *Estudios franciscanos* 306 (1959): 321–44.

57. See David Quint, *Origin and Originality in Renaissance Literature* (New Haven: Yale University Press, 1983), 17. For Spain, see M. Bataillon, "Charles-Quint bon pasteur, selon Fray Cipriano de Huerga," *Bulletin Hispanique* 50 (1948): 398–406; Margherita Morreale, "Carlos V, rex bonus, felix imperator; notas sobre Diálogos de Alfonso de Valdés," *Estudios y documentos. 2: Cuadernos de historia moderna*, no. 3 (Valladolid: Facultad de Filosofía y Letras de la Universidad, 1954), 7–20; Oreste Macrì, "La historiografía del barroco literario español," *Thesaurus* 15 (1960): 1–70.

58. The seminal study of this notion is of course Arthur O. Lovejoy's *The Great Chain of Being* (Cambridge: Harvard University Press, 1936).

59. Cf. E. M. W. Tillyard, *The Elizabethan World Picture* (New York: Vintage Books, n.d.), 29: "Another form of excellence, found in most accounts of the chain of being and certainly to be connected with it, is that within every class there was a primate."

60. Tillyard, 30.

form the longest of Calderón's circumstantial *autos*, *El Santo Rey don Fernando* (1671), in two parts, based on Fernando III's war of reconquest against the Moors in the thirteenth century. The *auto* is imbued with a theocentric and typological sense of nationhood. Castile and León are the weapons of the Church Militant: "Castellanos, y leoneses, / caballeros, en quien carga, / de eclesiástico y seglar / brazo hoy la Iglesia sus armas" ["Citizens of Castile and León, knights to whose charge falls today the weapons of the Church's ecclesiastical and secular arms"] (1298). Their monarch is the christic Crusader who will lead his vassals in rescuing the Church and restoring "the highest Sacrament":[61]

> Dilatar de la Fe el culto,
> y rescatar de tirana
> esclavitud las Iglesias,
> que hoy en Mezquitas profana
> impura bárbara Ley,
> restituyendo a sus aras
> los Sagrarios del más Alto
> Sacramento. . . .   (1299)

To diffuse the cult of the Faith, and to rescue her Churches from tyrannous enslavement (which today an impure, barbarous Law profanes in its mosques), by restoring to their rightful altars the tabernacle of the highest Sacrament.

Furthermore, Fernando's successors in Calderón's age— Philip III, Philip IV, and Charles II—are presented as typological "subfulfillments" of the saint's glorious promise, christic example, and theocratic mission.

Calderón brilliantly allegorizes the chain of being, primacy, and monarchial preeminence—correlative notions, which ground secular typology—in the *loa* to *El Santo Rey*, *Primera Parte*. This prologue dramatizes a logomachy designed to ex-

61. For Fernando III as moral and religious exemplar for his people, cf. 1300 and 1305.

press ". . . gran Devoción, / Celo, Amor y Reverencia" ["great Devotion, Zeal, Love, and Reverence"] (1265) for both the Eucharist and the sainted king of the title. Faith, explicitly invoking the primacy principle, summons ". . . cuantos el nombre / de reyes tengan" ["all those who bear the name of king"] (1265). Six actors come on stage in turn; each bears a placard with a painting on one side and a letter on the other. The emblems and associated logograms are *Sol* (S), *Aguila* (A), *León* (L), *Rosa* (R), *Oro* (O), and *Corazón* (C). Each explains that he is the "king" of his class (queen, in the case of Rose); thus, as "symbol" of both King Fernando and the Eucharist (the central or highest sacrament, hence another primate), s/he has come to acclaim ". . . [el] Misterio que en él [este día] celebran" ["the Mystery that today we celebrate"] (1264), and the excellence of the eponymous monarch. Before the assembled "monarchs," Faith declares that she, as queen or primate of the virtues, has appropriately convoked them. Faith's contention and preeminent status are disputed by Hope and Charity, who appear to assert rival claims to supremacy. The judge of "which of our Virtues conferred most glory and honor upon the World" ("cuál de las Virtudes nuestras / fue la que le adquirió [al Mundo] más / gloria y honor" [1268]) is, Faith tells the assemblage, implicit in the placards. She calls the five forward successively so that the cards spell out CARLOS (Charles II, king of Spain from 1665 to 1700, hence reigning monarch during the period of the *auto*). The *loa* ends with a musical tribute to the "Rey Angel" and the "Rey Santo."

The *loa* to *El Santo Rey* sacralizes Fernando III by linking him metonymically with the Corpus Christi festivities celebrated "this day" and by thus distinguishing him implicitly as a *typus Christi*.[62] The anagram formed by nature's primates

62. Cf.: "Si mi ejemplar os obliga / a honor de la Fe, en igual / Triunfo suyo, cada cual / tome su leño, y me siga" ["If my example," the King proclaims, "compels you, in Faith's honor, to a similar Triumph, take up your staff and follow me"] (1284). The monarch is likewise compared with God the Father, for he deliberately risks his

likewise establishes Charles II as "subfulfillment" of the national grandeur achieved in Fernando's age, a grandeur which is itself correlative antitype of hegemonic Christendom.[63] The logomachy as a whole materializes the chain of being and the correspondence of analogous primates: ". . . Misterios . . . concuerdan / entre sí" (1266), Faith says of the primates, "Mysteries agree among themselves." It furthermore links those notions to nationalistic typology. Calderón's logomachy thus allegorizes political theocentrism: the Spanish monarchy, and national hegemony, here manifest universal order and the typological fulfillment of providential history.

The politicized typology, which proclaims the monarch a *typus Christi* and national history an extension of sacred history, had firm roots in medieval political theory,[64] with its theological rationalization of secular stratagem.[65] Calderón's use of it in the circumstantial *autos* certainly reflects this tradition. However, his political typology is also an apologetic defense of the visionary, providentialist[66] goals of imperial poli-

---

son in battle for the good of nation and faith, an act equated with Divine Goodness: "¡Oh rasgo de aquella Inmensa / Divina Bondad de Dios!" ["Oh trace of that Immense, Divine Goodness of God!"] (1307). Fernando is also described as a type of both Moses and Joshua: "Moisés segundo, y segundo Josué . . ." ["second Moses, and second Joshua"] (1297).

63. In the *auto* Fernando's victories over the Moors and Albigensians are universalized as dominance over Islam, Judaism, and Apostasy.

64. See especially Kantorowicz.

65. Political typology had its analogy in Joachim di Fiore's writings in the later Middle Ages and Savonarola's prophecies of the fifteenth century, and its contemporaneous equivalent in the Reformation theology of Elizabethan England. See Zwicker, in Miner, ed., *Literary Uses of Typology,* 115–46.

66. On this imperial providentialism and similar themes in contemporaneous Spanish political thought, see especially Green, 3, Part 1, Ch. 4, "Political Expansion: The Idea of Empire." Green provides extensive bibliography on this theme. He also discusses alternate views of the king, monarchy, and nationhood propounded during this period.

cies in contemporary Spain, policies overwhelmingly popular, although not universally defended, in his day.[67]

It is undeniable that such historical analogizing, basic to the political allegory of the circumstantial *autos,* can seem at best facile and, at worst, expediential, to the modern reader. Even if we absolve Calderón of political opportunism or chauvinism, the dramatist still remains open to the charge that his analogizing, like that of other political typologists, is nothing more than that, nothing but the "discovery" of relationship where there is in fact none, the imposition of meaning rather than its disclosure. It must be recognized, however, that the Christian view of history implies, even necessitates, acceptance of a kind of Platonic historicism. This vision finds in particular historical events reflections of "persistent, recurrent patterns and themes . . . inherent in history or chronic to history"[68] and it asserts that those patterns and themes are divinely ordained and sacrally significant. Calderón's historical analogies (and allegoresis in general) thus implies that any perceived resemblance is not merely the expositor's presumption or heuristic construct; rather, it truly reflects reality as it is "out there," outside the mind, biases, and beliefs of the interpreter.[69] Secular typology is

---

67. Fray Juan de Salazar, for example, links Spanish imperialism, theocratic nationhood, and millenarianism: "Events, almost identical in every stage of time, and the remarkable way that God has selected and directed the Spanish nation, show that we are his chosen people in the New Dispensation, just as the Hebrews were in the time of the written Law." Fray Juan de Salazar, *Política española* (1619), quoted and translated by Green, 4, 5 n. 7.

68. J. V. Langmead Casserley, *Toward a Theology of History* (New York: Holt, Rinehart and Winston, 1965), 54.

69. It is perhaps Michel Foucault who has most eloquently explicated the potency of this conception for the Middle Ages and Renaissance: "Up to the end of the sixteenth century, resemblance played a constructive role in the knowledge of Western culture. It was resemblance that largely guided exegesis and the interpretation of texts; it was resemblance that organized the play of symbols, made possible knowledge of things visible and invisible, and controlled the art of representing them." Michel Foucault, *The Order of Things* (New York: Pantheon Books, 1970), 17.

thus no mere apologetic invention; if the parallels between the sacred and profane can be discerned, they must exist, and if they exist, they must be ultimately attibutable to divine purpose and providence.

But what, if anything, guarantees the validity of this central assumption?[70]

Calderón gives an implicit answer to this question in *El indulto general* (1680). Here World, like Culpa in *La vacante general,* attempts to obtain analogical knowledge of the Messiah by investigating a representable or dramatized metaphor: "careados a nuestro arbitrio, / veremos si entrambas líneas / van a dar a un punto fijo" ["we shall see whether both lines (historical fact and allegorical *argumento*), confronted or compared at our discretion, converge on one fixed point"] (1732).

This "fixed point," this numinous nexus of meaning, is the revelation. It is Calderón's view, and the belief of typologists in general, that universal history and contemporaneous event both derive their significance from the revelation, that unique event which confers transcendence upon history and confers interrelated meanings and significance upon the events of that history.[71] The revelation is thus the locus of significance, sacred and literary, for history as well as allegory, and guarantor of the legitimacy of secular typology.

The analogizing of individual, national, and Christological typology does far more than validate and rationalize mon-

70. Nancy F. Partner has written cogently of the significance of this hermeneutic problem for philosophy as well as literary studies; see p. 95.

71. See Boucher, 133:

Typology is continuous not simply because of the continuity of cause and effect in history, but because purpose is lent by history's author, God. According to this view God makes each event a partial revelation of his whole purpose and a term relative to the absolute fulfillment in Christ. God constructs history as a tightly written book where every episode depends on the episode before and refers to the episode ahead.

archial divine right; it also subtends the temporal realm and subsumes the individual, assimilating contemporaneous event and individual experience to universal history's patterns and sacral significance.[72] History in all its forms—sacred and contemporary, universal and individual, typologically legitimized and allegorically dramatized—is theophanic, revelatory of divine plan and presence. The *autos'* analogies, the plays' allegory of secular history, imply that that history is "post-figurative," that secular occasion can and must be assimilated to divinely sanctioned typology. Allegory in the Calderonian *auto* is thus commemorative in the potent sense of the term suggested by Eugene Vance.[73] That is, the allegorical *auto* is, for its dramatist and its public, a cultic re-creation and celebration of Christian faith's central mystery, a radical mimesis of the operations of typology, the contemporized kerygma of sacred history.[74]

In assessing the significance of Calderón's historical *autos* and typological vision it is to be noted that students of Christian typology and allegory frequently consider them utterly distinct

72. Cf. Lewalski: "Along with [the] legitimation of typological symbolism, the shift in emphasis in reformation theology from *quid agas* to God's activity in us made it possible to assimilate our lives to the typological design, recognizing the biblical stories and events, salvation history, not merely as exemplary to us but as actually recapitulated in our lives." Lewalski, "Typological Symbolism," 82. Lewalski is discussing the reformation literature of seventeenth-century England, primarily works by Donne, Traherne, Herbert, Vaughan, and Bunyan, but some of her conclusions are applicable as well in the thoroughly Catholic context of contemporaneous Spain.

73. "Par 'commémoration', j'entends tout geste, ritualisé, ou non, qui est destiné à récapituler, au nom de la collectivité, un événement soit antérieur, soit en dehors du temps, afin de rendre fécond, vivant, ou signifiant le *hic et nunc* du vécu." Eugene Vance, "Roland et la poétique de la mémoire," *Cahiers d'études médiévales* 1 (1975): 103.

74. José María Díez Borque considers the *auto* as cultic festivity and religious communication in *Una fiesta sacramental barroca*, especially 26–39.

classes of writing, totally different theological as well as literary approaches to sacred reality.[75] Jean Daniélou goes so far as to state that typology and allegory are "opposite," for allegory dissolves history into timeless generalities, whereas typology posits "a correspondence between historical realities at different stages in sacred history."[76] Basic to the distinction, and to Catholic hermeneutics in general, was the belief that the correspondences between Old and New Testaments were not merely verbal but were indeed divinely ordained to yield sacral significance, to manifest God's providential presence in history. Corollary to this central tenet was the principle that "[o]nly historical facts—persons, actions, events, and institutions—are material for typological interpretation; words and narratives can be utilized only insofar as they deal with such matters."[77] Thus typology alone had roots in a transcendent significance *in factis.* Allegory, on the contrary, was held to involve connections and analogies grounded *in verbis* only.[78]

The *locus classicus* for this distinction is perhaps Dante's differentiation in the *Convivio* II,i of the allegory of the poets and the allegory of the theologians. The allegorical sense found in "le favole de li poeti" (as an example of which Dante gives Ovid's story of Orpheus) is "quello che si nasconde sotto 'l manto di queste favole, ed è una veritade ascosa sotto bella men-

75. See, for example, David Aers, *Piers Plowman and Christian Allegory* (New York: St. Martin's, 1975), 1: "Frequently critics take 'typology' and 'allegory' as distinct classes of writing and ... the former is aligned with Judaeo-Christian historicity and realism, the later [*sic*] with a hellenistic-platonic flight from history."

76. Jean Daniélou, *Origen,* trans. Walter Mitchell (New York: Sheed and Ward, 1955), 327, n.2.

77. Goppelt, 17–18.

78. On the relationship of, and distinction between, allegory and typology, see especially Henri de Lubac, " 'Typologie' et 'Allégorisme,' " *Recherches de Science Religieuse* 34 (1947): 180–226, and A. Strubel, " 'Allegoria in factis' et 'Allegoria in verbis,' " *Poétique* 23 (1975): 342–57.

zogna."[79] Such *favole* hold no truth *in factis;* they are only non-historical stories invented by the poet. The hidden, moral truth discoverable in such a tale is to be carefully distinguished from the revealed truth of the Word of God, "which exists as actual truth in itself as a literal sense that is also historical":[80] "Veramente li teologi questo senso [allegorico] prendono altrimenti che li poeti."[81]

Yet the distinction of typology and allegory, as other scholars have demonstrated, is far more problematic than such a facile dichotomy would allow.[82] Henri de Lubac found that in the later Middle Ages, Christian typology was increasingly merged with "the allegory of the poets."[83] Auerbach and Singleton in their classic studies of Dante influentially extended the typological reading of history to the interpretation of secular allegory. In his seminal essay "Figura," Auerbach transferred typological hermeneutics from scriptural exegesis to the explication of the *Commedia.* He conceived of the great Christian poem as a figural schema according to which men's condition on earth, in all its historical reality, reveals God's cosmic plan of typological

79. Dante Alighieri, *Il convivio,* ed. G. Busnelli and G. Vandelli, 1 (Florence: F. Le Monnier, 1934–37): 240.

80. Robert Hollander, *Allegory in Dante's 'Commedia'* (Princeton: Princeton University Press, 1969), 36.

81. Dante, 240.

82. Singleton elucidated the distinction between the allegory of the poets and the allegory of the theologians, nowhere near a simple matter; see Charles S. Singleton, "Allegory," in *Dante Studies I. Commedia: Elements of Structure* (Cambridge: Harvard University Press, 1954), 15–16, and "The Irreducible Dove," *Comparative Literature* 9 (1957): 131. Singleton's figural reading of Dante, i.e., his contention that Dante's fiction is analogous to God's typology, has been forcefully disputed by a number of critics; see, for example, David Thompson, "Figure and Allegory in the *Commedia,*" *Dante Studies* 90 (1972): 1–10, and Richard Hamilton Green, "Dante's 'Allegory of Poets' and the Mediaeval Theory of Poetic Fiction," *Comparative Literature* 9 (1957): 118–28.

83. Henri de Lubac, *Exégèse médiévale,* 4 vols. (Paris: Aubier, 1959–63), 2.2, 350, 373–74, 491–93, 505–6.

prefigurations and recurrences, foreshadowings and fulfillments. Singleton's arguments are similar:

> For in this poem, the embodied, the real and the literal, the irre-
> ducible journey, "his" journey beyond, will time and again recall
> that other journey where the prologue scene placed us, our jour-
> ney here. And will do this, not by inviting us to "undo" the journey
> there, not by permitting us to see through the event there as if it
> were not there, not by washing out the literal; but by a kind of re-
> call more common in musical structure.[84]

Dante's writing in this view is analogous to God's typological
"writing" of history, for the *Commedia* maintains the "fiction
... that it is not fiction."[85] This is a vision of allegory, or more
precisely of Dante's allegory, that converts the Christian poet
into a *scriba Dei*.

Calderón's implicit claims for the ontological status of the
circumstantial *autos,* although similar to Dante's and to those of
some Dante scholars, would seem to go far beyond the contention that the poet, in treating sacred subjects, can imitate God's
way of writing. The dramatist's use of history reflects an apparent belief in the very homology of history and *auto* as manifestations of divine presence. Indeed, the discovery of the Eucharist,
coda of every *auto sacramental,* dramatizes the moment in
which divine grace is assumed to intervene in the quotidian affairs of men, including their literature. The Calderonian *auto*
thus becomes a virtual allegory of the supervention of divine
presence in the cosmos and of the divine warranty of the play as
contemporized kerygma.[86]

84. Singleton, "Allegory," 11.
85. Singleton, *Dante's 'Commedia': Elements of Structure* (Baltimore: Johns Hopkins University Press, 1954), 62.
86. Such divine ordination or warranty of interpretative success would presumably extend as well to the audience's interpretative endeavors. For more on this sacral
conception of the *auto,* see Ch. 4 and the Afterword of the present study. Díez
Borque considers the audience reception of the Calderonian *auto* in a different light;

This is a conception of the *auto* and its allegory that embodies an implicit metaphysics of history and allegorical discourse,[87] converting the Calderonian *autos* into true Christian
mysteries. Or, rather, the *autos*' typic approach to secular
event significantly extends the traditional Christian idea of
mystery. Mystery is no longer the events of sacred history
alone; it is also the copy or reflection throughout human history of the sacred prototype.[88] In the words of a Jesuit theologian of Calderón's day, Matthew Rader (1561–1634), "[T]here
are many more illustrations [of the great motions and affections of the soul] in our day than in Antiquity.[89] History
has generated new types, new examples of sacred history. Allegory exemplifies those types and, through the dramatic per-

---

see José María Díez Borque, "El auto sacramental calderoniano y su público: Funciones del texto cantado," in Kurt Levy, Jesús Ara, and Gethin Hughes, eds., *Calderón
and the Baroque Tradition* (Waterloo: Wilfrid Laurier University Press, 1985), 49–67,
and "Teatro y fiesta en el barroco español: El auto sacramental de Calderón y su público: Funciones del texto cantado," *Cuadernos hispanoamericanos* 396 (1983): 606–42.

87. Frei, in discussing biblical narrative, describes the process whereby figuration
or figural interpretation inevitably leads to, even demands, such temporal conflation,
and implies a holistic metaphysics of history:

> . . . if the real historical world described by the several biblical stories is a sin-
> gle world of one temporal sequence, there must in principle be one cumulative
> story to depict it. Consequently, the several biblical stories narrating sequential
> segments in time must fit together into one narrative. The interpretive means for
> joining them was to make earlier biblical stories figures or types of later stories
> and of their events and patterns of meaning.
>
> . . . since the world truly rendered by combining biblical narratives into one
> was indeed the one and only real world, it must in principle embrace the experi-
> ence of any present age and reader. Not only was it possible for him, it was also
> his duty to fit himself into that world in which he was in any case a member, and
> he too did so in part by figural interpretation and in part of course by his mode of
> life. He was to see his disposition, his actions and passions, the shape of his own
> life as well as that of his era's events as figures of that storied world.

Frei, 2–3.

88. On a similar relationship between Christian mystery and Christian literature,
see Raspa, *The Emotive Image,* 87–89.

89. Quoted by Raspa, 141.

formance of the allegorical *autos,* typologically participates in that history as contemporary witness.

It is not merely assimilation to a sacred past that sacralizes contemporary history and literature, however; it is also the prophecy of future event. Calderón's *auto sacramental* alludes incessantly in imagery and citation to the Book of Revelation. Such allusiveness to the Apocalypse most obviously integrates the totality of history into the *auto*'s dramatic compass and allegorical register: the play allegorizes not merely sacred past, but epiphanic future as well.

Of course, the prophetic, apocalyptic note is not unique to Calderón's *auto* or to the dramatist's vision of history. On the contrary, Christian allegories customarily, almost ceremonially, end with an epiphany or apocalypse: the *Commedia* concludes with the vision of the godhead, and *Pilgrim's Progress* with the passage into the Celestial City, to mention just two prominent examples. For modern (or perhaps merely secularized) readers such endings are an example of what Frank Kermode has called "the tick-tock plot."[90] Such a plot, by announcing its end, "enables us to see the middleness of what preceded it."[91] For an

90. John Frank Kermode, *The Sense of an Ending* (New York: Oxford University Press, 1967). It was Kermode in this highly influential book who, through a study of apocalyptic tendencies in literature, called attention to so-called "end-determined fictions" (6), of which the *auto sacramental* (which Kermode does not mention) is a preeminent example. On literary closure, see also Barbara Herrnstein Smith, *Poetic Closure* (Chicago: University of Chicago Press, 1968), and *Concepts of Closure, Yale French Studies* 67, ed. David F. Hult (New Haven: Yale University Press, 1984).

91. Partner, 109. This emphasis on the configurative significance of the end can perhaps be traced to Augustine:

Suppose I am about to recite a psalm which I know. Before I begin, my expectation is extended over the whole psalm. But once I have begun, whatever I pluck off from it and let fall into the past enters the province of my memory. So the life of this action of mine is extended in two directions—toward my memory, as regards what I have recited, and toward my expectation, as regards what I am about to recite. . . . And as I proceed further and further with my recitation, so the expectation grows shorter and the memory grows longer, until all the expec-

earlier (or entirely and knowledgeably Christian) audience such closings are an expression of faith, of reverence, of Christian hope.

However, they are something more as well. They reflect in miniature, in literary and allegorical form, the course and meaning of human life itself: of the individual life which ends in death redeemed by the promise of the soul's immortality, and of universal history—the life of humankind—which ends in the Second Coming.

Calderón's *autos,* plays that typically allegorize the history of man's fall and redemption, allegories that are therefore radically historical, likewise repeat this mythic pattern. The dramatic *argumento* of every *auto* is thus radically teleological, imitating the very patterns of sacred history. It is the ending, the Eucharist, that confers significance on everything that has come before, indeed, confers upon that "everything" its very power to signify, to manifest divine presence in the affairs of men.[92]

It is also the Eucharist that grounds the *auto*'s supervention of normal, quotidian temporal relationships. The sacrament as

---

tation is finished at the point when the whole of this action is over and has passed into the memory. And what is true of the whole psalm is also true of every part of the psalm and of every syllable in it. The same holds good for any longer action, of which the psalm may be a part. It is true also of the whole of a man's life, of which all his actions are parts. And it is true of the whole history of humanity, of which the lives of men are parts.

Augustine, *The Confessions of St. Augustine,* trans. Rex Warner (New York: New American Library, 1963), 282. Quoted and discussed by Mazzotta, 253. In Mazzotta, see also pp. 311–15.

92. It is significant in this regard that kerygma itself is intimately connected in Christian tradition with eschatology: "This announcement [of the preacher] was bracketed between that of the fulfillment of the Old Testament prophecies and the new Christian community's, or Church's, eschatological destiny in the Second Coming of the Savior to render judgment" ("Kerygma," *NCE* 168). The individual Christian, and the present historical moment in which the Christian bears witness to the faith, are implicated in all of providential history.

commemoration recapitulates sacred past and sacred mystery in the present moment. The *auto sacramental* does the same, or similarly: performance time, unfolding in "real" time, synopsizes "la duración del tiempo," the historical time of *Heilsgeschichte*. The *auto* also includes a sacramental epilogue—the Eucharistic "discovery"—which, besides being recapitulative typology, is also a "real" or nonallegorical event belonging to the world of "real" time and quotidian occurrence. The supervention of real event in allegory thus paradoxically allegorizes the very supersession of allegory, the moment in which *alegoría* becomes *historia,* in which performance participates in and partakes of an extraliterary world of numinous significance, the public ceremonial of communion.

Such a telescoping of temporal registers implies that those registers are analogates, and analogically sacred:

> . . . en su Providencia
> no hay tiempo para él pasado
> ni futuro, de manera
> que tiempo presente es todo,
> aunque varios nombres tenga,
> bien podrá hoy el Pensamiento,
> en metáfora de idea
> . . . .
> darle el del tiempo en común.　　　　　　(1637–38)

In God's Providence there is no past time, or future, so that everything is present time for Him. Although He has various names, Thought can today rightfully give Him, in ideated metaphor, the name of Time in Common.

God is identified with time, or with the temporal vision *sub specie aeternitatis,* and the *auto*'s metaphorization of time with this divine vision. Sacred time, the Eucharist's instantiation of past event in present moment, eternizes the *auto*'s *hic et nunc* of performance by endowing it with sacral meaning. And the here and now typologically recapitulates sacred history and, as analogically sacral synecdoche, it temporally synopsizes eternity.

Calderón's allegorical *auto* proclaims the homology of *Heilsgeschichte,* national history, contemporaneous event, *auto sacramental,* and the Eucharist—as well as past, present, and future—as theophanies, manifestations of and witnesses to divine providence.

Few, if any, allegorists have gone so far in secularizing typology and sacralizing allegory. Calderón's is a vision that implies a radical logocentrism, a belief in the ultimate divine ordination and sacramentalism of the *auto* and its allegory. The ramifications of that logocentrism for understanding and interpreting the Calderonian *auto* are the subject of the next chapter.

4. "In Imagined Space"
Auto as Spiritual Exercise

"... en espacio imaginado
al Laureto hemos llegado."
   (*A María el corazón*, 1664)

It is one of the peculiarities of allegorical writing that its authors frequently call attention to and write about the difficulties the mode poses for its readers. Edmund Spenser begins his famous expository letter to Sir Walter Raleigh with the admission, "... knowing how doubtfully all Allegories may be construed...."[1] Baltasar Gracián in the preface "To the reader" of *El Criticón* writes somewhat apprehensively of the "shadows," the metaphorical trappings, in which the work is clothed, to the possible detriment of his audience's understanding.[2] For his *Pilgrim's Progress,* John Bunyan penned a truly apologetic "Apology" that appeals to the reader to indulge the fancifulness of allegory while recognizing the pitfalls that lie ahead:

> This book is writ in such a dialect
> As may the minds of listless men affect:
> It seems a novelty, and yet contains

1. Edmund Spenser, in *The Faerie Queene,* "Letter of the Author expounding his whole intention in the course of this worke . . .," ed. J. C. Smith and E. de Selincourt (London: Oxford University Press, 1970), 407.

2. Baltasar Gracián, *El Criticón,* 2 vols., ed. Antonio Prieto, 1 (Madrid: Iter, 1970), 6.

Nothing but sound and honest gospel-strains.
Would'st thou divert thyself from melancholy?
. . . .
Would'st thou read riddles and their explanation,
Or else be drownded in thy contemplation?[3]

Despite the acknowledged difficulties, allegorists typically
have made rather large claims for their works' moral and/or
philosophical efficacy and for the impact their allegories are to
have on the reader. Spenser asserts as his end, "to fashion a gen-
tleman or noble person in vertuous and gentle discipline."[4] John
Amos Comenius, the seventeenth-century writer and educa-
tional reformer, describes his allegory *The Labyrinth of the
World* as "the kind of writing which is designed to inspire a soul
to courage and to bring peace in God."[5] Bunyan makes the
largest possible claims for his work:

My dark and cloudy words they do but hold
The truth. . . .
. . . .
This book will make a traveller of thee,
If by its counsel thou wilt ruled be;
It will direct thee to the Holy Land,
If thou wilt its directions understand:
Yea, it will make the slothful active be,
The blind also delightful things to see.[6]

Allegorists of various times, places, and religious, ethical,
and philosophical persuasions unite in asserting the problematic nature of reading allegorical texts, yet the spiritual and

3. John Bunyan, *The Pilgrim's Progress,* ed. Roger Sharrock (Harmondsworth,
Middlesex, England: Penguin Books, 1965), 37.

4. Spenser, 407.

5. John Amos Comenius, *The Labyrinth of the World and the Paradise of the Heart,*
"Dedication to Baron Charles Zerotin, Sr.," trans. Matthew Spinka (Ann Arbor:
The University of Michigan Press, 1972), xi.

6. Bunyan, 34 and 36–37.

moral benefits to be derived from the task. Implicit in much allegorical discourse is thus an obvious chasm to be bridged, a chasm between the writer's often obscure allegory and the reader's sometimes torturous interpretation. It is a bridge of interpretive activity that few allegorists attempt to describe in any detail. For example, Bunyan, who is usually charming rather than clear, unhelpfully tells his reader: "Would'st read thyself, and read thou know'st not what / And yet know whether thou are blest or not, / By reading the same lines? O then come hither, / And lay my book, thy head and heart together."[7] In other words, some unspecified catalysis of allegory and the reader's understanding is to bring about spiritual enlightenment and profit.

Within this tradition of obscurity, or even downright obfuscation, Calderón stands as a model of clarity and theoretical brilliance; the dramatist is, indeed, one of the most profound theoreticians ever to consider the workings and the import of allegorical discourse. Yet, as has already been observed,[8] Calderón has his peculiarities as a theoretician. He left no treatise on allegory; indeed, he produced no single, sustained piece of writing on the subject. What he did leave us are dozens of comments on allegory scattered throughout the *autos* themselves. It is by sifting and weighing such comments that a reconstruction of Calderón's allegorical theory is possible.[9]

In the face of the undeniable difficulties and limitations of using such excursuses, we are fortunate indeed to possess one relatively straightforward theoretical statement by the dramatist. In the prologue to the first printed volume of his *autos* (1677), Calderón offers an admonition concerning the plays

7. Bunyan, 37.

8. See discussion in the Introduction of the present study.

9. On the benefits and perils of this method, see also the Introduction to the present study.

that follow as well as some preliminary instructions to assist his audience in understanding them:

> Parecerán tibios algunos trozos; respecto de que el papel no puede dar de si ni lo sonoro de la música, ni lo aparatoso de las tramoyas, y si ya no es que el que lea haga en su imaginación composición de lugares. . . .   (42)

> Some passages may seem tepid, for paper can convey neither the sonority of the music nor the spectacle of the sets. So the reader should make in his imagination a composition of place."[10]

In suggesting a composition of place for capturing the dramatic power of the *autos,* Calderón is of course pointing out the reader's need to supply imaginatively those elements of dramatic production that are absent from the printed page. The "composition of place" in this light is simply a metaphor for the imaginative re-creation or compensation that every reader of dramatic texts must make.

However, Calderón's recommendation also contains a noteworthy and suggestive technicality: an apparent allusion to the famous *compositio loci* described by Ignatius of Loyola in the *Spiritual Exercises* (Rome, 1522) as a paradigm of meditative technique or mental prayer.[11] The use of such a technically pre-

---

10. For a further discussion of this passage, see above, Ch 1 of the present study.

11. On the content and history of the *Exercises,* see Ignacio Iparraguirre, S.I., *Historia de los Ejercicios de San Ignacio* (Bilbao: Bibliotheca Instituti Historici S.I., 1955), *Práctica de los Ejercicios de San Ignacio de Loyola en vida de su autor* (1522–1556), vol. 3 (Bilbao: Bibliotheca Instituti Historici S.I., 1946), and *Orientaciones bibliográficas sobre San Ignacio de Loyola,* 2d ed. (Rome: Institutum Historicum S.I., 1965); Pedro de Leturia, S.I., *Estudios ignacianos,* rev. P. Ignacio de Loyola, 2d ed. (Rome: Institutum Historicum S.I., 1957); Hugo Rahner, *Ignatius von Loyola als Mensch und Theologe* (Freiburg: Herder, 1964); Pedro Sainz Rodríguez, *Espiritualidad española* (Madrid: Rialp, 1961), Ch. 3, "Formación de la espiritualidad jesuítica"; Jesús Juambelz, *Bibliografía sobre la vida, obras y escritos de San Ignacio de Loyola, 1900–1950* (Madrid: Razón y Fe, 1956); Gaston Fessard, *La Dialectique des "Exercices Spirituels" de S. Ignacio de Loyola* (Paris: Aubier, 1966–). On the *compositio,* see especially the bibliography included by Iparraguirre in the *Orientaciones bibliográficas,* 163 ("Oración prepa-

cise term in his very instructions about how his works are to be understood suggests the possibility that Calderón's prolusion may be taken in a literal, and quite revealing, way: the dramatist's words may contain a veritable exhortation to true meditative reflection upon the *autos,* to a genuine use of meditative technique in apprehending and interpreting the plays.

This is a provocative hypothesis, to be sure. Ascetic exercise, designed to bring the soul closer to its God, is an activity apparently at the furthest possible remove in both intention and content from the emotionally intense but nonetheless wholly mundane (or at least secular) diversions of play going. Yet the investigations of Louis L. Martz, Anthony Raspa, and others have documented the potent appeal of the meditative paradigm for literary as well as ascetic writers of Calderón's age.[12] It is an

ratoria"). Especially useful among the sources mentioned by Iparraguirre is the article by Tomás Barreira, "La composición de lugar," *Manresa* 2 (1935): 158–69.

12. The bibliography in this area is enormous. Two fundamental works, which have been exceedingly helpful for this study, are Louis L. Martz, *The Poetry of Meditation* (New Haven: Yale University Press, 1964) and Anthony Raspa, *The Emotive Image* (Fort Worth: Texas Christian University Press, 1983); both contain useful bibliography. See also Melvin E. Bradford, "Henry Vaughn's 'The Night': A Consideration of Metaphor and Meditation," *Arlington Quarterly* 1 (1968): 209–22; Terence C. Cave, *Devotional Poetry in France c. 1570-1613* (Cambridge: Cambridge University Press, 1969); Joseph F. Chorpenning, "The Literary and Theological Method of the *Castillo interior,*" *Journal of Hispanic Philology* 3 (1979): 124–28; Ellen Eve Frank, *Literary Architecture* (Berkeley: University of California Press, 1979), Ch. 5, "The Analogical Tradition of Literary Architecture," *passim;* William H. Halewood, *The Poetry of Grace* (New Haven: Yale University Press, 1966); Barbara Kiefer Lewalski, *Donne's Anniversaries and the Poetry of Praise* (Princeton: Princeton University Press, 1973) and *Protestant Poetics and the Seventeenth-Century Religious Lyric* (Princeton: Princeton University Press, 1979); Anthony Low, *Love's Architecture* (New York: New York University Press, 1978); Martz, "The Action of the Self: Devotional Poetry in the Seventeenth Century," in *Metaphysical Poetry,* ed. M. Bradbury and D. Palmer (London: Edward Arnold, 1970), 101–21, *The Paradise Within* (New Haven: Yale University Press, 1964), and *The Poem of the Mind* (New York: Oxford University Press, 1966); Raspa, "Crashaw and the Jesuit Poetic," *University of Toronto Quarterly* 36 (1966): 37–54; Miriam Starkman, "Noble Numbers and the Poetry of Devo-

appeal rooted in a perceived common ground of meditative *compositio* and aesthetic design, of ascetic exercise and aesthetic response: the ground of shared metaphysical assumptions and similar psychological responses in both exercitant and audience to the sensorial imagery of *Exercises* and artistic artifact.

The hypothesized analogy of Ignatian *compositio* and Calderonian *auto* may, I hope to show, provide the key to a fresh understanding of Calderón's *autos sacramentales.* Calderón's recommendation concerning the composition of place, considered here in the context of contemporaneous theological and aesthetic doctrine regarding the work of art and its creation and apprehension, may adumbrate a veritable paradigm for the cognition of allegorical discourse itself, a cognitive model of profound significance for the dramatist's theory of allegory as well as the aesthetic and metaphysical import of that theory.

It might be objected at once that Calderón's prolusionary statement refers explicitly to the "reader" of the *autos,* and that it may thus be extreme, even erroneous, to extend the apprehensive paradigm to the plays' audience. I would argue in preemptive response that the careful distinction among various audiences of a text may be a modern preoccupation that would not have troubled Calderón and that, furthermore, evidence within the *autos* supports the contention that the dramatist had in mind for at least some of the plays the Ignatian meditative paradigm as both compositional model and paradigm for aesthetic apprehension.

---

tion," in *Reason and the Imagination,* ed. J. A. Mazzeo (New York: Columbia University Press, 1962), 1–27; John M. Wallace, "Thomas Traherne and the Structure of Meditation," *ELH* 25 (1958): 79–89; Frank Warnke, *Versions of Baroque* (New Haven: Yale University Press, 1972), Ch. 6, "Metaphysical and Meditative Devotion." On the relationship between Calderón's art and meditation, see Elizabeth S. Boyce, "Calderón's *Psalle et Sile:* The Meditative Art and the Metaphysical Mode," *Iberoromania* 6 (1977): 122–46.

That Calderón should have turned to the Ignatian meditative model for inspiration, or should have found in it an intrinsically affinitive and applicable doctrine, is scarcely surprising. The attraction for secular writers of such a recondite (for us) pursuit as meditative exercise can be almost prohibitively difficult to comprehend for the average inhabitant of the twentieth century, especially of twentieth-century academia; our artists, and even more our humanists, no longer typically experience abstruse religious doctrine as a crucial formative influence nor see it as a relevant touchstone of artistic creativity. However, in an age and a culture as thoroughly permeated by religious (and, naturally, Catholic) influence as were Calderón's, the entente of religious and aesthetic values was not merely facilitated but also in a certain sense mandated.

Ignatius's *Spiritual Exercises* were a landmark in the intellectual history of their time and a key influence on numerous writers, an influence attributable to the formidable authority of Jesuit religious directors and to the diffusion throughout Europe of the Jesuits' widely read treatises on meditation. In particular, Calderón's contacts with the Society were extensive and his knowledge of its teachings was profound. The dramatist studied for five years at the Company's Colegio Imperial in Madrid, where (his biographer Juan de Vera Tassis tells us) he became the most illustrious student of the day. Early in his career he took up the literary glorification of the Society and its greatest figures. In 1622, on the occasion of the canonization of Ignatius and Francisco de Javier, he entered and won a celebratory poetry contest with a *romance* in honor of Ignatius's penitence, and he took second place with *quintillas* on a miracle performed by Francisco.[13]

13. The literary impact on Calderón of this intense intellectual formation was doubtless enormous, and probably decisive. For example, there is a frequent coin-

Calderón's apparent evocation of the Ignatian *compositio* doubtless reflects these cultural and personal influences. However, the Ignatian allusion also suggests ramifications that transcend biographical curiosity. For Calderón, as for many other writers of his age, both the purpose and the practice of Ignatian or Jesuit meditation[14] suggested a veritable application of meditative technique to artistic endeavor, since the *Spiritual Exercises* utilize certain techniques intrinsically dramatic or narrative in nature.

Those techniques consist of several preliminary steps or preparatory prayers, followed by the meditation proper and concluded with prayers or "colloquies" between the soul and God. The first (sometimes second) prelude or preamble to meditation is the famous *compositio loci:* "El primer preámbulo es composición viendo el lugar. . . . [L]a composición será ver con la vista de la imaginación el lugar corpóreo donde se halla la

---

cidence of theme between the contemporaneous Jesuit theater and the Calderonian *auto;* see Balbino Marcos Villanueva, S.I., *La ascética de los jesuitas en los autos sacramentales de Calderón* (Bilbao: Universidad de Deusto, 1973). (The author does not consider the possible impact of the *Spiritual Exercises* on Calderón's art.) It is likewise suggestive that the Jesuits sponsored dramatic presentations, commonly based on sacred history, which were often developed through allegory. On this theater, see I. Elizalde, S.I., "San Ignacio de Loyola y el antiguo teatro jesuítico," *Razón y Fe* 153 (1956): 289–304, and Louise Fothergill-Payne, "The Jesuits as Masters of Rhetoric and Drama," *Revista canadiense de estudios hispánicos* 10 (1986): 375–87. Fothergill-Payne provides additional, valuable bibliography on Jesuit drama, 386, n. 2. There is no evidence that Calderón directly imitated any of these religious dramas.

14. Meditation, especially the Ignatian or Jesuit formulation, must be carefully distinguished from so-called "infused contemplation," with which it is frequently confused. Contemplation involves the soul's direct contact with "transcendental reality," that is, it is the unitive, noncognitive experience or intuition of the godhead. Meditation, on the other hand, "involves the disciplined but creative application of the imagination and discursive thought to an often complex religious theme or subject-matter." See Peter Moore, "Mystical Experience, Mystical Doctrine, Mystical Technique," in *Mysticism and Philosophical Awareness,* ed. Steven T. Katz (New York: Oxford University Press, 1978), 113.

cosa que quiero contemplar"[15] ["For a visual contemplation or meditation, the picture is an imaginative representation of the physical place where the event to be contemplated occurs"].[16]

To carry out the *compositio,* the visualization of the sacral place, the exercitant is to make use of an *applicatio sensuum,* or application of the so-called imaginary senses, to the mystery in question.[17] He is to call to mind, to "see" in his imagination, all the details of the sacred scene: its parts, dimensions, decor, and so forth. He is to imagine that he hears the accompanying sounds, smells the odors, tastes and even touches the scene. In a similar fashion, he is to "see" the personages, imagining not only their words, but also their voices, expressions, actions, and gestures. The workings of the "application" can be seen clearly in the famous meditation on hell:

> *1.° preámbulo.* El primer preámbulo, composición, que es aquí ver con la vista de la imaginación la longura, anchura y profundidad del infierno.
>
> *2.° preámbulo.* El segundo, demandar lo que quiero: será aquí pedir interno sentimiento de la pena que padescen los dañados, para que si del amor del Señor eterno me olvidare por mis faltas, a lo menos el temor de las penas me ayude para no venir en pecado.
>
> *1.° puncto.* El primer puncto será ver con la vista de la imaginación los grandes fuegos, y las ánimas, como en cuerpos ígneos.
>
> *2.° El 2.°:* oír con las orejas llantos, alaridos, voces, blas-

15. San Ignacio de Loyola, *Obras completas,* ed. Ignacio Iparraguirre and Candido de Dalmases, 4th ed. (Madrid: Biblioteca de Autores Cristianos, 1982), 221. Subsequent references will be indicated within the text by page numbers at the end of quotations. For the Latin version, see Sancti Ignatii de Loyola, *Exercitia Spiritualia,* ed. Iosephus Calveras (Rome: Institutum Historicum Societatis Iesu, 1969).

16. *The Spiritual Exercises of Saint Ignatius,* trans. Thomas Corbishley, S.J. (New York: P. J. Kennedy, 1963), 30. All subsequent English quotations from the *Exercises* are taken from this translation; page numbers will be indicated at the end of quotations.

17. On the *applicatio sensuum,* see José Calveras, "Los cinco sentidos de la imaginación en los Ejercicios de San Ignacio," *Manresa* 20 (1948): 47–70 and 125–36. See

femias contra Christo nuestro Señor y contra todos sus santos.

    3.° El 3.°: oler con el olfato humo, piedra azufre, sentina y cosas pútridas.

    4.° El 4.°: gustar con el gusto cosas amargas, así como lágrimas, tristeza y el verme de la consciencia.

    5.° El 5.°: tocar con el tacto, es a saber, cómo los fuegos tocan y abrasan las ánimas.   (226)

    First preliminary. The picture. In this case it is a vivid portrayal in the imagination of the length, breadth and depth of Hell.

    Second preliminary. Asking for what I want. Here it will be to obtain a deep-felt consciousness of the sufferings of those who are damned, so that, should my faults cause me to forget my love for the eternal Lord, at least the fear of these sufferings will help to keep me out of sin.

    First heading. To see in imagination those enormous fires, and the souls, as it were, with bodies of fire.

    Second heading. To hear in imagination the shrieks and groans and the blasphemous shouts against Christ our Lord and all the saints.

    Third heading. To smell in imagination the fumes of sulphur and the stench of filth and corruption.

    Fourth heading. To taste in imagination all the bitterness of tears and melancholy and a gnawing conscience.

    Fifth heading. To feel in imagination the heat of the flames that play on and burn the souls.   (36)

As can be deduced from this example, the *compositio* is based on a highly visualized re-creation or recollection of those concrete, vivid details of sacred people, places, and events most capable of stirring and inspiring the meditator.[18]

---

also the article "Application des sens" in the *Dictionnaire de Spiritualité* (Paris: Beauchesne, 1967), 1 (1937), 810–28.

    18. The *Exercises* are the culmination and synthesis of traditional affective or carnal meditation, a technique expounded in perhaps greatest detail in pseudo-Bonaventure's *Meditationes vitae Christi,* a manual of meditative models, which recommends again and again that the novice mentally dramatize every detail of Christ's

The *compositio* is sometimes developed through analogy or metaphor, as in the meditation on the temporal monarch: "El primer puncto es poner delante de mí un rey humano, eligido de mano de Dios nuestro Señor, a quien hacen reverencia y obedescen todos los príncipes y todos hombres christianos. . . . La segunda parte deste exercicio consiste en aplicar el sobredicho exemplo del rey temporal a Christo nuestro Señor" (231) ["I imagine a temporal king, chosen by our Lord God, revered and obeyed by the rulers and all the common men of Christendom. . . . The second part of this exercise consists in relating this illustration of the earthly king to Christ our Lord, point for point"] (42 and 43). That is, considering the regal qualities of the earthly monarch is to confer upon the exercitant analogical knowledge of Christ's preeminence.

As these examples reveal, the *compositio* is a rudimentary but nonetheless emotionally potent narrative or dramatic, hence artistic and aesthetic, elaboration of the central mysteries of Christian *Heilsgeschichte.* The meditator-spectator in effect strives mentally to "stage" those historical details most readily susceptible of sensory translation. Or, as Roland Barthes pointed out in his masterly consideration of the *Exercises,* "the 'mysteries' excerpted by Ignatius from the Christian narrative take on a theatrical quality which relates them to the medieval mysteries: they are 'scenes' the exercitant is called upon to live out, as in a psychodrama."[19]

The intrinsic dramatic qualities of Ignatian composition would have an obvious appeal for a dramatist working with the re-creation of that history. And in fact, it appears that Calderón did, indeed, make specific use of some descriptive techniques of

---

history as though he himself were present as witness to the scene; see the *Meditations on the Life of Christ,* trans. Isa Ragusa (Princeton: Princeton University Press, 1961).

19. Roland Barthes, *Sade/Fourier/Loyola,* trans. Richard Miller (New York: Hill and Wang, 1976), 61.

Ignatius's *compositio.* His long religious poem *Psalle et Sile* is, as some critics have noted, quite evidently based on the pattern of Ignatian mental prayer.[20] And his *romance* on Ignatius opens with a vision of the Saint's body, "helado, sangriento y roto": "Con el cabello erizado, / Pálido el color del rostro, / Bañado en un sudor frío, / Vueltos al cielo los ojos, / Más muerto que vivo" ["icy, bloodied, broken, with his hair bristling (with thorns), his face pale, bathed in cold sweat, his eyes turned heavenward, more dead than alive"].[21] This intensely physical vision of the penitential saint obviously and specifically recalls Ignatian *compositio,* based in analogous fashion on the emotionally intense visualization of sacred subjects.

Furthermore, a number of passages within the *autos sacramentales* similarly evoke in dramatic detail episodes of the Savior's life—for example, the pathetic (although highly allegorical) description of the Passion in the 1663 *El divino Orfeo:*

> No solo por ti al suelo
> quiso el Amor que baje,
> mas por ti también quiere
> que hasta el abismo pase.
> Para cuyo camino
> ha dispuesto que labre
> instrumento, que al hombro
> arrodillar me hace,
> siendo cada clavija
> un hierro penetrante,
> cada cuerda un azote
> y un golpe cada traste.
> Tan llena está de abrojos
> la senda que dejaste,

20. See E. M. Wilson, "A Key to Calderón's *Psalle et Sile,*" in *Hispanic Studies in Honour of I. González Llubera* (Oxford: Oxford University Press, 1959), 429–40, and Boyce.

21. Quoted and discussed by P. Juan Isern, *San Ignacio y su obra en el Siglo de Oro de la literatura castellana (1516-1700)* (Buenos Aires: S. de Amorrortu, 1924), 157–58.

que al pisarla la voy
regando con mi Sangre.[22]   (1852)

Love not only made me descend to earth for your [Eurydice's
or Human Nature's] sake; it also impels me, for you, to descend to
the very abyss. For this infernal journey Love has disposed that I
forge an instrument to be borne upon my shoulders, to crush me
to my knees. Each peg is a piercing iron, each string a lash, each
fret a blow. The pathway I must follow is so full of thorns that as
I tread it I bathe it in my blood.

Although such passages are intriguing evidence for Calderón's interest in the descriptive or dramatic techniques of Ignatian meditation, in and of themselves they are of only marginal
interest; incidental evocations or use of *compositio* might be little more than a sign of the pervasive topicality characteristic of
the Calderonian *auto* in general. However, a more profound affinity between *compositio* and *auto* can be deduced from the
very conception of the *auto* and its allegory adumbrated within
the plays: the *auto* as mental or imaginative conceptualization,

22. These and similar passages in their apparent use of Ignatian *compositio* resem-
ble so-called English meditative poetry of the seventeenth century, which likewise
drew its structure and imagery from contemporaneous meditative practice. Ignatian
compositio doubtless influenced as well numerous Spanish poets of the Golden Age.
On this influence, together with examples of poems inspired by it, see Arthur Terry,
ed., *An Anthology of Spanish Poetry, 1500-1700,* 2 (Oxford: Pergamon, 1968), xix–xxi.
Geoffrey Michael Voght sees in the cited passage from *El divino Orfeo* a possible rem-
iniscence or imitation of Ignatian composition. See Voght, "The Mythological *Autos*
of Calderón de la Barca" (Diss., University of Michigan, 1974), 64–65. He suggests
(325–26) as an additional example of Calderón's imitation of *compositio* a passage
from the 1654 *El laberinto del mundo* (1572). Voght calls attention to Calderón's adop-
tion of the term *compositio loci* in the 1677 anthology (125–26, n. 32), but he does not
consider any other possible ramifications of the dramatist's evident interest in Ignatian meditative technique. Ansgar Hillach also calls attention in passing to the possible analogy of such passages and the *Exercises;* see Hillach, "El auto sacramental calderoniano considerado en un relieve histórico-filosófico," in *Hacia Calderón: Quinto
Coloquio Anglogermano, Oxford 1978,* ed. Hans Flasche and Robert D. F. Pring-Mill
(Wiesbaden: Franz Steiner Verlag GMBH, 1982), 28–29.

or "imagined space." In *A María el corazón* (1664), for example, Thought explicitly refers to the sphere of the play's dramatic action as an "espacio imaginado," an imagined space: ". . . en espacio imaginado / al Laureto hemos llegado" ["in imagined space, we have reached Loreto"] (1142).

Of course, Calderón's *auto sacramental* is an "imagined space" in the sense that any dramatic production is. However, its action can also be seen as a very particular form of "imagined space"; for, the *auto*'s allegory frequently serves to dramatize the inner workings and theological and ethical implications of human thought itself, thought conceived as the interior site of the imagination and understanding.

One of the *autos*' most persistent definitions of allegory is that of the plays' symbolic action as the projection, externalization, or record of one or another character's ideation. Calderón frequently presents the Devil or one of his henchmen or doubles as a kind of dramatist who virtually invents the drama's allegorical action as a mental or imagined "industria," a conceptualization of his plans for bringing about man's fall.[23] In *La redención de cautivos* (1677?), for example, the Devil imagines himself a metaphorical corsair who reduces Man to the status of galley slave by tempting him to sin.

> . . . me he de valer de una industria,
> que en representable idea
> de sombras, visos y lejos
> . . . .
> en frase de alegoría
> uno diga y otro entienda.
> . . . .
> en metáfora de horrible
> monstruo de sañuda fiera,
> náutico horror de las ondas,

23. For further discussion of such contingent or subordinate "authorship" in Calderón's *autos,* see Barbara E. Kurtz, " 'No Word without Mystery': Allegories of Sa-

labre esa mental galera,
que en imaginado corso
le siguiese [al Hombre] a remo y vela.
. . . .
. . . para el concepto de hoy
. . . .
rastrear mis discurso [*sic*] intenta
o cómo, o cuándo o por dónde
vendrá el rescate. . . .   (1323–25)

I shall make use of a plan, which in a representable idea cast in
shadows, lights, and distances, in allegorical phrasing, will say one
thing and mean another. As metaphor of a horrible monster, of a
furious beast, a sea-born horror, let me forge that mental galley
which in an imagined course will follow Man by oar and sail. For
today's concept, my reasoning seeks to trace how or when or
whence the rescue will come.

In an "imagined scene," aboard a "mental galley," the Devil
will hypothetically test the efficacy of divine redemptive power
by awaiting the supervention in the allegory of the messianic
"rescue" of Man.

The motif of the allegorical "industria" recurs in *El jardín de
Falerina* (1675). Fearing scriptural "shadows" (typological adumbrations of the Messiah's advent), and wanting to discredit
the Savior, Lucifer formulates an allegorical "idea" or *fábula,*
an experiment that will enable him to take appropriate precau-
tions against the redemption of man. Lucifer's experiment is
the allegorical *auto* itself. In similar fashion, the 1665 *Psiquis y
Cupido* represents Hate (the Devil's alter ego) concocting an
"allegory of poetical fiction" in which he will attempt to bring
about the demise of Psyche (soul):

. . . con la conexión
que hay entre divinas letras

cred Truth in the *Autos Sacramentales* of Pedro Calderón de la Barca," *Publications
of the Modern Language Association* 103 (1988): 262–73.

> y humanas mi presunción
> intente en alegoría
> de poética ficción
> ver si antes que a estado llegue,
> consiguiese mi rencor
> el verla al mar arrojada.   (369)

Given the connection that obtains between divine and human letters, let my presumption attempt in an allegory of poetical fiction to see if, before she reaches married state, my rancor can see her hurled into the sea.

In *Las órdenes militares* (1662) Culpa (Sin or Guilt, another diabolic double)[24] plots an examination of the significance of Christ, the scriptural promises of whom she cannot comprehend:

> . . . tengo
> procurando apurar este
> místico sentido . . .
> . . . .
> de reducir a un dictamen,
> a un discurso, a un pensamiento
> la experiencia para ver
> si en representable objeto
> de metafórica frase
> tantas confusiones venzo.   (1019)

I must try, by probing this mystical sense, to convert experience to surmise, to reasoning, to thought, so that I can see whether I can resolve this confusion in the representable object of a metaphorical phrase.[25]

For this test Culpa makes use of a metaphorical hypothesis: she conceives of the world as a "supreme monarch" and the Messiah as a young soldier of fortune who comes to the royal court

---

24. Because the acceptation of Culpa as proper noun, as personified figure, is not univocal, hence not accurately translatable, the Spanish name is retained.

25. On this passage, see also above, Ch. 3.

to seek reward for his deeds. This claim will permit, even require, the desired investigation of the metaphorized Christ's background within the *auto*'s allegory.[26]

What are we to make of all this? Characters within the *autos* frequently assert that the plays are the projection or elaboration of a seminal idea or conjecture couched in metaphorical form. The *auto* itself in this view is a prolepsis, the representation or assumption of some future act or development as though it were presently existing or accomplished, a hypothesis whose allegorical form permits analogical investigation and understanding of sacral, hence intellectually inaccessible, reality. The play is thus an "imagined space," the dramatized projection of the step-by-step working out of a character's imaginative, speculative activity.[27]

26. It is significant that in this play Culpa makes use of the lexicon of rhetoric and oratory, referring to herself specifically as "orador" and presenting the entire metaphorical experiment as a "conjecture" or *"causa."* The Greek rhetorician Hermagoras of Temnos discussed hypothesis (the Latin term for which, "causa," Culpa notably utilizes) as one of the categories of rhetoric. Boethius in Book IV of the *Topica* distinguishes in similar fashion between thesis, or "question without circumstances"—the province of dialectic—and hypothesis, "question attended by many circumstances"—the province of rhetoric. On hypothesis in Hermagoras, see George A. Kennedy, *Classical Rhetoric and Its Christian and Secular Tradition from Ancient to Modern Times* (Chapel Hill: University of North Carolina Press, 1980), 88. It is interesting that Hermagoras's system was designed for use in the law courts, a juridical tradition that Calderón explicitly evokes in *Las órdenes.* The entire rhetorical and juridical framework of *Las órdenes* underscores the hortatory and suasive ends of the Calderonian *auto* as a whole. A somewhat different interpretation of the use of rhetorical *suppositio* in a Calderonian *auto* is offered by Leslie J. Woodward, *"Suppositio* in Calderón's *No hay más fortuna que Dios,"* in Kurt Levy, Jesús Ara, and Gethin Hughes, eds., *Calderón and the Baroque Tradition* (Waterloo: Wilfrid Laurier University Press, 1985), 41–46. For further dicussion of *Las órdenes,* see Ch. 3 of the present study.

27. In particular, the conceptualization of the *auto*'s allegorical action as the Devil's imaginary activity converts the allegory into a conjectural method for testing man's virtue. This is an experimental/allegorical method that always fails, of course, because of Christ's timely intervention on man's behalf. Angel L. Cilveti studies this

Such passages, such references to the *auto* as imaginative or mental representation, as "imagined space," suggest that the *auto* as a whole may be in some ways analogous to an Ignatian *compositio*. The *compositio* was, after all, an "imagined space" to be ideated within the exercitant's imagination, and, like many of the *autos*, it was based on the characters and *res gestae* of sacred mystery. In both cases the object of the mental representation is often developed through point-by-point elaboration of an analogy or metaphor between the sacred and profane realms.[28]

The equation of *compositio* and *auto* thus implies not only a shared structural basis in dramatized analogy, but also a logically consequent correspondence of exercitant and the *auto*'s ideative personages: in both cases, allegorical *auto* and Ignatian *compositio*, an "imagined space" of visualized, dramatized analogy leads to insight into sacral reality.[29]

The *auto* as medium or vehicle of analogical understanding is one of Calderón's most persistently reiterated definitions of the *auto sacramental*.[30] Ignatius posits a similar effect for the spiritual exercise: to make the sacral, intangible, and transcendental at least partially accessible to human understanding: "Aquí es de notar que en la contemplación o meditación visible, así como contemplar a Christo nuestro Señor, el qual es visible, la composición será ver con la vista de la imaginación el lugar

---

speculative or suppositional process briefly, but clearly, in "Dramatización de la alegoría bíblica en *Primero y Segundo Isaac* de Calderón, in *Critical Perspectives on Calderón de la Barca*, Frederick A. de Armas, David M. Gitlitz, and José A. Madrigal, eds. (Lincoln, NE: Society of Spanish and Spanish-American Studies, 1981), 40–41.

28. On the role of metaphor in Calderón's *auto*, see Ch. 1 of the present study.

29. Of course, there are numerous and crucial differences between *compositio* and *auto*. To mention just one, the role of the religious director is explicitly supervisory; the dramatist who writes the words in which the "authorial character" expresses his creative or ideational role is exercising a more indirect but nonetheless even more potent control. Some of the aesthetic and religious implications of this hierarchy of authorial authority are discussed in the Afterword to the present study.

30. See discussion in Ch. 1 of the present study.

corpóreo donde se halla la cosa que quiero contemplar. Digo el lugar corpóreo, así como un templo o monte, donde se halla Jesu Christo o Nuestra Señora, según lo que quiero contemplar. En la invisible . . . la composición será ver con la vista imaginativa y considerar mi ánima ser encarcerada en este cuerpo corruptible y todo el compósito de este valle, como desterrado entre brutos animales; digo todo el compósito de ánima y cuerpo" (221–22) ["For a visual contemplation or meditation, the picture is an imaginative representation of the physical place where the event to be contemplated occurs. By physical place I mean, e.g., a temple or mountain where Jesus Christ our Lord is, as demanded by the subject matter. Where the subject matter is not something visible, the 'picture' will be the idea, produced by an effort of the imagination, that my soul is a prisoner in this corruptible body and that my whole self, body and soul, is condemned to live amongst animals on this earth, like someone in a foreign land" (30). In both *auto* and *compositio* the imagination's particular limitations and possibilities demand recourse to "human categories of thought"[31] in approaching and elucidating sacred mystery. In both cases, furthermore, an authoritative ideational or creative control (the religious director on the one hand, the dramatist on the other) subtends or directs the imaginative activity of the exercitant or "authorial" character.[32] The control over or channeling of the imagination, explicit in the

31. Frederick Ferré, *Language, Logic and God* (Chicago: University of Chicago Press, 1961), 67: "Human language, all admit, is best suited for dealing with familiar objects, qualities, and relations. The very meanings of the terms in our speech . . . have grown up through the needs and experiences of ordinary life. Since our language is thus firmly rooted in human purpose, it would seem inevitable that wherever it is applied it must express its ancestry by imposing human categories of thought on everything it touches."

32. There are differences, of course. The role of the director is explicitly supervisory; the dramatist who writes the words in which the "authorial" character expresses his creative or ideational role is exercising a more indirect but nonetheless even more potent control. Some of the theological and allegorical implications of this

compositio, implicit in the *auto,* suggests that in both spiritual exercise and play the object is "directed vision"[33] aimed at conferring knowledge of sacred mystery.

More provocatively, the analogy of *compositio* and *auto,* in light of Calderón's prefatory allusion to the reader's "composición de lugares," would also seem to imply a certain equivalence of exercitant and the drama's reader or spectator. The reader who is to "make in his imagination a composition of place" in order to understand the plays is doubtless to participate vicariously in the analogical insight achieved within the *auto* by his dramaturgical counterpart. Specifically, the diabolical mental theater in which man's virtue is examined can be considered in this light a conjectural allegorical composition that is to have its analogue in the reader's own "composition of place," that is, his own apprehension or imaginative construing of the eternal drama of mankind's temptation, fall, and redemption re-created in the *auto.* That the Devil's allegorical composition is to have (rather oddly in our eyes) its counterpart in the reader's own composition of place may seem odd to modern eyes. Yet such an analogy is not only enabled but also demanded by Calderón's ultimately Thomistic conception of the Devil: the Devil's knowledge is, according to Thomas, only conjectural or speculative with respect to the future.[34] And in this limitation, the Devil's knowledge resembles man's. The hypothesized identification of reader and Culpa in particular is especially appropriate: what better ar-

---

hierarchy of authorial authority are discussed in Ch. 2 and the Afterword of the present study.

33. On "directed vision," see Stephen G. Nichols, Jr., *Romanesque Signs* (New Haven: Yale University Press, 1983), 14: ". . . an image of the force of Scripture on everyday reality demonstrating how God's word shaped the universe. . . ."

34. On the limited nature of the Devil's knowledge, and the Thomistic origin of the conception, see Ch. 3 ("Conocimiento diabólico") of Angel L. Cilveti, *El demonio en el teatro de Calderón* (Javea, Valencia: Albatros, 1977).

chetype of the universal drama of fall and redemption, what more compelling icon of the individual drama of sin and salvation, than a personification that conflates the original sin of all mankind and the particular sins of the individual Christian?[35]

Calderón's apparent equation of analogates—exercitant, dramatic character, audience member—is all very interesting, but it may strike us as somewhat crude, an analogy perhaps so broad as to be only debatably useful. However, it may be possible to refine and extend the analogy's implications by examining more closely the desired impact of *compositio* and *auto* as posited respectively in contemporaneous Jesuit writings and within the *autos* themselves.

The exact nature of the *Exercises'* spiritual benefits, Ignatius affirms, is "quitar de [el ánima] todas las affecciones desordenadas" (207), a purgation from the soul of all "disordered affections." A treatise on the *Exercises,* the *De religione S.I.* (written 1597, printed 1625) by Francisco Suárez, is more explicit: ". . . mediante ella uno contemple con la mente algún hecho . . . cuyo peso pondere, para moverse con ella . . ." [". . . by means of (the application of the senses) the meditator will mentally contemplate some deed . . . whose import he will ponder, *to be moved thereby*"] (emphasis mine).[36] In other words, the application of the senses in the *compositio loci* has as its aim a very particular spiritual effect: the movement of the soul's affections,

35. It is interesting, although ultimately, of course, bootless, to speculate that Calderón's singular use of the Devil and his doubles or deputies (especially Culpa) in such a dramatically and theologically central role likewise reflects the dramatist's undeniably heterodox cosmology; in particular, the ubiquitously pivotal role of Culpa may at least partially incarnate Calderón's uneasiness or guilt about his Manicheistic leanings and thus represent the projection of an essentially personal psychodrama or psychomachia.

36. Quoted by J. Calveras, "Los cinco sentidos de la imaginación en Los Ejercicios de San Ignacio," *Manresa* 20 (1948): 52.

defined by the Jesuit Alexander Donati in the *Ars Poetica* of
1631 as "those things ... by which men are moved to change
their dispositions, resulting in either pain or delight."[37]

The theoretical basis and psychological and moral efficacy of
the *applicatio* are perhaps no more explicitly expounded than by
the Jesuit Luis de la Puente, who posits a definite sequence of
psychological events and their spiritual and moral consequences. "[W]ith the memory" the exercitant is "to be mindefull of God our Lorde ... and to be mindefull also, of the mysterie that is to bee meditated, passing thorough the memorie,
with clearnesse, and distinction, that which is to be the matter
of the meditation [. . .]." "[W]ith the understanding" he is then
"to make severall discourses, and considerations about that
mysterie, inquyring, and searching out the Verities compre-
hended therein, with all the causes, properties, effectes, and circumstances that it hath, pondering them very particularly" so
that "the Understanding may forme a true, proper, and entire
conceipt of the thing that it meditateth, and may remaine convinced, and persuaded to receive, and to embrace, those truthes
that it hath meditated, to propound them to the Will, and to
move it thereby to exercize its Actions." Finally, "with the freedom of our will" the devotee will "draw forth sundry Af-

37. Quoted by Raspa, "Crashaw and the Jesuit Poetic," 45. Cf. Miguel de Salinas,
Retórica en lengua castellana: "Afecto es un movimiento o perturbación que más pro-
piamente decimos las pasiones del ánima, porque según las mudanzas que se ofrecen,
así se inclinan a dolor, alegría, misericordia, crueldad, amor, odio, etc. De estas nin-
guno carece, pero si se mueven con razón son virtudes y si no, son vicios. Toda la
victoria del bien decir ponen los retóricos en saber mover estas afecciones a los oy-
entes según la cualidad de la causa" ["Affection is a movement or perturbation more
properly called the passions of the soul, because depending on the changes that occur,
those passions incline to sorrow, happiness, compassion, cruelty, love, hate, etc. Of
these no one lacks, but if they are moved with good reason, they are virtues, and if
not, they are vices. Rhetoricians attribute the success of good speaking to knowing
how to move these affections in their listeners as the case requires"]. In *La retórica en
España,* ed. Elena Casas (Madrid: Editora Nacional, 1980), 156.

fections, or vertuous Actes, conformable to that which the Understanding hath meditated [. . .]."[38]

De la Puente propounds a clear sequence or hierarchy of both communication and value: memory submits its impressions to be examined by the understanding, the highest rational and judicial power of the soul. The understanding in its turn informs the will, which is moved thereby to the performance of "vertuous Actes."

Ignatian *compositio* implies and is veritably grounded in such psychological tenets, which represent an elaboration or application of Aristotelian-Scholastic faculty psychology. The Calderonian *auto* as well contains precise echoes of this underlying psychological paradigm. For example, in the *loa* or prologue to *El maestrazgo de Toisón* (1659), Understanding calls attention to sacred music's magnetic appeal to the senses and the resultant attraction of Understanding to the contemplation of divine mystery: "Y así, oh coro de la Fe, / que, atraído de los ecos, / cuyas consonancias son / boreal imán de mi afecto, / tras ti me llevas . . ." ["And so, chorus of Faith, you draw me, attracted by the echoes that are a harmonious magnet for my affections"] (890).

The soul's affections themselves actually appear as personified actors in a number of *autos*. *El primer refugio del hombre y probática piscina* (1661), for instance, represents Pilgrim's (Christ's) gradual conversion and ultimate conquest of the Affections. An emissary Angel first attempts to awaken the Affections to that moral "motion" discussed in Scholastic psychology: "Despertad, dormidos Afectos, / que ya la moción se empieza a sentir" ["Awaken, sleeping Affections, for your motion is now perceptible"] (973). Pilgrim later completes the conversion by giving the Affections "testimonies" from the Gospel, which the personifications proceed to read aloud to each other.

38. Quoted by Martz, 34–35.

In effect, sensory appeal is used to attract the affections to spiritual steadfastness and emendation. In *La serpiente de metal* (1676) the Affections are at first tempted by the beauty of Idolatry:

> AFECTO 1°: ¿Qué es lo que miro?
> No es este el prodigio bello
> que, al verle, me robó el alma?
> AFECTO 5°: ¿No es este el raro portento
> que abrasó mi corazón?   (1542)

FIRST AFFECTION: "What is this I see? Is this not the beauteous prodigy that robbed me of my soul when first I saw it?" FIFTH AFFECTION: "Is this not the rare portent that scorched my heart?"

Finally, however, the Affections are humbled and converted by the sight of Moses' staff, which displays as "mysterious insignia" the metallic serpent (mentioned in Numbers 21) that is a traditional symbol of the Redemption.

A number of passages in the *autos* explicitly discuss the general usefulness of sensory appeal, for example:

> lo invisible no es
> posible que se comprenda;
> y solo para rastrearlo
> da a lo visible licencia
> de que en ejemplos visibles,
> lo no visible se entienda   (1187)

It is impossible to comprehend the invisible; and merely to trace [or imperfectly grasp] it, visible examples permit understanding of the unseen.

The *auto,* like the *Exercises,* is to bridge the gap between known and unknown, human and divine, concrete and ineffable, by means of sensorially apprehensible examples from sacred history. The drama is thus a practicable concept or visible example, like De la Puente's "discourses"—or the Ignatian *compositio*—which, by enabling analogical comprehension of

Christian mystery and sacred history and by awakening the soul's affections to contemplation of sacred exemplarity, is to lead to "a true, proper, and entire conceipt" of divine mystery, and thence to spiritual reflection and redemption.

Calderón's prefatory invocation of the Ignatian precedent can thus be seen to have definite aesthetic and moral or spiritual implications in light of additional theoretical statements throughout the plays. The *auto* is a structure analogous in many respects—use of dramatized analogy and metaphor, sensory appeal—to a *compositio*. And like the *compositio,* the *auto* is to appeal to the understanding through the movement of the soul's affections. The *auto* is therefore to serve an ascetic role equivalent to the function performed by the preludial image re-created within the exercitant's imagination.[39]

The conceptualization of the Calderonian *auto* hypothesized here makes of this dramatic form an example of what Judson Boyce Allen in another context has termed an "ethical poetic," that is, poetry conceived as the inevitable embodiment of ethical concerns and doctrine.[40] Indeed, just such an inextricable inter-relationship of aesthetic and spiritual or ethical concerns was a hallmark of contemporaneous aesthetic speculation, particularly among the Jesuits, who created a body of theory and practice so coherent as to constitute virtually a Jesuit poetic, grounded in the prevailing psychological/aesthetic theories.[41] For example, the art of the emblem book, in the vast contemporaneous production of which members of the Society played the leading role, had its roots in the same philosophy, and it exploited the same basic methodology, as the Ignatian *Exercises:*

39. Cf. discussion by Raspa, *The Emotive Image,* 39.

40. Judson Boyce Allen, *The Ethical Poetic of the Later Middle Ages* (Toronto: University of Toronto Press, 1982).

41. On the existence and content of a distinct and distinctive Jesuit poetic, see Raspa, *The Emotive Image,* 2.

"the application of the senses, to help the imagination to picture to itself in the minutest detail circumstances of religious import. . . ."[42] In his bibliography of unpublished manuscripts of six-teenth- and seventeenth-century Jesuit writers, Simon Díaz lists a number of theoretical treatises whose very titles suggest their reliance on the dominant ethical and psychological/aes-thetic speculation, for example: "Memoria, Entendimiento, y Voluntad. Empresas, que enseñan, y persuaden su buen uso en lo Moral, y en lo Político"; "Ver, Oir, Oler, Gustar, Tocar. Em-presas que enseñan, y persuaden su buen Uso, en lo Político, y en lo Moral" ["Memory, Understanding, and Will. Emblems that instruct and persuade to good usage in morality and in pol-itics"; "Seeing, Hearing, Smelling, Tasting, Touching. Em-blems that instruct and persuade to good usage in morality and in politics"].[43] Beyond doubt, the Jesuit elaboration of fac-ulty psychology and of the *applicatio sensuum* was having fruit-ful aesthetic and theoretical consequences throughout the pe-riod of Calderón's intellectual formation and literary pro-duction.

We also possess more accessible evidence of the impact of Ig-natian techniques and theory on aesthetic doctrine. For exam-ple, the poetical theorist Famianus Strada maintained in the *Prolusiones Academicae* (1617) that poetry ideally should awaken

---

42. Mario Praz, *Studies in Seventeenth-Century Imagery* (London: The Warburg Institute, 1939), 156. Cf. the discussion of religious imagery by the Jesuit Louis Ri-cheome: "Il n'y a rien qui plus delecte et qui fasse glisser plus suavement une chose dans l'ame che la peinture, ni qui plus profondement la grave en la memoire, ni qui plus efficacement pousse la volonte pour lui donner branle et l'emouvoir avec ener-gie." Quoted by Praz, 159. On the contemporaneous emblem books and their under-lying philosophy, see also Robert J. Clements, *Picta Poesis* (Roma: Edizioni di Storia e Letteratura, 1960) and Rosemary Freeman, *English Emblem Books* (New York: Oc-tagon, 1966).

43. José Simon Díaz, *Jesuitas de los siglos XVI y XVII* (Madrid: Universidad Pon-tificia de Salamanca, 1975), 265–66.

"currents of desire in the soul."[44] The English Jesuit John Floyd
in a theoretical justification of poetry points out the similarity
in structure between Charles Scribani's *Amphitheatrum Honoris*
and Ignatian meditation, both of which, he says, are "apprehen-
sions" that arouse the affections of the reader or exercitant.[45]
The Society's Henry Hawkins in the *Partheneia Sacra* (1633)
makes an even more direct application of the *Exercises* to poetical theory. He opens this emblem book with a true *compositio
loci,* commending his Genius "to enter into the large, spacious,
and ample GARDEN of our SACRED PARTHENES" and then
giving a lengthy description of the garden and its contents, a description comparable to the descriptive amplification of an Ignatian *compositio.*[46] More significant than this initial *compositio*

44. Quoted by Raspa, "Crashaw," 51.

45. "When we apprehend, and imagine ourselves in prayer to be before the
throne of God, to be kneeling in heaven among the blessed Angells . . . this apprehension is not false, because we do not iudg [*sic*], and thinke indeed we are in heaven,
but so frame our imaginations, thoughts, affections, prayers and inward speaches
unto God, as if we were in Heaven." Quoted by Raspa, "Crashaw," 41–42.

46. ". . . survey her GARDEN, beset with the bashful ROSE, the candid LILLIE,
the purple VIOLET, the goodlie HELIOTROPION, sprinckled al with
DEWES, which the busie BEE gathers as it falles from the HEAVENS, dressed
with an IRIS, as with a silver MOON, instead of a torch, and enameled with miri-
ads of STARRES, as lesser lamps, to afford it light, in the obscuritie of the night;
enclosed round, and compassed-in with a wal, where on an OLIVE, you may behold the iollie PHILOMEL to pearch, chanting her Roundelayse; and on the
other side, a flourishing and statelie PALME; and likewise see a goodlie HOUSE
of pleasure, standing therein before you; and if you mark it wel, you shal dicerne
that domestical and almost inseparable companion thereof, the HEN, there
scraping in the dust for food, wherein She finds a precious Margarit or PEARL;
and on top therof espy an innocent and meek DOVE, as white and candid, as the
driven snow; for in this GARDEN are al things pure. Where likewise in a place
more eminent and conspicuous than the rest, you may behold a faire and beautiful FOUNTAIN, artificiously contrived with pipes so under ground, as waters
al, when need requires. And if, my *Genius,* al these wil not suffise, to make up ful
thy Quire of Laudes, to magnify thy SACRED PARTHENES, ascend upon that
MOUNT before thy face; and with an Opticon discover thence, the Ocean SEA,

is Hawkins's theoretical formulation of the program the reader is to follow in perusing the work. The author's Genius is to lead "thy Reader into the Maze or Labyrinth of the beauties therein contained," along a pathway of constant contemplation of various aspects of the "Symbol itself, . . . expressing the allusion to the SACRED PARTHENES herself, in some mysterie of hers, or attribute belonging to her."[47] In effect, Hawkins proposes a series of meditative models designed to address through sensory appeal the reader's intellectual and spiritual needs.

It would be difficult indeed to overstate the significance of this ethico-poetic speculation. The intrinsic aesthetic qualities of an Ignatian *compositio* recommended it not only to literary

---

and invite it likewise with the rest, to beare a part; and for a fuller complement of al, wave but a little banner to some SHIP or other, to come-in with al her fraught of magnificent prayses. For al within ken or view of that same MOUNT, are subiects and deare Devotes of our Sacred and Incomparable PARTHENES." Henry Hawkins, *Partheneia Sacra,* introd. Iain Fletcher (Aldington, KY: Hand and Flower, 1950), 1–2.

47. First then shalt thou presente him with the Symbol itself, set-forth in the manner of a Devise, with an Imprese and Motto, expressing the allusion to the SACRED PARTHENES herself, in some mysterie of hers, or attribute belonging to her. Then shalt thou take the Imprese being the Symbol by itself, and dallie as it were with some natural and apt Character upon it; being no more, than certain superficial Glances, deciphering it in some sort, but lightly only, for a first entertainment of thy Reader. Then with Moral, on the Mottos, shalt thou but touch or reflect upon the Paragon herself for the present, and no more. Then looking back with a fresh review on the Symbol itself, by way of an Essay, shalt thou make a fuller Survey therof, discoursing on the Paragon herself, to match, compare, and paralel them together to find out some Elogies or other, in prayse of our SACRED PARTHENES. Thence to satisfy the Eye as wel as the Understanding, for his greater delight, thou shalt pause a while, to leade him to behold, as in a Tapestrie the Symbol turned into an Embleme, piously composed; where for the clearer understanding therof, the same shal be indicatively expressed in a Poesie, made for the purpose. Then shalt thou make him sit downe a while, to ponder, consider, and contemplate some things besides, conducing to further discoverie of the hidden mysterie, contained in the Symbol itself, to the honour of our SACRED PARTHENES, as certain Speculations or Theories thereon. Hawkins, 3.

artists but to literary theoreticians as well. Such writers as
Strada and Hawkins took the Ignatian meditative paradigm as
the point of departure in developing an entire aesthetic theory,
a theory grounded in an Aristotelian-Scholastic psychological
doctrine that implies a whole metaphysics capable of explaining
the production and aesthetic apprehension or cognition of artistic works and of justifying the ethical validity and import of art
itself.[48]

It is within the context of such interrelated metaphysical,
cognitive, and aesthetic doctrines that Calderón's allegorical
theory should be placed and can best be understood. Like contemporary Jesuits writing on poetical theory, Calderón apparently appropriated not merely the techniques but also, and
more significantly, the underlying psychological doctrine of Ignatian *compositio;* he used both techniques and doctrine to give
theoretical coherence to his *autos* and to their implicit theory of
allegory.

For both meditative exercise and *auto sacramental,* it is the
exercitant or audience, respectively, that is central to the significance and the signification of the paradigmatic text; both
seek what Raspa in a different context has termed "a common
meditative effect."[49] According to the Ignatian paradigm, the
exercitant, in focussing his attention and his soul's affections on
the suggested sacred mysteries, achieves prudential reflection
and spiritual emendation.[50] In Calderón's view, the reader of

48. The relation of the Ignatian conception of the *compositio* to Thomistic doctrine is amply discussed by Barreira. A good, brief introduction to faculty psychology
and its influence on literature, particularly that of the Renaissance, is Phillips Salman's "Instruction and Delight in Medieval and Renaissance Criticism," *Renaissance
Quarterly* 32 (1979): 303–32. Salman's essay also provides valuable additional bibliography.

49. Raspa, *The Emotive Image,* 37.

50. This is a theory grounded in a recognition of the human limitations of perception and intellection themselves. Aristotle in various places, but especially in *De
Anima,* discusses the soul's need of phantasms for understanding and even for

the *auto* "concretizes" the text (in modern critical parlance), a text that receives its significance principally through its aesthetic, moral, and spiritual impact on the audience.[51]

The Jesuit and certain twentieth-century versions of aesthetic response[52] both assume that the reader's activity is in some sense "programmed" by the text itself, determined by structures put there by the author. The difference lies in the nature of the realization or concretization the reader is to carry out. In Wolfgang Iser's view, to cite a pioneering and influential example, texts contain "indeterminacies," impasses of meaning or intelligibility that the reader must fill in to render the text consistent and assimilable. For the seventeenth-century theoreticians, the existence of such indeterminacies would most probably be not merely inconceivable, but literally impossible. Implicit in their view of aesthetic response is the assumption that the work of art is a perfect conduit of the artist's meaning, and that that meaning is an adjunct of a transcendental meaning in

thought: "the soul never thinks without a mental picture"; "no one could learn or understand anything, if he had not the faculty of perception; even when he thinks speculatively, he must have some mental picture with which to think." Quoted by Yates, *The Art of Memory*, 32. In their development of Aristotelian psychology, Albertus Magnus and Thomas Aquinas in similar fashion recognized the human need for similitudes and corporeal images that begin with the concrete and the particular in order to reach some understanding, no matter how incomplete and imperfect, of the transcendent and universal. On Magnus and Aquinas, see discussion by Yates, 61–77. On the general influence of Aquinas on Calderón, see especially R. W. Newman, "Calderón and Aquinas" (Diss., Boston University, 1956). Rosemond Tuve also makes some illuminating observations concerning Renaissance writers' conception of the affections and the role of literature in moving them in *Elizabethan and Metaphysical Imagery* (Chicago: University of Chicago Press, 1947), especially Ch. 14, "Images and a Redefined Didactic Theory."

51. It is interesting in this regard that reading (specifically, the reading of Augustine) is explicitly used as an instrument of conversion in *La protestación de la fe* (1656). See especially 736.

52. On reception aesthetics, see especially Roman Ingarden, *The Cognition of the Literary Work of Art,* trans. Ruth Ann Crowly and Kenneth R. Olsen (Evanston: Northwestern University Press, 1973) and Wolfgang Iser, *The Act of Reading* (Baltimore: Johns Hopkins University Press, 1978).

reality itself. For the rationale of neo-Scholastic theories of ideation and cognition, of which Calderón is one of the supreme representatives and practitioners, is theological; rooted in a perceived homology of divine and human ideational and creative abilities, the conceptualization of which was basic to Scholastic doctrine.[53]

It was Thomas Aquinas's vision of the creative process that established the theoretical model followed by many later thinkers. His model of artistic creation was based on the notion of the "exemplary idea" regarded as basis for the artist's work.[54] According to this theory, "as the artificer proceeds with his constructive endeavors, he has in his mind an idea of the object he is making":[55]

> Et tunc intellectus operativus, praeconcipiens formam operati, habet ut ideam ipsam formam rei imitatae, prout est illius rei imitatae.

> The operative intellect, when preconceiving the form of what is made, possesses as an idea the very form of the thing imitated, precisely as the form of the thing made.[56]

Thus "[t]he artificer discovers within his own mind an idea of the thing to be made":[57] "Dicimus enim formam artis in artifice esse exemplar vel idea artificiati" ["For we say that the form of art in the artist is the exemplar or idea of the artistic product"].[58]

---

53. On Calderón and neo-Scholasticism in general, see Robert L. Fiore, "Neo-Scholasticism in Calderón's Autos: 'No hay más fortuna que Dios,' 'El gran teatro del mundo,' 'A Dios por razón de estado' " (Diss., University of North Carolina, 1967).

54. On Aquinas's theory of art, see Umberto Eco, *The Aesthetics of Thomas Aquinas,* trans. Hugh Bredin (Cambridge: Harvard University Press, 1988), especially Ch. 6, 163–89.

55. Eco, 169.

56. Quoted and translated by Eco, 167.

57. Eco, 169.

58. Quoted and translated by Eco, 167.

From this exemplary form the artificer can proceed with material creation: "... sicut domus praeexistit in mente aedificatoris: et haec potest dici idea domus, quia artifex intendit domum assimilare formae, quam mente concepit" ["... thus the house preexisted in the mind of the architect: and this can be designated as the Idea of the house, because the artist intends to assimilate the house to the same form that he has conceived in his mind."[59] Scholastic aesthetic theory held, in other words, "that the artist worked, even if not from an Idea in the real, metaphysical sense, at least from an inner notion of form, or 'quasi-idea,' that preceded the work."[60]

The question arises, of course, where do these exemplary ideas come from in the first place? Where does the artificer get the idea for the material object, such as a house, he wishes to fabricate?

Aquinas, not surprisingly, is ready with an answer: "[T]he idea of a house exists inchoately in the divine exemplar and becomes determinate in the intellect of the artist who conceives it."[61] In other words, "The labors of the artist confer actuality upon a preexisting formal design in his mind,"[62] a design that has its origin in the godhead:

> Omnes creaturae sunt in mente divina sicut arca in mente artificis. Sed arca in mente artificis est per suam similitudinem et ideam.

---

59. *Summa Theol.*, I.15.1. Quoted and translated by Erwin Panofsky, *Idea,* trans. Joseph J. S. Peake (New York: Harper and Row, 1968), 40 and 41. The provenance of this conception can be traced in Aristotle, *Metaphysics,* Bk. VII, Ch. 7, in *The Basic Works of Aristotle,* ed. Richard McKeon (New York: Random House, 1941), 792: "... from art proceed the things of which the form is in the soul of the artist." Dante discusses these Aristotelian ideas, as well as this conception of artistic creation, in the *Convivio,* 2, chapter 10.

60. Panofsky, 41.

61. Eco, 170.

62. Eco, 180.

All creatures are in the divine mind, just as a piece of furniture is in the mind of its maker. But a piece of furniture is in its maker's mind because of its idea and its likeness.[63]

Speculation about the role and function of such preexisting and configurative "ideas" and their divine origin was in Calderón's age especially intense and fruitful, particularly among theoreticians of Scholastic and neo-Scholastic persuasion.[64] Federico Zuccari, in *L'Idea de' pittori, scultori et architetti* (1607), "proceeds from the premise that whatever is to be revealed in a work of art must first be present in the mind of the artist."[65] This mental notion Zuccari designates *designo interno,* or idea: "per Disegno interno intendo il concetto formato nella mente nostra per poter conoscere qualsivoglia cosa, ed operar di fuori conforme alla cosa intesa" ["a concept formed in our mind, that enables us explicitly and clearly to recognize any thing, whatever it may be, and to operate practically in conformance with the thing intended"].[66] The Spanish painter and art theoretician Francisco Pacheco in discussing invention advances a similar theory of the idea: "Que para mover la mano a la execución se necesita de exemplar o idea interior, la cual reside en su imaginación y entendimiento, del exemplar exterior y objetivo que se ofrece a los ojos" ["To move the hand to execution, one has need of an exemplar or interior idea, resident in the imagination and understanding, of the exterior and objective exemplar available to sight"].[67] In short, of some "exterior exemplar" the artist

63. Quoted and translated by Eco, 167.

64. On the concept of "idea" in artistic creation, especially in this period, see Panofsky, whom I follow closely in what follows. See also Salman, especially his discussion of the notions of "Idea or foreconceit" in Sir Philip Sidney, 327 ff. Aurora Egido makes some brief although suggestive remarks on this theme in *La fábrica de un auto sacramental: "Los encantos de la Culpa"* (Salamanca: Ediciones Universidad de Salamanca, 1982), 99 and 132–33.

65. Panofsky, 85.

66. Quoted by Panofsky, 226, n. 30, and translated, 85.

67. Francisco Pacheco, *Arte de la pintura,* in 2 vols., ed. F. J. Sánchez Cantón, 2 (Madrid: Instituto de Valencia de don Juan, 1956): 259. The translation is mine.

forms an "interior idea" in the imagination. He then executes
the work of art itself in conformity with this internal design or
idea.

In discussions of poetic creation, the indispensability of such
prior, formative ideas is likewise a commonplace. "Necesse
enim est arteficem earum rerum, quae a se fiunt, priusquam
manum admoveat, precognitam habere notitiam; animoque
praevidere formam, cuius exemplo opus quoque informet,"
Francesco Pedemonte points out in his *Ecphrasis in Horatii Ar-
tem poeticam* (1546).[68] Julius Caesar Scaliger conflates Platonic
and Aristotelian doctrine in positing a threefold configurative
idea: "l'idea immutevole per se stante"; "la cosa mutevole, deri-
vante dall'idea ed esistente come immagine dell'idea stessa";
and "la rappresentazione della cosa ovvero la parola" ["the im-
mutable idea in and of itself"; "the mutable thing, deriving
from the idea and existing as image of the idea itself"; and "the
representation of the thing or the word"]. He further posits the
embodiment of this informative idea in material artistic form:
"Come l'idea costituirà dunque l'essenza delle cose di questo
mondo, così la cosa dovrà ritenersi l'elemento informatore della
rappresentazione, della statua, del linguaggio. . . . Il che è pure
in conformità alla prova addotta da Aristotele: grazie alla quale
ci rendiamo conto che l'immagine di un bagno esiste nella
mente dell'architetto anche prima ch'egli costruisca il bagno"
["As the idea will then constitute the essence of the things of this
world, thus the thing should retain the informative element of
the representation, of the statue, of language. Which is also in
conformity with the proof adduced by Aristotle: thanks to
which we realize that the image of a bath exists in the mind of
the architect even before he constructs it"].[69]

68. Quoted by Rose Mary Ferraro, *Giudizi critici e criteri estetici nei poetices libri
septem (1561) di Giulio Cesare Scaligero rispetto alla teoria letteraria del rinascimento*
(Chapel Hill: University of North Carolina Press, 1971), 17, n. 32.

69. Quoted by Ferraro, 65–66.

A similar conception of the necessary prior presence of such "ideas" recurs throughout Calderón's *autos*. Most often, allusions to the underlying configurative "concept" of the *auto* mention an "idea" to which the allegory is to give concrete, visible, representable form: "... en esta nueva idea / es fuerza usar del estilo / de alegóricas figuras" ["in this new idea it is necessary to use the style of allegorical figures"] (541); "Ya habéis visto en las ideas / que fantásticas os finjo / cómo es el Hombre viador,/ cómo es la vida camino" ["You have already seen in the fantastical ideas I simulate that Man is a sojourner and his life a roadway"] (1415); "La industria y la idea que dije / ... / en una fábula intento / fundarla ..." ["The plan and the idea I mentioned I plan to base on a fable"] (1509); "Y pues lo caduco no / puede comprender lo eterno, / y es necesario que para / venir en conocimiento / suyo haya un medio visible / que en el corto caudal nuestro / del concepto imaginado / pase a práctico concepto" ["And since the transitory cannot understand the eternal, it has need for its understanding of a visible medium that, within the limited compass of our intellectual ken, turns the imagined concept into a practicable conceit"] (1215).

This idea of the "idea" has a number of telling aesthetic and theological ramifications, primarily, perhaps, the implicit analogy of human and divine ideational or creative powers. This is an analogy rooted in the originary divine source of all exemplary or formative ideas, as Aquinas suggested.[70] Zuccari's "idea" is analogous, albeit imperfectly so, to the original image immanent in God's intellect according to which he created the world: " ... e ... diremo quello spiraculo di luce infuso nell' anima nostra, come immagine del Creatore, è quella virtù formativa, che noi chiamiamo anima del Disegno, concetto, idea. Questo concetto e quest' idea uniti all' anima, come specie ed

70. See above, 195.

immagine divina, immortale, che è quella, che avviva i sensi e tutti i concetti nell'intelligenza dell'intelletto" ["and we shall say that that glimmer of light (the 'scintilla divina,' or 'divine spark') infused in our soul, as image of the Creator, is that formative virtue, which we call the spirit of the Design, concept, idea. This concept and this idea united to the soul, as species and divine, immortal image, is that which gives life to the senses and all the concepts in the intellect's intelligence"].[71] Pacheco finds a similar correspondence: "Es pues, según lo dicho, la idea un conceto o imagen de lo que se à de obrar, i a cuya imitación el artifice haze otra cosa semjante, mirando como a dechado la imagen, que tiene en el entendimiento. . . . Sacó Dios a luz, cuanto vemos, imitando su idea; en tanto pintor, en cuanto dirigido de su viva imagen dava ser a lo exterior a semejança de su interior modelo, favoreciendo tanto las imágines, objeto i fin de la Pintura" ["Thus, according to what we have said, the idea is a concept or image of what is to be done, in imitation of which

71. Quoted by Panofsky, 229, n. 33. Cf. as well the following passage, quoted by Panofsky in the original Italian, 86–87, and translated as follows, 87–88: "I say, therefore, that God, all-bountiful and almighty, and first cause of everything, in order to act externally necessarily looks at and regards the Interal Design in which He perceives all things that He has made, is making, will make, and can make with a single glance; and that this concept by which He internally proposes, is of the same substance as He, because in Him there is not nor can there be any accident, He being the purest act. In a similar way, because of his goodness and to show in a small replica the excellence of His divine art, having created man in His image and likeness with respect to the soul, endowing it with an immaterial, incorruptible substance and the powers of thinking and willing, with which man could rise above and command all the other creatures of the World except the Angel and be almost a second God, He wished to grant him the ability to form in himself an inner intellectual Design; so that by means of it he could know all the creatures and could form in himself a new world, and internally could have and enjoy in a spiritual state that which externally he enjoys and commands in a natural state; and, moreover, so that with this Design, almost imitating God and vying with Nature, he could produce an infinite number of artificial things resembling natural ones, and by means of painting and sculpture make new Paradises visible on Earth."

the artificer makes another, similar thing, by looking in his understanding to the image as a model. God created all that we see by imitating his idea (of possible things); as a painter, directed by his image, he gave existence to the external according to his interior model, giving thereby favor to imagery, object and end of Painting"].[72]

Calderón in similar fashion posits a theologically validated hierarchy of artistic expression. As Truth explains the origin of allegory in *El laberinto del mundo* (1654?), the concept (understood as the abstract or universal created by God) engenders truth, the authorial mind conceives or conceptualizes it, the idea (understood here in a sense analogous to Zuccari's *disegno interno*) nurtures it, and the tongue gives it birth: ". . . a la Verdad también / el Concepto es quien la engendra, / la Mente quien la concibe, / la Idea quien la alimenta" ["It is Concept that engenders Truth, Mind that conceives it, Idea that gives it nourishment"] (1562).[73]

Analogizing human and divine ideation permits, even demands, the assimilation of the products of that ideation, the analogy of divine and human letters, of the parabolic mode of Scripture and the allegory of the *auto,* a connection explicitly formulated in *El jardín de Falerina* (1675): ". . . la autoridad de Pablo [dice] / [. . .] / que las más puras verdades / en fábulas se conviertan. / Y . . . para una fingida / o representable escena / la Retórica nos da / alegórica licencia" ["Paul's authority states that the purest truths are converted into fables. And for a simulated or representable scene, Rhetoric gives us license for allegory"] (1509).[74] In other words, the allegorization of "feigned" or "representable" scenes contains, converted

72. Quoted by Panofsky, 226. The translation is mine.

73. For further discussion of this key passage, see Kurtz, " 'No Word without Mystery,' " as well as Ch. 2 of the present study.

74. For other examples of this vision of myth, see Ch. 2 of the present study.

into "fábulas," the "purest truths" of Christian history and Christian mystery.

Calderón's conception of the idea and its role in artistic creation, like that formulated in contemporaneous neo-Scholastic aesthetic speculation, acquires its most profound implications through its role in his overall vision of human imagination and readerly cognition, a vision that can now be illuminated by the newly explicated meaning of the dramatist's prolusion on the readers' "composición de lugares." The *auto* in this vision is an analogical or allegorized "representable" of sacred mystery, a "visual medium" that translates the artist's "imagined concept" of that mystery into representable terms. To apprehend the sacral and divinely ordained concept, the reader is to ideate a *compositio,* an imaginative, meditative re-creation of the sacral/authorial idea, much as, in Iser's view, the reader imaginatively constitutes what the modern theoretician terms an integrated gestalt.[75] Indeed, the idea embodied by the text acquires its true functionality only through such a *compositio,* which permits analogical contemplation and comprehension of divine mystery and which through the consequent movement of the soul's affections enables the soul's new reflective and prudential disposition.

Calderón's prefatory dictum concerning his *autos* can thus be said to constitute nothing less than an entire, albeit implicit, theory of allegory itself, or at least allegory as utilized in the dramatist's own *auto sacramental.* It is a theory that posits an apprehensive, creational, and ultimately sacral paradigm of allegory and allegorical text, a paradigm apparently grounded in certain contemporaneous theories regarding the way in which we perceive and the ethical, prudential, and fundamentally

75. On Iser's conception of the reader's formation of gestalten in grasping a literary text, see Wolfgang Iser, *The Act of Reading* (Baltimore: Johns Hopkins University Press, 1978), especially 118–34.

spiritual and theological, implications of that perceptive act.[76] It is likewise a theory that implies what Walter Ong has called the pipeline conception of artistic creation and readerly cognition, the assumption of "the prior presence of an extramental referent which the word presumably captures and passes on through a kind of pipeline to the psyche."[77]

The analogy of human and divine, basic to this assumption and to the Calderonian conception of allegory, extends much further than the resemblance of divine and human ideation and creation. Analogy in this vision is a principle, perhaps *the* principle, of universal order. Indeed, our very apprehension of reality is enabled by man's analogical relation to the godhead.[78] Furthermore, it is a curious and potent fact that Christ himself is described in the *autos* in terms remarkably similar to those used to define allegory. In *El verdadero Dios Pan* (1670) the titular deity, conflation of the pagan god and Jesus Christ, defines himself and his mission in the following terms: ". . . corriendo /

76. The relationship between allegory and audience or reader response is also discussed by Michael Murrin, *The Veil of Allegory* (Chicago: University of Chicago Press, 1969), chapters 5 and 6, and Maureen Quilligan, *The Language of Allegory* (Ithaca: Cornell University Press, 1979), *passim*.

77. Walter J. Ong, *Orality and Literacy* (London: Methuen, 1982), 166.

78. In the Augustinian view, which determined so much later thinking:
. . . in that realm of eternal truth from which all things temporal were made, we behold with our mind's eye the pattern upon which our being is ordered, and which rules all to which we give effect with truth and reason, in ourselves or in the outer world. Thence we conceive a truthful knowledge of things.
See (Saint) Augustine, *The Trinity,* in *Augustine: Later Works* ed. John Burnaby (Philadelphia: Westminster, 1955), 65. On the philosophical/literary conception of universal analogy, see especially Joseph A. Mazzeo, "Metaphysical Poetry and the Poetic of Correspondence," *Journal of the History of Ideas* 14 (1953): 221–34, "Universal Analogy and the Culture of the Renaissance," *Journal of the History of Ideas* 15 (1954): 299–304, and *Renaissance and Seventeenth-Century Studies* (New York: Columbia University Press, 1964); also D. C. Allen, *Mysteriously Meant.* On the currency of such ideas in the Spanish literature of the period, see Voght, "The Mythological Autos," 120, n. 24.

a la oscura confusión / de humanas letras el velo / del fabuloso dios Pan / en el Pan Dios verdadero" ["By drawing a veil over the obscure confusion of human letters, I am turning the fabled god Pan into the true God 'Pan' "] (1261). If allegory analogizes and conflates the divine and the human, Christ himself is the ultimate and originative "allegory," the hypostatized union of two apparently irreconcilable natures.

Authorial invention, human cognition, the world or universe—and the allegorical *auto* itself—are thus homologous structures, the homology rooted in a universal and immanent analogy to divine ideation and creation themselves.[79]

This is logocentrism with a vengeance, of course. Yet Calderón's vision of allegory and its role within universal order is scarcely naive. Kenneth Burke has remarked that the methodological hub of every system of thought is what he calls a "godterm," an originative principle that orders its discourse.[80] Calderón's godterm was God—God as the enabling postulate, not just of the universe and of life, but of allegorical discourse as

79. The apparently comprehensive implications of the above analysis to the contrary, it is not suggested here that the *compositio loci* in particular or meditative techniques and philosophy in general were wholly determinative of either Calderón's dramatic formulation or theoretical conceptualization of the *auto sacramental*. Furthermore, hypothetical analogizing of *compositio* and *auto* does not, cannot, imply the entire equation of meditative exercise, executed within the imagination of the exercitant, and literary text, a communicative act between author and audience which, in the case of the dramatic *auto,* involves as well the participation of producers, directors, performers, etc. Cf. Raspa's comments on the meditative poem and its similarities to and dissimilarities from meditation proper (*The Emotive Image,* 37).

80. Kenneth Burke, *The Rhetoric of Religion* (Berkeley: University of California Press, 1961), 2–3: "As for a unitary concept of God, its linguistic analogue is to be found in the nature of any name or title, which sums up a manifold of particulars under a single head. . . . Any such summarizing word is functionally a 'godterm.' What, then, might be the relation between such a term and the countless details classifiable under its 'unifying' head? Is there not a sense in which the summarizing term, the overall name or title, could be said to 'transcend' the many details subsumed under that head, somewhat as 'spirit' is said to 'transcend matter'?"

well. And the dramatist was well aware of the consequences of the loss of such a godterm, or its substitution by false godterms. He explored the consequences of such a loss to both human morality and human discourse in such secular dramas as "The Surgeon of His Honor" and "The Painter of His Dishonor."[81] But that is another story—or, perhaps, another allegory.

81. In "The Surgeon of His Honor," for example, the protagonist Don Gutierre, on the mere suspicion of his wife's infidelity, constitutes himself the "surgeon" of his dishonor and hires a bloodletter to open her veins, with the result that she bleeds to death. Calderón presents Gutierre's values as a perversion of Christian *caritas,* as the substitution of a false "godterm"—a twisted and inordinate sense of honor—for Christian reverence. The protagonist himself in his symbolical role is an inversion of *Christus medicus;* the play thus becomes at least to some extent the allegorization of a particular sort of apostasy. On the tradition of the "good physician," see Rudolf Arbesmann, "The Concept of *Christus Medicus* in St. Augustine," *Traditio* 10 (1954): 1–28.

Afterword

...en cuanto
hay alegoría, hay misterio
   (*El nuevo palacio del Retiro,* 1634)

Calderón very seldom represents directly, or has his characters explicitly discuss, the personage who is at the center of the *autos sacramentales* and their dramatic and theological meaning. Christ the Redeemer, despite his central significance for the *auto,* almost always appears in metaphorical guise: as knight, as merchant, as monarch, as any one of numerous allusive, sometimes ingenious, and occasionally farfetched analogues.

Metaphorizing the literary character is of course scarcely to be wondered at in allegory; metaphor is, after all, a standard, salient feature of the mode. For Calderón as for other writers of the Christian tradition of allegory, analogizing the godhead in human terms represents a condescension to the limitations and the possibilities of human understanding. Chastity says as much in *Sueños hay que verdad son* (1670):

> ...quiere Dios
> que para rastrear lo inmenso
> de su amor, poder y ciencia,
> nos valgamos de los medios
> que, a humano modo aplicados,
> nos puedan servir de ejemplo"   (1215)

In order for us to fathom the immensity of God's love, power, and wisdom, He wants us to make use of those measures that can serve us example when applied in the human mode.

Calderón's metaphorization of Christ thus participates in a well-established allegorical and homiletic tradition; it reflects as well the suasive, educative function the dramatist envisioned for his *autos*. However, if Calderón's treatment of the Savior is conventional, the significance he repeatedly gives that metaphorization decidedly is not. In *El nuevo palacio del Retiro* (1634), the King-Christ asserts that as divine monarch he "co-equally occupies two places at one time" ["... ocupando iguales / dos lugares en un tiempo"] (151): he is coextensively present in Heaven and in the species of the Eucharist as transubstantiated presence.

Christ's self-definition, or, rather, his explanation of his real presence in the Eucharist, resembles in a telling way the Calderonian definition of allegory itself.[1] The resemblance suggests that allegory in the *auto sacramental* is, for Calderón, fundamentally sacramental, a veil for sacral, transcendent reality, and the manifestation or conduit for divine intentionality and divine grace.

Calderón's constant emphasis on the *auto*'s veiled nature also suggests as inevitable corollary the necessity of interpretation for understanding the plays. This necessity is of course implicit in the requirements of an inherently oblique mode of discourse. However, Calderón also explicitly thematizes interpretation as the very genesis of the *auto* considered as both metaphorical conceptualization and performance.

1. "La alegoría no es más / que un espejo que traslada / lo que es con lo que no es; / y está toda su elegancia / en que salga parecida / tanto la copia en la tabla, / que el que está mirando a una / piense que está viendo a entrambas" ["Allegory is only a mirror which translates what is through what is not; and all its beauty consists in its capacity to bring out so artfully the copy's resemblance to the original that the onlooker will think that he is simultaneously seeing both"] (1242). See above, Ch. 1.

As already noted,[2] the *auto* is often described within the plays as the Devil's "industria" or imaginative representation of his plans for effecting man's fall. This diabolical mental theater for testing man's virtue becomes a kind of allegorized, conjectural "composition of place" that is to have its analogue in the spectator's own "composition," his apprehension or imaginative recreation of the eternal drama of mankind's temptation and ultimate redemption. The thematization of the *auto* as imaginative "industria" highlights the suasory and exemplary function that Calderón elsewhere explicitly attributes to these liturgical plays.

However, presenting the *auto* as the Devil's allegorized conjecture or speculation has ramifications that transcend the devotional exemplarity of the *auto* conceived as *compositio* in the Ignatian sense. The fuller implications of the conception can be seen in one of the more complex *autos,* the 1665 *Psiquis y Cupido.*[3] Hate, we may recall, is reading Apuleius's fable as the *auto* opens. He interprets, or allegorizes, the tale as a veiled allusion to the traditional Christian conception of sacred history's three successive ages: the ages of natural law, written law, and the law of grace. To prevent the promised marriage of Psyche (Third Age or Soul) to a divine monarch, and thus the feared inception of the law of grace, Hate conceives an "alegoría de poética ficción" ["allegory of poetical fiction"] (369), in which the girl will be thrown into a symbolic sea of tribulations.

Hate fails in his malignant plot, of course, because Cupid-Christ intervenes to rescue Psyche-Third Age and make her his bride within the Church of his faithful. Hate's discomfiture at this turn of events most obviously allegorizes the subordinate, contingent power of the Devil in the affairs of man. More pro-

2. See Ch. 4 of the present study.

3. See Ch. 2 for a full discussion of this *auto.* See also Barbara E. Kurtz, "'No Word without Mystery': Allegories of Sacred Truth in the *Autos Sacramentales* of Calderón de la Barca," *Publications of the Modern Language Association* 103 (1988): 262–71.

vocatively, Hate's inefficacy also reflects a failure in proper reading and enlightened interpretation. In describing his perusal of Apuleius, Hate mentions that he did not finish reading the tale:

> en la fábula de Psiquis
> . . . .
> leí, que un alto, un superior
> monarca tuvo tres hijas,
> que a las dos estado dio,
> y a la tercera echó al mar
> por envidia de las dos;
> hasta aquí no más leí,
> porque en llegando a ver yo
> lo era él, de allí adelante
> me sobraba la lección.   (368)

In the fable of Psyche I read that a high, a supreme monarch had three daughters, that for two he arranged marriage and the third he threw into the sea because of the envy of her sisters. No more did I read, for when I saw that it was about him (whom I hate and fear), the rest of the reading was superfluous to me.

Hate read just enough, in other words, to warrant his own interpretation of the fable as allegorizing the inception of the Third Age or age of grace. Without knowing how the pagan writer ended the story, Hate attempts to constitute himself a coauthor, composing for the tale an ending that suits his own desires and purpose.

In this ingenious passage Calderón is doubtless playing with and against the centuries-old tradition of moralizing or divinizing secular literature.[4] Hate's "diabolization" of Apuleius

---

4. On the tradition of divinizing or Christianizing secular literature, see, for example, Fabio Planciades Fulgentius, in *Fulgentius the Mythographer*, trans. Leslie George Whitbread (Columbus: Ohio State University Press, 1971); Bernardus Silvestris, *Commentary on the First Six Books of Virgil's Aeneid*, trans. Earl B. Schreiber and Thomas E. Maresca (Lincoln: University of Nebraska Press, 1979); John Gar-

(Calderón would, I hope, approve of the coinage) constitutes an interpretive gloss or diabolical allegoresis that adumbrates the glossator's own perverse values and serves as pretext for and taxonomy of his malignant moral and philosophical truisms.

Hate's failure to read carefully and interpret correctly is a failure both epistemological and moral, reflective of his diabolic limitations, as well as literary and hermeneutical. The Devil's allegorical experiment must go awry and slip out of his control, yielding before the higher textual authority of the dramatist's controlling hand and, of course, before the preeminent ontological, theological, and literary authority of the Supreme Author.

In this allegorical vision Calderón's (presumed) success in the *autos* should be seen as similar in range though opposite in implications. The discovery of the Eucharist, conclusion of every *auto sacramental,* represents (in the dramatist's view) the supervention in the play of that grace which sanctions the playwright's hermeneutical and creative enterprise and guarantees the interpretative and authorial success denied to his diabolical counterpart. The discovery sacramentalizes the *auto* and makes it the allegory of the supervention of divine presence and purpose in the cosmos and of the divine warranty of valid, illumined intepretation.[5] The allegorist, in this view, is the exposi-

---

land, "The Integumenta on the Metamorphoses of Ovid," ed. and trans. Lester Kruger Born (Diss., University of Chicago, 1929); and the *Ovide moralisé*, ed. C. de Boer *et al.* (Amsterdam: Verhandelingen Koninklijke Akademie van Wetenschappen, 1915–38). For the Hispanic tradition, see Bruce W. Wardropper, *Historia de la poesía lírica a lo divino en la cristiandad occidental* (Madrid: Revista de Occidente, 1958).

5. The necessity of such a guarantee of interpretation is expounded by Augustine in *De doctrina Christiana*, Book 2, Ch. viii:

He will be the most expert investigator of the Holy Scriptures who has first read all of them and has some knowledge of them, at least through reading them if not through understanding them. That is, he should read those that are said to be canonical. For he may read the others more securely when he has been instructed in the truth of the faith so that they may not preoccupy a weak mind nor,

tor of a canonical original, a glossator or mystagogue rather than creator in his own right. In the case of Calderón, that original is sacred history (commemorated in the Eucharist), whose "author" is the Supreme Creator himself; and divine intentionality is the presumed source of any and all sacred meaning.

Calderón's *autos sacramentales* may be the ultimate logocentric literature (at least in theory), the perfect embodiment of religio-aesthetic creationism or *theosis:* that is, the belief in the possibiilty of perfect coincidence among human creative activity and communication, human perception, and divine intentionality, and the concomitant conviction that the human author can give "new testimony to God's continuing presence by praising Him in [his] own form."[6] Anything that man contemplates or about which he writes will thus "reveal the latent presence of God, not least of all in the re-creative discourse itself."[7]

The *auto* may thus constitute a "disclosure model" as defined by Ian T. Ramsey in his studies of theological language.[8] Ramsey sees theological discourse as an attempt to be articulate about an insight into structures and patterns of existential and universal significance. Such an insight he calls a "cosmic disclosure." The religious writer wishing to communicate his insight relies on various models from which he hopes the "cosmic disclosure" may be generated for his reader. In such a model, met-

---

deceiving it with vain lies and fantasies, prejudice it with something contrary to sane understanding. In the matter of canonical Scriptures he should follow the authority of the greater number of catholic Churches, among which are those which have deserved to have apostolic seats and to receive epistles.

(Saint) Augustine, *On Christian Doctrine*, trans. D. W. Robertson, Jr. (Indianapolis: Bobbs, 1958), 40–41. For further discussion of this issue, see above, Ch. 2.

6. Stephen G. Nichols, Jr., *Romanesque Signs* (New Haven: Yale University Press, 1983), 26.

7. Nichols, 20.

8. See Ian T. Ramsey, *Religious Language* (London: SCM Press, 1957), *Models and Mystery* (London: Oxford University Press, 1964), and *Christian Discourse* (London: Oxford University Press, 1965).

aphor is neither adventitious nor whimsical. It is, on the contrary, inherently functional, intrinsic to the very process of understanding:

> A memorable metaphor has the power to bring separate domains into cognitive and emotional relation by using language directly appropriate to the one as a lens for seeing the other.... Metaphorical thought is a distinctive mode of achieving insight, not to be construed as an ornamental substitute for plain thought.[9]

The metaphors of the *autos*' allegorical discourse are thus innately performative,[10] "a language not so much concerned with imparting information as with getting things done."[11] What the metaphors most obviously "get done" is to make manifest, concrete and visible, the sacral mystery embodied in the *autos*' personified abstractions and in the allegorical action those personifications actualize. Most of Calderón's personifications are abstractions who verbally realize their existence, who constantly actualize their figurative import through their words. With the partial exception of such characters as Man or Soul, most possess no inner life, no affectivity in the conventional sense. For example, the advisory characters which abound in Calderón's *autos*—Prudence, Care, Innocence, Gratitude, Understanding, Conscience, Memory, Consolation, Disillusionment, and so forth—are dramatically limited to giving advice. Their words exhibit neither the expressivity nor the variety we associate with the dialogue of characters in nonallegorical drama. To a certain extent their statements are tautological, defining and making explicit the abstract acceptations, the theological and/or moral referents, that their words materialize.

9. Ramsey, *Models and Mystery*, 236–37.

10. On the whole notion of "performative utterance," see especially J. L. Austin, *How to Do Things with Words* (New York: Oxford University Press, 1962). See also John R. Searle, *Speech Acts* (Cambridge: Cambridge University Press, 1969).

11. John MacQuarrie, *God-Talk* (New York: Harper and Row, 1967), 45.

What the dramatized metaphors of the allegorical *auto* "get done," less obviously but more significantly, is that sensory appeal to the audience which will elicit movement of the soul's affections and, thereby, spiritual reflection, emendation, and redemption.[12] The primary goals of the Calderonian *auto,* like personification allegory in general, are not aesthetic or ludic. Rather, the *auto*'s social function and communicative achievement implicitly posit as aim a *conversio morum* in the spectator or reader.[13]

The "discovery" of the Eucharistic host and chalice at every *auto*'s conclusion is no mere cultic celebration integrating *auto* into religious ceremonial and conferring upon it quasi-liturgical status. Nor is the "human mode" of these plays a mere anthropocentric distortion,[14] a condescension to human percep-

12. On this affectional process, see above, Ch. 4.

13. These observations are based on Hans R. Jauss's work with what he terms "the communcative achievement and social function of preautonomous art." In a treatise on *Negativität und Identifikation* Jauss develops a "typology of the hero" based on "levels of identification of hero and audience." He discusses the aesthetic perception of literary texts and the "prereflective level of aesthetic perception [as] the communicative framework for an imaginative consciousness which is prepared to enter into emotional identification with the action and situation of the character." But there are other possible modes of interaction with a literary text, responses that reflect the implicit assumptions of premodern, Christian art:

> The authority of the Christian church and its doctrine, to the extent that it gained power over everyday life, . . . gradually developed arguments which gave aesthetic experience a new framework. The exemplary was opposed to the imaginary, pity leading to action was opposed to purgation by catharsis, the hortatory principle of emulation was opposed to the aesthetic pleasure derived from imitation.

The goal of such art, according to Jauss, was a *conversio morum* in the spectator or reader, its subject an *"imitabile* . . . which appeals to our rational insight and thus avoids the seductiveness of the senses," that *concupiscentia oculorum* or mere sensory enjoyment criticized by Augustine. All quotations here have been taken from Jauss's English synopsis of his own work, "Levels of Identification of Hero and Audience," *New Literary History* 5 (1974): 283–317.

14. ". . . human speech brings with its use unavoidable anthropocentric distortion. . . ." Frederick Ferré, *Language, Logic and God* (Chicago: University of Chicago Press, 1961), 67.

tual and intellective limitations. Rather, the mysterious and numinous "discovery" suggests that the preceding performance serves as testimony to God's continuing presence and participation in the affairs of men, including their literature. It is also the embodiment of a metaphysics that sees language as intrinsically efficacious and numinous and literature as the conduit of divine intentionality.[15] In similar fashion, the apparent anachrony of registers in the *auto*—what seems to be the conflation of "levels" as the personifications momentarily step out of their metaphorical story line to talk about personification, allegory, and sacred truth—such stunning moments are no lapse of dramaturgical decorum or skill. They represent more properly the supersession of dramatic (hence quotidian), limited, and emotionally and theologically unsatisfying verisimilitude, as well as the implicit conceptualization of allegory and allegorical text as a *manifestatio* of sacramentalism.[16]

Positing the text as revelatory of sacred truth, as kerygma, as

15. Cf. the comments of David Quint: "Renaissance allegory . . . normatively posits a metaphysical source of authority for its meaning—as if God were the ideal reader as well as the ultimate author of the sign. . . . Allegory locates the text's value in a source of truth and authority that lies outside the text itself—normally in an earlier text or series of texts that have been granted an authoritative or sacred status." Quint, *Origin and Originality in Renaissance Literature* (New Haven: Yale University Press, 1983), 20 and 22.

16. I use the term *manifestatio* in the sense first suggested, as far as I know, by Erwin Panofsky in his discussion of Gothic architecture and its philosopical presuppositions: "*Manifestatio*, then, elucidation or clarification, is what I would call the first controlling principle of Early and High Scholasticism. . . . Hence the much derided schematicism or formalism of Scholastic writing which reached its climax in the classic Summa with its three requirements of (1) totality (sufficient enumeration), (2) arrangement according to a system of homologous parts and parts of parts (sufficient articulation), and (3) distinctness and deductive cogency (sufficient interrelation). Panofsky, *Gothic Architecture and Scholasticism* (Cleveland: World Publishing, 1951), 29. Eugene Vinaver points out in *The Rise of Romance* (New York: Oxford University Press, 1971), 23, that Panofsky, despite his brilliant insight, erred only through incompleteness; it could easily be extended as a general principle to much of medieval thought and letters and, of course, to later literature and theory imbued with such medievalism.

spiritual exercise, as conduit of divine intentionality, confers upon the *auto* a truly sacramental character. The Eucharist is semiotic, the *auto* is sacramental, and allegory exemplifies *theosis.*

The complex and subtle homologies of allegory, *auto,* and sacrament do not in Calderón's conception so much legitimize the *auto*'s theory and practice as irradiate them, implicate them in the very patterns and intentionality of the cosmos and its creator. Calderón wrote allegory, I am convinced, because at a certain point in his literary and religious development he could conceive of no other way to write. For a man of his sensibility, his beliefs, and his time, the endless analogies and correspondences of creation used as basis of the *auto sacramental* are not random coincidence but truth. Allegory is thus not aesthetic choice or linguistic convenience; rather, it is a philosophical, theological, linguistic, even cognitive necessity.

This is heady stuff, indeed, a philosophy and a literature to which the twentieth-century reader may feel an instinctive reaction of doubt and denial. As man's orderly paradigm of the universe comes to an end, as randomization and chance increasingly appear as the hallmarks of the day, as our texts, both literary and critical, proclaim and incarnate a new era of discontinuity and entropy,[17] it may be difficult for us to approach with true sympathy the austerity and sacramentalism of Calderón's allegory, where words and Word meet and fuse. Perhaps this is a sign of our intellectual progress. But it is a register as well of our spiritual and emotional loss.

17. For a similar, and interesting, discussion, see Vincent B. Leitch, *Deconstructive Criticism* (New York: Columbia University Press, 1983), 263. Cf. as well similar comments by Murray Krieger, "'A Waking Dream': The Symbolic Alternative to Allegory," in Morton W. Bloomfield, ed., *Allegory, Myth, and Symbol* (Cambridge: Harvard University Press, 1981), 8.

Works Cited

Aers, David. *Piers Plowman and Christian Allegory*. New York: St. Martin's, 1975.

Allen, Don Cameron. *Mysteriously Meant: The Rediscovery of Pagan Symbolism and Allegorical Interpretation in the Renaissance*. Baltimore: Johns Hopkins University Press, 1970.

Allen, Judson Boyce. *The Ethical Poetic of the Later Middle Ages: A Decorum of Convenient Distinction*. Toronto: University of Toronto Press, 1982.

Allers, Rudolf. "*Microcosmos*, from Anaximandros to Paracelsus." *Traditio* 2 (1944): 319–407.

"Application des sens." *Dictionnaire de Spiritualité, ascetique et mystique, doctrine et histoire*. Paris: Beauchesne, 1967.

Arbesmann, Rudolf. "The Concept of *Christus Medicus* in St. Augustine." *Traditio* 10 (1954): 1–28.

Arias, Ricardo. *The Spanish Sacramental Plays*. Boston: Twayne Publishers, G. K. Hall, 1980.

Aristotle. *The Basic Works of Aristotle*. Ed. Richard McKeon. New York: Random House, 1941.

Asensio, Eugenio. "El *Auto dos quatro tempos* de Gil Vicente." *Revista de filología española* 33 (1949): 350–70.

Auerbach, Erich. *Mimesis: The Representation of Reality in Western Literature*. Trans. Willard R. Trask. Princeton: Princeton University Press, 1953.

———. *Scenes from the Drama of European Literature*. New York: Meridian Books, 1959.

Augustine (Saint). *Concerning the City of God Against the Pagans*. Trans. David Knowles. Middlesex, England: Penguin Books, 1972.

———. *The Confessions of St. Augustine*. Trans. Rex Warner. New York: New American Library, 1963.

———. *Later Works*. Ed. John Burnaby. Philadelphia: Westminster, 1955.

———. *On Christian Doctrine*. Trans. D. W. Robertson, Jr. Indianapolis: Bobbs, 1958.

Austin, J. L. *How to Do Things with Words*. New York: Oxford University Press, 1962.

Balthasar, Hans Urs von. *A Theology of History*. New York: Sheed and Ward, 1963.

Barkan, Leonard. *Nature's Work of Art: The Human Body as Image of the World*. New Haven: Yale University Press, 1975.

Barney, Stephen A. *Allegories of History, Allegories of Love*. Hamden, CT: Archon Books, 1979.

Barreira, Tomás. "La composición de lugar." *Manresa* 2 (1935): 158–69.

Barthes, Roland. *Sade/Fourier/Loyola*. Trans. Richard Miller. New York: Hill and Wang, 1976.

Bataillon, Marcel. "Charles-Quint bon pasteur, selon Fray Cipriano de Huerga." *Bulletin Hispanique* 50 (1948): 398–406.

———. "Ensayo de explicación del 'auto sacramental.'" *Varia lección de clásicos españoles*. Madrid: Gredos, 1964. 183–205.

———. "Essai d'explication de l'auto sacramental." *Bulletin Hispanique* 42 (1940): 193–212.

Bayley, Peter. *French Pulpit Oratory 1598–1650: A Study in Themes and Styles*. Cambridge: Cambridge University Press, 1980.

Beardsley, Theodore S., Jr. *Hispano-Classical Translations Printed between 1482 and 1699*. Duquesne Studies Philological Series 12. Pittsburgh: Duquesne University Press, 1970.

Berchem, Theodor, and Siegfried Sudhof, eds. *Pedro Calderón de la Barca: Vorträge anlässlich der Jahrestagung der Görres-Gesellschaft 1978*. Berlin: Erich Schmidt, 1983.

Bernardus Silvestris. *Commentary on the First Six Books of Virgil's Aeneid*. Trans. Earl B. Schreiber and Thomas E. Maresca. Lincoln: University of Nebraska Press, 1979.

Biadene, L. "'Carmina de Mensibus' di Bonvesin de la Riva." *Studi di Filologia Romanza* 4 (1903): 1–130.

Bloesch, Donald B. "The Primacy of Scripture." *The Authoritative Word: Essays on the Nature of Scripture*. Ed. Donald K. McKim. Grand Rapids, MI: Wm. B. Eerdmans, 1983. 117–53.

Bloomfield, Morton W. "Allegory as Interpretation." *New Literary History* 3 (1972): 301–17.

Boccaccio, Giovanni. *Genealogiae deorum gentilium libri*. Ed. Vincenzo Romano. Bari: G. Laterza, 1951.

Boethius. *Tracts and De Consolatione Philosophiae*. Trans. H. F. Stewart and E. K. Rand, rev. S. J. Tester. Cambridge: Harvard University Press, 1973.

Born, Lester K. "Ovid and Allegory." *Speculum* 9 (1934): 362–79.

Boucher, Holly Wallace. "Metonymy in Typology and Allegory, with a Consideration of Dante's *Comedy*." *Allegory, Myth, and Symbol*. Ed. Morton W. Bloomfield. Cambridge: Harvard University Press, 1981. 129–45.

Bower, Maurice. "Orpheus and Euridice." *Classical Quarterly*, n.s. 2 (1952): 113–26.

Boyce, Elizabeth S. "Calderon's *Psalle et Sile*: The Meditative Art and the Metaphysical Mode." *Iberoromania* 6 (1977): 122–46.

Bradford, Melvin E. "Henry Vaughan's 'The Night': A Consideration of Metaphor and Meditation." *Arlington Quarterly* 1 (1968): 209–22.

Bright, John. "Typological Interpretatation of the Old Testament." *Essays on Old Testament Hermeneutics*. Ed. Claus Westermann, English trans. and ed. James Luther Mays. Richmond, VA: John Knox, 1963. 17–39.

Brown, Jonathan, and John H. Elliott. *A Palace for a King: The Buen Retiro and the Court of Philip IV*. New Haven: Yale University Press, 1980.

Buelow, Kenneth Dale. "A Semi-Critical and Annotated Edition of *El Divino Orfeo, Segunda Parte*, by Pedro Calderón de la Barca." Diss., University of Wisconsin, Madison, 1976.

Bultmann, D. Rudolf. *History and Eschatology*. Edinburgh: Edinburgh University Press, 1975.

———. "Ursprung und Sinn der Typologie als hermeneutischer Methode." *Theologische Literaturzeitung*. Vol. 75–76. 1950–51. 205–12.

Bunyan, John. *The Pilgrim's Progress*. Ed. Roger Sharrock. Harmondsworth, England: Penguin Books, 1965.

Burke, Kenneth. *The Rhetoric of Religion: Studies in Logology*. Berkeley: University of California Press, 1961.

Bush, Douglas. *Mythology and the Renaissance Tradition in English Poetry*. rev. ed. New York: W. W. Norton, 1963.

Cabañas, Pablo. *El mito de Orfeo en la literatura española*. Madrid: Consejo Superior de Investigaciones Científicas, Instituto Miguel de Cervantes de Filología Hispánica, 1948.

Cabrera, Alonso de. *Sermones*. Ed. Miguel Mir. Vol. 3. Madrid: Bailly- Baillère, 1906. 3 vols.

Cabrol, Fernand, and Henri Leclercq, eds. *Dictionnaire d'archéologie chrétienne et de liturgie*. Paris: Letouzey, 1936.

Calderón de la Barca, Pedro. *Obras completas 3: Autos sacramentales*. Ed. Angel Valbuena Prat. Madrid: Aguilar, 1967.

———. *El pleito matrimonial del cuerpo y el alma*. Ed. Manfred Engelbert. Hamburg: Cram, de Gruyter, 1969.

Calveras, José. "Los cinco sentidos de la imaginación en los Ejercicios de San Ignacio." *Manresa* 20 (1948): 47–70.

Camón Aznar, J. "Teorías pictóricas de Lope y Calderón." *Velázquez* 1 (1964): 66–72.

Casas, Elena, ed. *La retórica en España*. Madrid: Editora Nacional, 1980.

Cascardi, Anthony J. "Calderón's Encyclopaedic Rhetoric." *Neophilologus* 16 (1982): 56–65.

Casserley, J. V. Langmead. *Toward a Theology of History*. New York: Holt, Rinehart and Winston, 1965.

Cave, Terence C. *Devotional Poetry in France c. 1570–1613*. Cambridge: Cambridge University Press, 1969.

Chamberlin, John S. *Increase and Multiply: Arts-of-Discourse Procedure in the Preaching of Donne*. Chapel Hill: University of North Carolina Press, 1976.

Charity, A. C. *Events and Their Afterlife: The Dialectics of Christian Typology in the Bible and in Dante*. Cambridge: Cambridge University Press, 1966.

Chew, Samuel. *The Pilgrimage of Life: An Exploration into the Renaissance Mind*. New Haven: Yale University Press, 1962.

Chorpenning, Joseph F. "The Literary and Theological Method of the *Castillo interior*." *Journal of Hispanic Philology* 3 (1979): 124–28.

Cilveti, Angel L. *El demonio en el teatro de Calderón*. Javea, Valencia: Albatros, 1977.

———. "Dramatización de la alegoría bíblica en *Primero y Segundo Isaac* de Calderón." *Critical Perspectives on Calderón de la Barca*. Ed. Frederick A. de Armas, David M. Gitlitz and José A. Madrigal. Lincoln, NE: Society of Spanish and Spanish-American Studies, 1981. 39–52.

Cinquemani, A. M. "Henry Reynolds' *Mythomystes* and the Continuity of Ancient Modes of Allegoresis in Seventeenth-Century England." *Publications of the Modern Language Association* 85 (1970): 1041–49.

Clements, Robert J. *Picta Poesis: Literary and Humanistic Theory in Renaissance Emblem Books*. Rome: Edizioni di Storia e Letteratura, 1960.

Colish, Marcia. *The Mirror of Language: A Study in the Medieval Theory of Knowledge*. rev. ed. Lincoln: University of Nebraska Press, 1983.

Comenius, John Amos. *The Labyrinth of the World and the Paradise of the Heart*. Trans. Matthew Spinka. Ann Arbor: University of Michigan, 1972.

Comparetti, Domenico. *Vergil in the Middle Ages*. Trans. E. F. M. Benecke. rept. 1929. New York: G. E. Stechert, 1929.

Cooke, J. D. "Euhemerism: A Mediaeval Interpretation of Classical Paganism." *Speculum* 2 (1927): 396–410.

Cossío, José María de. *Fábulas mitológicas en España*. Madrid: Espasa-Calpe, 1952.

Cotarelo y Mori, E. *Bibliografía de las controversias sobre la licitud del teatro en España*. Madrid: Revista de archivos, bibliotecas y museos, 1904.

Coulter, C. C. "The Genealogy of the Gods." *Vassar Mediaeval Studies*. Ed. C. F. Fiske. New Haven: Yale University Press, 1923. 317–41.

Cox, R. Merritt. "Calderón and the Spanish Neoclassicists." *Romance Notes* 24 (1983): 43–48.

Cro, Stelio. "Calderón y la pintura." *Calderón and the Baroque Tradition*. Ed. Kurt Levy, Jesús Ara, and Gethin Hughes. Waterloo: Wilfrid Laurier University Press, 1985. 119–24.

Cummins, John G. "Methods and Conventions in the 15th-Century Poetic Debate." *Hispanic Review* 31 (1963): 307–23.

———. "The Survival in the Spanish *Cancioneros* of the Form and Themes of Provençal and Old French Poetic Debates." *Bulletin of Hispanic Studies* 42 (1965): 9–17.

Curtius, Ernst Robert. *European Literature and the Latin Middle Ages*. Trans. Willard R. Trask. Princeton: Princeton University Press, 1973.

Damiani, Bruno M. *Moralidad y didactismo en el Siglo de Oro (1492–1615)*. Madrid: Orígenes, 1987.

Daniélou, Jean. "The Conception of History in the Christian Tradition." *Journal of Religion* 30 (1950): 171–79.

———. *The Lord of History: Reflections on the Inner Meaning of History*. Trans. Nigel Abercrombie. London: Longmans, Green, 1963.

———. *Origen*. Trans. Walter Mitchell. New York: Sheed and Ward, 1955.

———. "The Problem of Symbolism." *Thought* 25 (1950): 423–40.

———. "The Ship of the Church." *Primitive Church Symbols*. Trans. Donald Attwater. London: Burns and Oates, 1964. 58–70.

Dante Alighieri. *Il convivio*. Ed. B. Busnelli and G. Vandelli. Vol. 1. Florence: F. Le Monnier, 1934–37.

David, Pierre. "Notes sur deux motifs introduits par Gil Vicente dans l'Auto da Embarcação da Gloria." *Bulletin des Etudes portugaises*, n.s. (1945): 189–203.

de Armas, Frederick A., David M. Gitlitz, and José A. Madrigal, eds. *Critical Perspectives on Calderón de la Barca*. Lincoln, NE: Society of Spanish and Spanish American Studies, 1981.

de Boer, C., ed. *Ovide moralisé, poème du commencement du quatorzième siècle. publié d'après tous les manuscrits connus*. Verhandelingen der Koninklijke Academie van Wetenschappen. Afdeeling Letterkunde. Nieuwe Reeks, 15 (1915), 21 (1920), 30 (1931), 37 (1936), 43 (1938).

de Lubac, Henri. *Exégèse médiévale*. 2 vols. Paris: Aubier, 1959–64.

———. " 'Typologie' et 'Allégorisme,' " *Recherches de Science Religieuse* 34 (1947): 180–226.

de Osma, José María. "Apostilla al tema de la creación en el auto *El divino Orfeo* de Calderón de la Barca." *Hispania* 34 (1951): 165–71.

de Pisan, Christine. *The Epistle of Othea to Hector*. Ed. James D. Gordon. Diss. University of Pennsylvania, 1942.

Deyermond, A. D. *A Literary History of Spain: The Middle Ages*. London: Ernest Benn, 1971.

Dietz, Donald T. *The Auto Sacramental and the Parable in Spanish Golden Age Literature*. Chapel Hill: University of North Carolina Dept. of Romance Languages, 1973.

———. "Conflict in Calderón's *Autos Sacramentales*." *Approaches to the Theater of Calderón*. Ed. Michael D. McGaha. Washington, DC: University Press of America, 1982. 175–86.

———. "Liturgical and Allegorical Drama: The Uniqueness of Calderón's *Auto Sacramental*." *Calderón de la Barca at the Tercentenary: Comparative Views*. Ed. Wendell M. Aycock and Sydney P. Cravens. Lubbock: Texas Tech University Press, 1982. 71–88.

———. "Toward Understanding Calderon's Evolution as an *Auto* Dramatist." *Studies in Honor of Ruth Lee Kennedy*. Ed. Vern G. Williamsen and A. F. Michael Atlee. Chapel Hill, NC: Estudios de Hispanófila, 1977. 51–55.

Díez Borque, José María. "El auto sacramental calderoniano y su público: Funciones del texto cantado." *Calderón and the Baroque Tradition*. Ed. Kurt Levy, Jesús Ara, and Gethin Hughes. Waterloo: Wilfrid Laurier University Press, 1985. 49–67.

———. "Teatro y fiesta en el barroco español: El auto sacramental de Calderón y su público: Funciones del texto cantado." *Cuadernos hispanoamericanos* 396 (1983): 606–42.

———. *Una fiesta sacramental barroca*. Madrid: Taurus, 1983.

Dolan, Kathleen. "Eurydice and the Imagery of Redemption: Calderón's *Auto del divino Orfeo*." *Proceedings of the Pacific Northwest Council on Foreign Languages* 26 (1975): 196–98.

Dondaine, A. "La Vie et les oeuvres de Jean de San Gimignano." *Archivum Fratrum Praedicatorum* 2 (1939): 128–83.

Donne, John. *Devotions Upon Emergent Occasions*. Ann Arbor: University of Michigan Press, 1965.

Durán, Manuel, and Roberto González Echevarría. *Calderón y la crítica: Historia y antología*. 2 vols. Madrid: Gredos, 1976.

Eco, Umberto. *The Aesthetics of Thomas Aquinas*. Trans. Hugh Bredin. Cambridge:

Harvard University Press, 1988. Previously published as *Il problema estetico in Tommaso d'Aquino*. Milan: Gruppo Editoriale Fabbri, Bompiani, Sonzogno, Etas S.p.A., 1970.

Egido, Aurora. *La fábrica de un auto sacramental: "Los encantos de la Culpa."* Salamanca: Universidad de Salamanca, 1982.

Elizalde, I., S.I. "San Ignacio de Loyola y el antiguo teatro jesuítico." *Razón y Fe* 153 (1956): 289–304.

———. "El papel de Dios verdadero en los autos y comedias mitológicos de Calderón." *Calderón: Actas del Congreso internacional sobre Calderón y el teatro español del Siglo de Oro*. Ed. Luciano García Lorenzo. Madrid: Consejo Superior de Investigaciones Científicas, 1983, 999–1012.

Elliott, J. H. *Imperial Spain: 1469–1716*. New York: New American Library, 1963.

Farrar, Frederic W. *History of Interpretation*. Grand Rapids, MI: Baker Book House, 1961.

Feldman, Burton, and Robert D. Richardson, eds. *The Rise of Modern Mythology, 1680–1860*. Bloomington: Indiana University Press, 1972.

Ferraro, Rose Mary. *Giudizi critici e criteri estetici nei poetices libri septem (1561) di Giulio Cesare Scaligero rispetto alla teoria letteraria del rinascimento*. Chapel Hill: University of North Carolina Press, 1971.

Ferré, Frederick. "Design Argument." *Dictionary of the History of Ideas*. Ed. Philip P. Wiener. New York: Scribner's, 1968.

———. *Language, Logic and God*. Chicago: University of Chicago Press, 1961.

Fessard, Gaston. *La Dialectique des 'Exercises Spirituels' de S. Ignacio de Loyola*. Paris: Aubier, 1966–.

Fichte, Jörg O. *Expository Voices in Medieval Drama: Essays on the Mode and Function of Dramatic Exposition*. Erlanger Beiträge zur Sprach- und Kunstwisssenschaft 53. Nuremberg: Hans Carl, 1975.

Fiore, Robert L. "Neo-Scholasticism in Calderon's Autos: 'No hay más fortuna que Dios,' 'El gran teatro del mundo,' 'A Dios por razón de estado.' " Diss. University of North Carolina, 1967.

Flasche, Hans. "Antiker Mythos in christlicher Umprägung: Andromeda und Perseus bei Calderón." *Romanistisches Jahrbuch* 16 (1965): 290–317.

———. "El arte de poner ante los ojos en el auto *La segunda esposa o triunfar muriendo*." *Calderón and the Baroque Tradition*. Ed. Kurt Levy, Jesús Ara and Gethin Hughes. Waterloo: Wilfrid Laurier University Press, 1985. 93–108.

———. "Calderón als 'magister religionis' im Auto Sacramental." *Sonderdruck aus Europäische Lehrdichtung: Festschrift für Walter Naumann zum 70. Geburtstag*. Darmstadt: Wissenschaftliche Buchgesellschaft, 1981. 143–58.

———. "Calderón y San Agustín." *Homenaje a Pedro Sainz Rodríguez*. Vol. 2: *Estudios de Lengua y Literatura*. Madrid: Fundación Universitaria Española. 195–207. 2 vols.

———. "Elementos teológicos constitutivos en el auto sacramental *El sacro Parnaso*." *Calderón: Actas del Congreso internacional sobre Calderón y el teatro español del Siglo de Oro*. Ed. Luciano García Lorenzo. Madrid: Consejo Superior de Investigaciones Científicas, 1983. 37–49.

———. "Die Struktur des Hof-Laudatio in den *Loas* der *Autos* Calderóns." *Euro-*

*päische Hofkultur im 16. und 17. Jahrhundert: Vorträge und Referate gehalten anläss-
lich des Kongresses des Wolfenbütteler Arbeitskreises für Renaissanceforschung und
des Internationalen Arbeitskreises für Barockliteratur in der Herzog August Bibliothek Wolfenbüttel vom 4. bis 8. September 1979*. Ed. August Buch, Georg Kauffmann, Blake Lee Spahr, and Conrad Wiedemann. Hamburg: Hauswedell, 1981.
277–86.

Flasche, Hans, Karl-Hermann Körner, and Hans Mattauch, eds. *Hacia Calderón:
Cuarto Coloquio Anglogermano, Wolfenbüttel 1975*. Berlin: De Gruyter, 1979.

Flecniakoska, Jean-Louis. *La Formation de l'auto religieux en Espagne avant Calderón*.
Montpellier: P. Déhan, 1961.

Fletcher, Angus. *Allegory: The Theory of a Symbolic Mode*. Ithaca: Cornell University
Press, 1964.

Flew, Anthony. "Aquinas." *A Dictionary of Philosophy*. New York: St. Martin's,
1979.

————. "Argument from (or to) Design." *A Dictionary of Philosophy*. New York:
St. Martin's, 1979.

Fothergill-Payne, Louise. *La alegoría en los autos y farsas anteriores a Calderón*. London: Tamesis, 1977.

————. "Doble historia de la alegoría (unas observaciones generales sobre el modo
alegórico en la literatura del Siglo de Oro)." *Actas del Sexto Congreso Internacional
de Hispanistas*. Ed. Alan M. Gordon and Evelyn Rugg. Toronto: Dept. of Spanish
and Portuguese, University of Toronto, 1980. 261–64.

————. "The Jesuits as Masters of Rhetoric and Drama." *Revista canadiense de estudios hispánicos* 10 (1986): 375–87.

————. "The World Picture in Calderón's *Autos Sacramentales*." *Calderón and the
Baroque Tradition*. Ed. Kurt Levy, Jesús Ara and Gethin Hughes. Waterloo:
Wilfrid Laurier University Press, 1985. 33–40.

Foucault, Michel. *The Order of Things: An Archaeology of the Human Sciences*. New
York: Pantheon Books, 1971. New York: Vintage Books, 1973.

Frank, Ellen Eve. *Literary Architecture: Essays Toward a Tradition (Walter Pater, Ge-
rard Manley Hopkins, Marcel Proust, Henry James)*. Berkeley: University of California Press, 1979.

Franzbach, Martin. *El teatro de Calderón en Europa*. Madrid: Fundación Universitaria Española, 1982.

Freeman, Rosemary. *English Emblem Books*. New York: Octagon, 1966.

Frei, Hans W. *The Eclipse of Biblical Narrative: A Study in Eighteenth and Nineteenth
Century Hermeneutics*. New Haven: Yale University Press, 1974.

Friedman, John Block. *Orpheus in the Middle Ages*. Cambridge: Harvard University
Press, 1970.

Friedman, Lionel J. Rev. of *Etudes sur le poème allégorique en France au Moyen Age*,
by Marc-René Jung. *Speculum* 47 (1972): 316–20.

Frutos, Eugenio. *La filosofía de Calderón en sus Autos Sacramentales*. Saragossa: Institución "Fernando el Católico," 1952.

Frye, Northrop. *Anatomy of Criticism: Four Essays*. Princeton: Princeton University
Press, 1957.

Fulgentius. *Fulgentius the Mythographer*. Ed. Leslie George Whitbread. Columbus:
Ohio State University Press, 1971.

García Lorenzo, Luciano, ed. *Calderón: Actas del Congreso internacional sobre Calderón y el teatro español del Siglo de Oro*. Madrid: Consejo Superior de Investigaciones Científicas, 1983.

García Soriano, Justo. "El teatro de colegio en España." *Boletín de la Real Academia Española* 14 (1927): 235–77, 374–411, 535–65, 620–50; 15 (1928), 62–93, 145–87, 396–446, 651–69; 16 (1929), 80–106, 223–43; 19 (1932), 485–98, 608–24.

Garland, John. *The Integumenta on the 'Metamorphoses' of Ovid*. Ed. and trans. Lester K. Born. Diss. University of Chicago, 1929.

Gewecke, Frauke. *Thematische Untersuchungen zu dem vor-calderonianischen Auto Sacramental*. Kölner Romanistische Arbeiten n.s. 42. Geneva: Droz, 1974.

Ghisalberti, F. "L' 'Ovidius Moralizatus' di Pierre Bersuire." *Studi Romanzi* 23 (1933): 5–136.

Gilson, E. "Poésie et vérité dans la *Genealogia* de Boccace." *Studi sul Boccaccio*. Ed. Vittore Branca. 2 vols. Firenze: Sansoni, 1963–. 253–82.

Glaser, Edward A., ed. *Imagen de la vida cristiana*. By Héctor Pinto. Espirituales españoles. Ser. B: Lecturas. Vol. 1. Barcelona: Juan Flores, 1967.

Goldberg, Michael. *Theology and Narrative: A Critical Introduction*. Nashville: Parthenon, 1981.

González de la Riva, D. "Cristocentrismo en los autos sacramentales de Calderón, por Gabriel de Sotiello." *Estudios franciscanos* 306 (1959): 321–44.

González Pedroso, Eduardo, ed. *Autos sacramentales desde su origen hasta fines del siglo XVII*. Vol. 58. Madrid: Biblioteca de Autores Españoles, 1865.

Goppelt, Leonhard. *Typos: The Typological Interpretation of the Old Testament in the New*. Trans. Donald H. Madvig. Grand Rapids, MI: William B. Eerdmans, 1982.

Gracián, Baltasar. *El Criticón*. Ed. Antonio Prieto. Vol. 1. Madrid: Iter, 1970. 2 vols.

Green, Otis H. "'Fingen los poetas': Notes on the Spanish Attitude toward Pagan Mythology." *Estudios dedicados a Menéndez Pidal* 1. Madrid: Consejo Superior de Investigaciones Científicas, 1950. 275–88.

———. *Spain and the Western Tradition*. Vol. 3. Madison: University of Wisconsin Press, 1968. 4 vols.

Green, Richard Hamilton. "Dante's 'Allegory of Poets' and the Mediaeval Theory of Poetic Fiction." *Comparative Literature* 9 (1957): 118–28.

Greer, Margaret Rich. "Art and Power in the Spectacle Plays of Calderón de la Barca." *Publications of the Modern Language Association* 104 (1989): 329–39.

Guillaume de Lorris and Jean de Meun. *Le Roman de la Rose*. Ed. Daniel Poirion. Paris: Garnier-Flammarion, 1974.

Hahn, Juergen H. *The Origins of the Baroque Idea of 'Peregrinatio'*. Chapel Hill: University of North Carolina Press, 1973.

Haight, Elizabeth. *Apuleius and His Influence*. New York: Longmans, Green, 1927.

Halewood, William H. *The Poetry of Grace: Reformation Themes and Structures in English Seventeenth-Century Poetry*. New Haven: Yale University Press, 1966.

Hanson, R. P. C. *Allegory and Event: A Study of the Sources and Significance of Origen's Interpretation of Scripture*. Richmond, VA: John Knox, 1959.

Hartland, Edwin Sidney. *The Legend of Perseus*. London: D. Nuff, 1894–96.

Hauvette, Henri. *Boccace*. Paris: A. Colin, 1914.

Hawkins, Henry. *Partheneia Sacra*. Ed. Iain Fletcher. Aldington, KY: Hand and Flower, 1950.

Heitman, Klaus. "Orpheus im Mittelalter." *Archiv für Kulturgeschichte* 45 (1963): 253–94.

———. "Typen der Deformierung antiker Mythen im Mittelalter: Am Beispiel der Orpheussage." *Romanistisches Jahrbuch* 14 (1963): 45–77.

Helm, R., ed. *Fabii Planciadis Fulgentii Opera*. Leipzig: Bibliotheca Teubneriana, 1898.

Hersman, Anne Bates. *Studies in Greek Allegorical Interpretation*. Chicago: Blue Sky, 1906.

Highet, Gilbert. *The Classical Tradition: Greek and Roman Influences on Western Literature*. London: Oxford University Press, 1949.

Hillach, Ansgar. "El auto sacramental calderoniano considerado en un relieve histórico-filosófico." *Hacia Calderón: Quinto Coloquio Anglogermano Oxford 1978*. Ed. Hans Flasche and Robert D. F. Pring-Mill. Wiesbaden: Franz Steiner Verlag GMBH, 1982. 20–29.

Hoefer, Hartmut. *Typologie im Mittelalter: Zur Übertragbarkeit typologischer Interpretation auf weltliche Dichtung*. Göttingen: A. Künmerle, 1971.

Hollander, Robert. *Allegory in Dante's 'Commedia'*. Princeton: Princeton University Press, 1969.

———. "Typology and Secular Literature: Some Medieval Problems and Examples." In Earl Miner, ed., *Literary Uses of Typology from the Late Middle Ages to the Present*. Princeton: Princeton University Press, 1977.

Hortis, Attilio. *Studi sulle opere latine del Boccaccio*. Trieste: J. Dase, 1879.

"Hortus." *Dictionnaire de Spiritualité et mystique, doctrine et histoire*. Paris: Beauchesne, 1967.

Hugh of St. Victor. *Soliloquy on the Earnest Money of the Soul*. Trans. Kevin Herbert. Milwaukee: Marquette University Press, 1956.

Hult, David F., ed. *Concepts of Closure*. Yale French Studies 67. New Haven: Yale University Press, 1984.

Ingarden, Roman. *The Cognition of the Literary Work of Art*. Trans. Ruth Ann Crowly and Kenneth R. Olsen. Evanston: Northwestern University Press, 1973.

Iparraguirre, Ignacio, S.I. *Historia de los Ejercicios de San Ignacio*. Bilbao: Bibliotheca Instituti Historici S. I., 1955.

———. *Orientaciones bibliográficas sobre San Ignacio de Loyola*. 2nd ed. Rome: Institutum Historicum S. I., 1965.

———. *Práctica de los Ejercicios de San Ignacio de Loyola en vida de su autor (1522–1556)*. Vol. 3. Bilbao: Bibliotheca Instituti Historici S. I., 1946.

Iser, Wolfgang. *The Act of Reading: A Theory of Aesthetic Response*. Baltimore: Johns Hopkins University Press, 1978.

Isern, P. Juan. *San Ignacio y su obra en el Siglo de Oro de la literatura castellana (1516–1700)*. Buenos Aires: S. De Amorrortu, 1924.

Jauss, Hans Robert. "Levels of Identification of Hero and Audience." *New Literary History* 5 (1974): 283–317.

Jeffrey, David L. *By Things Seen: Reference and Recognition in Medieval Thought*. Ottawa: University of Ottawa Press, 1979.

Juambelz, Jesús. *Bibliografía sobre la vida, obras y escritos de San Ignacio de Loyola, 1900–1950*. Madrid: Razón y Fe, 1956.

"Justification." *The Catholic Encyclopedia*. New York: Encyclopedia Press, 1913.

Kantorowicz, Ernst H. *The King's Two Bodies: A Study in Medieval Political Theology*. Princeton: Princeton University Press, 1957.

Keating, E. F. "El diablo en Calderón de la Barca y John Milton." *Cuadernos hispánicos* 333 (1978): 417–34.

Kennedy, George A. *Classical Rhetoric and Its Christian and Secular Tradition from Ancient to Modern Times*. Chapel Hill: University of North Carolina Press, 1980.

Kermode, Frank. *The Sense of an Ending: Studies in the Theory of Fiction*. New York: Oxford University Press, 1967.

"Kerygma." *New Catholic Encyclopedia*. New York: McGraw-Hill, 1967.

Kirk, G. S. *Myth: Its Meaning and Functions in Ancient and Other Cultures*. Berkeley and Los Angeles: Cambridge University Press and University of California Press, 1970.

Knowlton, Edgar C. "Notes on Early Allegory." *Journal of English and Germanic Philology* 29 (1930): 159–81.

Kolve, V. A. *The Play Called Corpus Christi*. Stanford: Stanford University Press, 1966.

Korshin, Paul J. "The Development of Abstracted Typology in England, 1650–1820." *Literary Uses of Typology from the Late Middle Ages to the Present*. Ed. Earl Miner. Princeton: Princeton University Press, 1977. 147–203.

Krieger, Murray. "'A Waking Dream': The Symbolic Alternative to Allegory." *Allegory, Myth, and Symbol*. Ed. Morton W. Bloomfield. Cambridge: Harvard University Press, 1981. 1–22.

Kurtz, Barbara E. "'In imagined space': Allegory and the *Auto Sacramental* of Pedro Calderón de la Barca." *Romanic Review* 79 (1988): 647–64.

———. "'No Word without Mystery': Allegories of Sacred Truth in the *Autos Sacramentales* of Pedro Calderón de la Barca." *Publications of the Modern Language Association* 103 (1988): 262–73.

———. "'With Human Aspect': Studies in European Personification Allegory with Special Reference to the Hispanic Contribution." Diss. University of Chicago, 1983.

Lacosta, F. C. "Los autos sacramentales de Pedro Calderón de la Barca." *Archivo hispalense* 42 (1965): 9–26.

Lampe, David. "Middle English Debate Poems: A Genre Study." Diss. University of Nebraska, 1969.

Latham, C. S. *A Translation of Dante's Eleven Letters*. Ed. George Rice Carpenter with a preface by Charles Eliot Norton. Boston: Houghton, Mifflin, 1891.

Latour, Antoine de. *Psyché en Espagne*. Paris: Charpentier, 1879.

Le Gentil, Pierre. *La Poésie lyrique espagnole et portugaise à la fin du Moyen Age*. 2 vols. Rennes: Plihon, 1949–53.

Lea, Henry Charles. *A History of Auricular Confession and Indulgences in the Latin Church*. 1968 ed. Vol. 2. New York: Greenwood, 1968. 2 vols.

Ledesma, Alonso de. *Conceptos espirituales y morales*. Ed. Eduardo Juliá Martínez. Madrid: Consejo Superior de Investigaciones Científicas, 1969.

Lee, M. O. "Orpheus and Euridice: Myth, Legend and Folklore." *Classica et Mediaevalia* 26 (1965): 198–215.

Leitch, Vincent B. *Deconstructive Criticism: An Advanced Introduction*. New York: Columbia University Press, 1983.

León, Pedro R. "*El divino Orfeo* ca. 1634: Paradoja teológico-poética." *Calderón: Actas del Congreso internacional sobre Calderón y el teatro español del Siglo de Oro*. Ed. Luciano García Lorenzo. Madrid: Consejo *Superior de Investigaciones Científicas*, 1983. 687–99.

————. "Sobre el manuscrito autógrafo de *El divino Orfeo*, 1663, de Calderón." *Revista canadiense de estudios hispánicos* 5 (1981): 321–37.

————. "Un manuscrito de la loa para *El divino Orfeo*, 1663, de Calderón." *Revista canadiense de estudios hispánicos* 9 (1985): 228–50.

Leturia, Pedro de, S. I. *Estudios ignacianos*. Ed. P. Ignacio de Loyola. 2d ed. Rome: Institutum Historicum S.I., 1957.

Levin, Samuel R. "Allegorical Language." *Allegory, Myth, and Symbol*. Ed. Morton W. Bloomfield. Cambridge: Harvard University Press, 1981. 23–38.

Levy, Kurt, Jesús Ara, and Gethin Hughes, eds. *Calderón and the Baroque Tradition*. Waterloo: Wilfrid Laurier University Press, 1985.

Lewalski, Barbara K. *Donne's* Anniversaries *and the Poetry of Praise*. Princeton: Princeton University Press, 1973.

————. "Typological Symbolism and the 'Progress of the Soul' in Seventeenth-Century Literature." *Literary Uses of Typology from the Late Middle Ages to the Present*. Ed. Earl Miner. Princeton: Princeton University Press, 1977. 79–114.

————. "Typology and Poetry: A Consideration of Herbert, Vaughan, and Marvell." *Illustrious Evidence: Approaches to English Literature in the Early Seventeenth Century*. Ed. Earl Miner. Berkeley: University of California Press, 1975. 41–69.

————. *Protestant Poetics and the Seventeenth-Century Religious Lyric*. Princeton: Princeton University Press, 1979.

Lida de Malkiel, María Rosa. "La tradición clásica en España." Rev. of *The Classical Tradition*, by Gilbert Highet. *Nueva revista de filología hispánica* 5 (1951): 183–223.

Liebschütz, Hans. *Fulgentius Metaforalis: Ein Beitrag zur Geschichte der antiken Mythologie im Mittelalter*. Leipzig: B. G. Teubner, 1926.

Llompart, Gabriel. "La nave de la iglesia y su derrotero en la iconografía de los siglos XVI y XVII." *Gesammelte Aufsätze zur Kulturgeschichte Spaniens*. Ed. Johannes Vincke et al. Spanische Forschungen der Görresgesellschaft 25. Munster: Aschendorff, 1970. 309–35.

Lorinser, Franz, trans. *Don Pedro Calderón de la Barca, Geistliche Festspiele: In deutscher Ubersetzung mit erklärendem Commentar und einer Einleitung über die Bedeutung und den Werth dieser Dichtungen* 5. Regensburg: G. J. Manz, 1856–72. 18 vols.

Lovejoy, Arthur O. *The Great Chain of Being: A Study of the History of an Idea*. Cambridge: Harvard University Press, 1936.

Low, Anthony. *Love's Architecture: Devotional Modes in Seventeenth-Century English Poetry*. New York: New York University Press, 1978.

Loyola, Ignacio de (San). *Exercitia Spiritualia*. Ed. Iosephus Calveras. Roma: Institutum Historicum Societatis Iesu, 1969.

————. *Obras Completas*. Ed. Ignacio Iparraguirre and Cándido de Dalmases. 4th ed. Madrid: Biblioteca de Autores Cristianos, 1982.

————. *The Spiritual Exercises of Saint Ignatius*. Trans. Thomas Corbishley, S.J. New York: P. J. Kennedy & Sons, 1963.

McGaha, Michael D., ed. *Approaches to the Theater of Calderón*. Washington, DC: University Press of America, 1982.

McGarry, M. Francis de Sales (Sister). *The Allegorical and Metaphorical Language in the Autos Sacramentales of Calderón*. Washington, DC: Catholic University of America Press, 1937.

McIntyre, John. *The Christian Doctrine of History*. Grand Rapids, MI: W. B. Eerdmans, 1957.

MacQuarrie, John. *God-Talk: An Examination of the Language and Logic of Theology* New York: Harper and Row, 1967.

Macri, Oreste. "La historiografía del barroco literario español." *Thesaurus* 15 (1960): 1–70.

Manuel, Frank E. *The Eighteenth Century Confronts the Gods*. Cambridge: Harvard University Press, 1959.

Marcos Villanueva, Balbino, S.I. *La ascética de los jesuitas en los autos sacramentales de Calderón*. Bilbao: Universidad de Deusto, 1973.

Martín Acosta, María Inés (Sister), C.S.J. "The Mythological *Autos* of Calderón de la Barca." Diss. Columbia University, 1969.

Martínez Torrón, Diego. "El mito de Circe y *Los encantos de la culpa*." *Calderón: Actas del Congreso internacional sobre Calderón y el teatro español del Siglo de Oro*. Ed. Luciano García Lorenzo. Madrid: Consejo Superior de Investigaciones Científicas, 1983. 701–12.

Martz, Louis L. "The Action of the Self: Devotional Poetry in the Seventeenth Century." *Metaphysical Poetry*. Ed. M. Bradbury and D. Palmer. London: Edward Arnold, 1970. 101–21.

————. *The Paradise Within: Studies in Vaughan, Traherne, and Milton*. New Haven: Yale University Press, 1964.

————. *The Poem of the Mind: Essays on Poetry, English and American*. New York: Oxford University Press, 1966.

————. *The Poetry of Meditation: A Study in English Religious Literature of the Seventeenth Century*. New Haven: Yale University Press, 1964.

Maury, Alfred. *Essai sur les légendes pieuses du Moyen Age*. Paris: Librairie Philosophique de Ladrange, 1843.

Mazzeo, Joseph A. "Metaphysical Poetry and the Poetic of Correspondence." *Journal of the History of Ideas* 14 (1953): 221–34.

————. *Renaissance and Seventeenth-Century Studies*. New York: Columbia University Press, 1964.

————. "Universal Analogy and the Culture of the Renaissance." *Journal of the History of Ideas* 15 (1954): 299–304.

Mazzotta, Giuseppe. *Dante, Poet of the Desert: History and Allegory in the 'Divine Comedy.'* Princeton: Princeton University Press, 1979.

Migne, Jacques Paul, comp. *Patrologiae cursus completus*. Series latina. Paris: J. P. Migne, 1844–82.

Miner, Earl, ed. *Literary Uses of Typology from the Late Middle Ages to the Present*. Princeton: Princeton University Press, 1977.

Momigliano, Arnaldo. *Studies in Historiography*. London: Weidenfeld and Nicolson, 1966.

Mommsen, Theodore. "Petrarch and the Story of the Choice of Hercules." *Medieval and Renaissance Studies*. Ed. E. Rice. Ithaca: Cornell University Press, 1959. 175–96.

Moore, Peter. "Mystical Experience, Mystical Doctrine, Mystical Technique." *Mysticism and Philosophical Awareness*. Ed. Steven T. Katz. New York: Oxford University Press, 1978. 101–31.

Morreale, Margherita. "Carlos V, rex bonus, felix imperator; notas sobre Diálogos de Alfonso de Valdés." *Estudios y documentos*. 2: *Cuadernos de historia moderna 3*. Valladolid: Facultad de Filosofía y Letras de la Universidad, 1954. 7–20.

Murrin, Michael. *The Veil of Allegory: Some Notes Towards a Theory of Allegorical Rhetoric in the English Renaissance*. Chicago: University of Chicago Press, 1969.

Neumeister, Sebastian. "Las bodas de España: Alegoría y política en el auto sacramental." *Hacia Calderón: Quinto Coloquio Anglogermano Oxford 1978*. Ed. Hans Flasche and Robert D. F. Pring-Mill. Wiesbaden: Franz Steiner Verlag GMBH, 1982. 30–41.

———. "Calderón y el mito clásico: *Andromeda y Perseo*, auto sacramental y fiesta de corte." *Calderón: Actas del Congreso internacional sobre Calderón y el teatro español del Siglo de Oro*. Ed. Luciano García Lorenzo. Madrid: Consejo Superior de Investigaciones Científicas, 1983. 713–21.

Newman, R. W. "Calderón and Aquinas." Diss. Boston University, 1956.

Nichols, Stephen G., Jr. *Romanesque Signs: Early Medieval Narrative and Iconography*. New Haven: Yale University Press, 1983.

Niebuhr, H. Richard. *The Meaning of Revelation*. New York: Macmillan, 1941.

O'Malley, John W. *Praise and Blame in Renaissance Rome: Rhetoric, Doctrine, and Reform in the Sacred Orators of the Papal Court, c. 1450–1521*. Durham, NC: Duke University Press, 1979.

Oakley, Francis. "Jacobean Political Theology: The Absolute and Ordinary Powers of the King." *Journal of the History of Ideas* 29 (1968): 323–46.

Ong, Walter J. *Orality and Literacy: The Technologizing of the Word*. London: Methuen, 1982.

Pacheco, Francisco. *Arte de la pintura*. Ed. F. J. Sánchez Cantón. 2 vols. Madrid: Instituto de Valencia de don Juan, 1956.

Panofsky, Erwin. *Gothic Architecture and Scholasticism*. Cleveland: World Publishing, 1951.

———. *Hercules am Scheidewege und andere antike Bildstoffe in der neuren Kunst*. Studien der Bibliotek Warburg, vol 18. Leipzig-Berlin: B. G. Teubner, 1930.

———. *Idea: A Concept in Art Theory*. Trans. Joseph J. S. Peake. New York: Harper & Row, 1968.

Páramo Pomareda, Jorge. "Consideraciones sobre los 'autos mitológicos' de Calderón de la Barca." *Thesaurus* 12 (1957): 51–80.

Parker, Alexander A. *The Allegorical Drama of Calderón: An Introduction to the Autos Sacramentales*. Oxford: Dolphin, 1943.

———. "The Devil in the Drama of Calderón." *Critical Essays on the Theatre of Calderón*. Ed. Bruce W. Wardropper. New York: New York University Press, 1965. 3–23.

————. "Notes on the Origins of the 'Auto Sacramental'" *Modern Language Review* 30 (1935): 170–82.

Partner, Nancy F. "Making up Lost Time: Writing on the Writing of History." Rev. art. *Speculum* 61 (1986): 90–117.

Patrides, C. A. *The Phoenix and the Ladder*. Berkeley: University of California Press, 1964.

Patterson, L. G. *God and History in Early Christian Thought: A Study of Themes from Justin Martyr to Gregory the Great*. London: Adam and Charles Black, 1967.

Pépin, Jean. *Mythe et allégorie: les origines grecques et les contestations judéo-chrétiennes*. Paris: Aubier, 1958.

Philo of Alexandria. *Philo*. Trans. F. H. Colson and G. H. Whitaker. Vol. 1. Cambridge: Harvard University Press, 1971. 10 vols.

Plato. *The Collected Dialogues*. Ed. Edith Hamilton and Huntington Cairns. Princeton: Princeton University Press, 1969.

Pollin, Alice M. "'Cithara Iesu': La apoteosis de la música en *El divino Orfeo* de Calderón." *Homenaje a Casalduero: Crítica y poesía ofrecido por sus amigos y discípulos*. Ed. Rizel Pincus Sigele and Gonzalo Sobejano. Madrid: Gredos, 1972. 419–31.

Praz, Mario. *Studies in Seventeenth-Century Imagery*. London: The Warburg Institute, 1939.

Preiss, T. "The Christian Philosophy of History." *Journal of Religion* 30 (1950): 157–70.

Preminger, Alex, O. B. Hardison, Jr., and K. Kervante, eds. *Classical and Medieval Literary Criticism: Translations and Interpretations*. New York: F. Ungar, 1974.

Preto-Rodas, Richard A. "Anchieta and Vieira: Drama as Sermon, Sermon as Drama." *Luso-Brazilian Review* 7 (1970): 96–103.

Preus, J. S. *From Shadow to Promise: Old Testament Interpretation from Augustine to the Young Luther*. Cambridge: Harvard University Press, 1969.

"Probabilism." *The Catholic Encyclopedia*. New York: Encyclopedia Press, 1913.

Prudentius. *Prudentius*. Ed. and trans. H. J. Thomson. Cambridge: Harvard University Press, 1949.

Pseudo-Bonaventure. *Meditations on the Life of Christ*. Trans. Isa Ragusa. Princeton: Princeton University Press, 1961.

Quacquarelli, Antonio. *La concezione della storia nella società dei primi secoli dopo Cristo*. Bari: Adriatica, 1968.

Quain, Edwin A. "The Medieval *Accessus ad Auctores*." *Traditio* 3 (1945): 223–24.

Quilligan, Maureen. *The Language of Allegory: Defining the Genre*. Ithaca: Cornell University Press, 1979.

Quint, David. *Origin and Originality in Renaissance Literature: Versions of the Source*. New Haven: Yale University Press, 1983.

Raby, F. J. E. *A History of Secular Latin Poetry in the Middle Ages*. 2d ed. Oxford: Clarendon, 1953, 1967.

Rahner, Hugo. *Greek Myths and Christian Mystery*. Trans. Brian Battershaw. London: Burns and Oates, 1963.

————. *Ignatius von Loyola als Mensch und Theologe*. Freiburg: Herder, 1964.

Ramsey, Ian T. *Christian Discourse: Some Logical Explorations*. London: Oxford University Press, 1965.

————. *Models and Mystery*. London: Oxford University Press, 1964.

————. *Religious Language: An Empirical Placing of Theological Phrases*. London: SCM, 1957.

Raspa, Anthony. "Craspa and the Jesuit Poetic." *University of Toronto Quarterly* 36 (1966): 37–54.

————. *The Emotive Image: Jesuit Poetics in the English Renaissance*. Fort Worth: Texas Christian University Press, 1983.

Reichenberger, Kurt. "Calderóns Welttheater und die Autos Sacramentales." *"Theatrum Mundi": Götter, Gott und Spielleiter im Drama von der Antike bis zur Gegenwart*. Ed. Franz Link and Gunter Niggl. Berlin: Duncker & Humbolt, 1981. 161–75.

Reichenberger, Kurt, and Roswitha Reichenberger, eds. *Bibliographisches Handbuch der Calderón-Forschung*. 3 vols. Kassel: Thiele, 1979.

Rico, Francisco. *El pequeño mundo del hombre: varia fortuna de una idea en las letras españolas*. Madrid: Castalia, 1970.

Ricoeur, Paul. "Toward a Hermeneutic of the Idea of Revelation." *Harvard Theological Review* 70 (1977): 1–37.

Ripandelli, Carol Janet. "The Tropological Model of the Fall in *El divino Orfeo* and *El mágico prodigioso* by Calderón de la Barca." Diss. Florida State University, 1979.

Robertson, D. W., Jr. *A Preface to Chaucer: Studies in Medieval Perspectives*. Princeton: Princeton University Press, 1962.

Rodríguez Puértolas, Julio. "La transposición de la realidad en los autos sacramentales de Calderón." *Calderón: Actas del Congreso internacional sobre Calderón y el teatro español del Siglo de Oro*. Ed. Luciano García Lorenzo. Madrid: Consejo Superior de Investigaciones Científicas, 1983. 751–58.

Rossi, Giuseppe Carlo. "Calderón en la crítica española del XVIII." *Estudios sobre las letras en el siglo XVIII*. Trans. Jesús López Pacheco. Madrid: Gredos, 1967. 41–96.

————. "Calderón en la polémica del XVIII sobre los 'autos sacramentales.' " *Estudios sobre las letras en el siglo XVIII*. Trans. Jesús López Pacheco. Madrid: Gredos, 1967. 9–40.

Rouanet, Léo, ed. *Colección de autos, farsas y coloquios del siglo XVI*. Madrid: Biblioteca Hispánica, 1901.

Rozas, Juan Manuel. "La licitud del teatro y otras cuestiones literarias en Bances Candamo, escritor límite." *Segismundo* 1 (1965): 247–74.

Rudwin, Maximilian. *The Devil in Legend and Literature*. La Salle, IL: Open Court Publishing, 1931.

Ruiz-Lagos de Castro, Manuel. *Estética de la pintura en el teatro de Calderón*. Granada: Gráficas del Sur, 1969.

Rupp, Stephen. "Allegory and Diplomacy in Calderón's *El lirio y la azucena*." *Bulletin of the Comediantes* 41 (1989): 107–25.

Rust, Eric Charles. *The Christian Understanding of History*. London: Lutterworth, 1947.

Sainz Rodríguez, Pedro. *Espiritualidad española*. Madrid: Rialp, 1961.

Salman, Phillips. "Instruction and Delight in Medieval and Renaissance Criticism." *Renaissance Quarterly* 32 (1979): 303–32.

Salter, Elizabeth. "Medieval Poetry and the Figural View of Reality." *Proceedings of the British Academy* 54 (1968): 73–92.

San Miguel, Angel. "*La humildad coronada de las plantas* de Calderón. Contribución al estudio de sus fuentes." *Hacia Calderón. Cuarto Coloquio Anglogermano. Wolfenbüttel 1975.* Ed. Hans Flasche, Karl- Hermann Körner and Hans Mattauch. Berlin-New York: Walter de Gruyter, 1979. 117–22.

———. "*La humildad coronada de las plantas*: Ein aussergewöhnliches 'Auto sacramental' Calderóns?" *Pedro Calderón de la Barca: Vorträge anlässlich der Jahrestagung der Görres-Gesellschaft 1978.* Ed. Theodor Berchem and Siegfried Sudhof. Berlin: Erich Schmidt, 1983. 114–23.

Sánchez Mariana, Manuel. *La humildad coronada.* Madrid: Espasa-Calpe, 1980.

Sarolli, Gian Roberto. "Dante e la teologia politica: simbolismo cristologico cristomimetico." *Prolegomena alla 'Divina Commedia.'* Florence: Olschki, 1971. 248–88.

Scobie, Alexander. *Aspects of the Ancient Romance and Its Heritage.* Beiträge zur klassischen Philologie 30. Meisenheim am Glan: Anton Hain, 1969. 93–95.

———. "The Dating of the Earliest Printed European Translation of Apuleius's *Metamorphoses.*" *More Essays on the Ancient Romance and Its Heritage.* Beiträge zur klassischen Philologie 46. Meisenheim am Glan: Anton Hain, 1973. 47–52.

Searle, John R. *Speech Acts: An Essay in the Philosophy of Language.* Cambridge: Cambridge University Press, 1969.

Seznec, Jean. *The Survival of the Pagan Gods: The Mythological Tradition and Its Place in Renaissance Humanism and Art.* Trans. Barbara F. Sessions. Bollingen Series 38. Princeton: Princeton University Press, 1972.

Shergold, N. D. *A History of the Spanish Stage from Medieval Times until the End of the Seventeenth Century.* Oxford: Oxford University Press, 1967.

Shergold, N. D., and J. E. Varey. *Los autos sacramentales en Madrid en la época de Calderón, 1637–1681: Estudios y documentos.* Madrid: Ediciones de Historia, Geografía y Arte, 1961.

Sheridan, Richard Brinsley. *The Dramatic Works of Richard Brinsley Sheridan.* Ed. Cecil Price. Oxford: Clarendon, 1973.

Simón Díaz, José. *Jesuitas de los siglos XVI y XVII.* Madrid: Universidad Pontificia de Salamanca, 1975.

Singleton, Charles. *Dante Studies I. Commedia: Elements of Structure.* Cambridge: Harvard University Press, 1954.

———. "The Irreducible Dove." *Comparative Literature* 9 (1957): 129–35.

Smith, Barbara Herrnstein. *Poetic Closure: A Study of How Poems End.* Chicago: University of Chicago Press, 1968.

Smith, Hilary Dansey. *Preaching in the Spanish Golden Age: A Study of Some Preachers of the Reign of Philip III.* Oxford: Oxford University Press, 1978.

Smith, Macklin. *Prudentius' 'Psychomachia': A Reexamination.* Princeton: Princeton University Press, 1976.

Smith, T. V., ed. *From Aristotle to Plotinus.* Chicago: University of Chicago Press, 1934.

Snyder, Joel. "Picturing Vision." *The Language of Images.* Ed. W. J. T. Mitchell. Chicago: University of Chicago Press, 1974. 219–46.

Soons, Alan. "Calderón's Augustinian *Auto*: *El sacro Parnaso.*" *What's Past Is Pro-*

logue: A Collection of Essays in Honour of L. J. Woodward. Ed. Salvador Bacarisse, Bernard Bentley, Mercedes Clarasó, and Douglas Gifford. Edinburgh: Scottish Academic, 1984. 124-31.

Spenser, Edmund. *Poetical Works.* Ed. J. C. Smith and E. de Selincourt. London: Oxford University Press, 1970.

Spicq, C. *Esquisse d'une histoire de l'exégèse latine au moyen âge.* Paris: J. Vrin, 1944.

Spitzer, Leo. "Classical and Christian Ideas of World Harmony." *Traditio* 2 (1944): 409-64. Republished in book form, ed. Anna Granville Hatcher. Baltimore: Johns Hopkins University Press, 1963.

Starkman, Miriam. "Noble Numbers and the Poetry of Devotion." *Reason and the Imagination.* Ed. Joseph A. Mazzeo. New York: Columbia University Press, 1962. 1-27.

Starnes, DeWitt T., and E. W. Talbert. *Classical Myth and Legend in Renaissance Dictionaries.* Chapel Hill: University of North Carolina Press, 1955.

Strubel, A. "'Allegoria in Factis' et 'Allegoria in Verbis.'" *Poétique* 23 (1975): 342-57.

Sullivan, Henry W. *Calderón in the German Lands and the Low Countries: His Reception and Influence, 1654-1980.* Cambridge: Cambridge University Press, 1983.

———. "Calderón's Appeal to European Audiences in the Enlightenment and Romantic Eras: 1738-1838." *Ottawa Hispánica* 5 (1983): 41-58.

———. "Calderón's Reception in Spain during the Romantic Era, 1800-59." *Ottawa Hispánica* 4 (1982): 27-54.

———. "The Problematic of Tragedy in Calderón's *El médico de su honra.*" *Revista canadiense de estudios hispánicos* 5 (1981): 355-72.

———. "A Select Bibliography of Calderón's Reception in Holland and Germany." *Ottawa Hispánica* 3 (1981): 91-101.

———. *Tirso de Molina and the Drama of the Counter Reformation.* Amsterdam: Rodolfi, 1976.

Tate, J. "The Beginnings of Greek Allegory." *The Classical Review* 41 (1927): 214-17.

———. "On the History of Allegorism." *Classical Quarterly* 28 (1934): 105-14.

———. "Plato and Allegorical Interpretation." *Classical Quarterly* 23 (1929): 142-54 and 24 (1930): 1-10.

Terry, Arthur. "Introduction." *An Anthology of Spanish Poetry 1500-1700, Part II 1580-1700.* Vol. 2. Oxford: Pergamon, 1968. xiii-xlvi. 2 vols.

Thomas, Lucien-Paul. "Les jeux de scène et l'architecture des idées dans le théâtre de Calderón." *Homenaje ofrecido a Menéndez Pidal.* Vol. 2. Madrid: Hernando, 1925. 501-30. 2 vols.

Thomas, Mary Lorene. "A Critical Edition of Pedro Calderón de la Barca's *Tu prójimo como a ti.*" Diss. University of Michigan, 1984.

Thompson, David. "Figure and Allegory in the *Commedia.*" *Dante Studies* 90 (1972): 1-10.

Tillyard, E. M. W. *The Elizabethan World Picture.* New York: Vintage Books, n.d.

Timoneda, Juan de. *Juan de Timoneda, Obras.* Ed. Eduardo Juliá Martínez. Madrid: Sociedad de Bibliófilos Españoles, 1947-48.

Torres Esquer, Ramón. "Las prohibiciones de comedias y autos sacramentales en el siglo XVII." *Segismundo* 2 (1965): 187-226.

Tuve, Rosemond. *Allegorical Imagery: Some Mediaeval Books and Their Posterity*. Princeton: Princeton University Press, 1966.

————. *Elizabethan and Metaphysical Imagery: Renaissance Poetic and Twentieth-Century Critics*. Chicago: University of Chicago Press, 1947.

Valdivielso, José de. *Teatro completo*. Ed. Ricardo Arias y Arias and Robert V. Piluso. Madrid: Isla, 1975.

Van Dyke, Carolynn. *The Fiction of Truth: Structures of Meaning in Narrative and Dramatic Allegory*. Ithaca: Cornell University Press, 1985.

Vance, Eugene. "Roland et la poétique de la mémoire." *Cahiers d'etudes médiévales* 1 (1975): 103–15.

Varey, J. E. "Calderón's *Auto Sacramental, La vida es sueño*, in performance." *Iberoromania* 14 (1981): 75–86.

Vázquez, Dionisio. *Sermones*. Ed. Felix G. Olmedo. Madrid: Espasa-Calpe, 1943.

Vega Carpio, Lope de. *Obras completas de Lope de Vega*. Ed. Marcelino Menéndez y Pelayo. Vol. 3. Madrid: Real Academia Española, 1892. 15 vols. 1890–1913.

Vinaver, Eugene. *The Rise of Romance*. New York: Oxford University Press, 1971.

Voght, Geoffrey Michael. "Calderón's *El cubo de la Almudena* and Comedy in the *Autos Sacramentales*." *Critical Perspectives on Calderón de la Barca*. Ed. Frederick A. de Armas, David M. Gitlitz, and José A. Madrigal. Lincoln, NE: Society of Spanish and Spanish American Studies, 1981. 141–60.

————. "The Mythological *Autos* of Calderón de la Barca." Diss. University of Michigan, 1974.

Waites, M. C. "Some Aspects of the Ancient Allegorical Debate." *Studies in English and Comparative Literature*. Radcliffe College Monographs, no. 15. Boston: Radcliffe College Monographs, 1910.

Wallace, John M. "Thomas Traherne and the Structure of Meditation." *ELH* 25 (1958): 79–89.

Walther, Hans. *Das Streitgedicht in der lateinischen Literatur des Mittelalters, Quellen und Untersuchungen zur lateinischen Philologie des Mittelalters*. Vol. 5, pt. 2. Munich: Beck, 1920.

Warden, John, ed. *Orpheus: The Metamorphoses of a Myth*. Toronto: University of Toronto Press, 1982.

Wardropper, Bruce W., ed. *Critical Essays on the Theatre of Calderón*. New York: New York University Press, 1965.

————. *Historia de la poesía lírica a lo divino en la cristiandad occidental*. Madrid: Revista de Occidente, 1958.

————. *Introducción al teatro religioso del Siglo de Oro: Evolución del Auto Sacramental antes de Calderón*. Salamanca: Anaya, 1967.

————. "The Search for a Dramatic Formula for the *Auto Sacramental*." *Publications of the Modern Language Association* 65 (1950): 1196–1211.

Warnke, Frank. *Versions of Baroque: European Literature in the Seventeenth Century*. New Haven: Yale University Press, 1972.

Weir, Lucy E. *The Ideas Embodied in the Religious Drama of Calderón*. Lincoln, NE: The University, 1940.

Wille, Jutta. *Calderóns Spiel der Erlösung: eine spanische Bilderbibel des 17. Jahrhunderts*. Munich: C. Kaiser, 1932.

Wilson, E. M. "A Key to Calderón's *Psalle et Sile*." *Hispanic Studies in Honour of I. González Llubera*. Oxford: Oxford University Press, 1959. 429–40.

Wilson, Edward M. "Nuevos documentos sobre las controversias teatrales: 1650–1681." *Actas del Segundo Congreso de la Asociación Internacional de Hispanistas*. Nijmegen: University of Nimega, 1967. 155–70.

Wind, Edgar. *Pagan Mysteries in the Renaissance*. New Haven: Yale University Press, 1958.

"Witness." *New Catholic Encyclopedia*. New York: McGraw-Hill, 1967.

"Witness." *The New International Dictionary of New Testament Theology*. Ed. Colin Brown, trans., with additions and revisions, from *Theologisches Begriffslexikon zum Neuen Testament*, ed. Lothar Coenen et al., 3. Grand Rapids, MI: Regency Reference Library, 1978. 1038–51.

Woodward, Leslie J. "La dramatización del tiempo en el auto *Los alimentos del hombre*." *Hacia Calderón, Cuarto Coloquio Anglogermano Wolfenbüttel 1975*. Ed. Hans Flasche, Karl-Hermann Körner, and Hans Mattauch. Berlin: Walter de Gruyter, 1979. 123–28.

———. "*Suppositio* in Calderón's *No hay más fortuna que Dios*." *Calderón and the Baroque Tradition*. Ed. Kurt Levy, Jesús Ara, and Gethin Hughes. Waterloo: Wilfrid Laurier University Press, 1985. 41–46.

Yates, Frances A. *The Art of Memory*. Chicago: University of Chicago Press, 1966.

Zwicker, Steven N. *Dryden's Political Poetry: The Typology of King and Nation*. Providence: Brown University Press, 1972.

———. "Politics and Panegyric: The Figural Mode from Marvell to Pope." *Literary Uses of Typology from the Late Middle Ages to the Present*. Ed. Earl Miner. Princeton: Princeton University Press, 1977. 115–46.

Index